"In these beautifully crafted essays, Siedell brings the eye of the curator, the intellect of the critic, and the passion of the believer to a much-misunderstood subject. The reader is rewarded with a clear, sharply critical, theologically astute, and decisive apologia for the essential contribution of contemporary art to the life of faith."

—Robin Jensen, Luce Chancellor's Professor of the History of Christian Art and Worship, Vanderbilt University Divinity School

"We've been waiting for this book for nearly forty years. Finally, a robust and unapologetically Christian engagement with contemporary art by an 'insider' to its world and conversation. Though Siedell invites us beyond the wooden ideal of 'the Christian artist,' at the same time he articulates a vision of artistic practice and criticism rooted in the church. He provides much-needed wisdom, modeling how Christians can charitably engage modern art. He also provides much-needed guidance for how Protestants can—and should—incorporate the arts in worship beyond the eclectic pastiche of the 'hip.' Required reading for emerging artists—and their teachers."

—James K. A. Smith, associate professor of philosophy, Calvin College; author of *Who's Afraid of Postmodernism?*

"Finally! A book for contemporary Protestant communities that drinks deeply from the christological dogmas that arose out of the Byzantine iconoclastic controversy (eighth and ninth centuries). In a masterful way, Siedell shows the contemporary relevance of Nicaea II (AD 787) for modern artists and the worship practices of Western Christianity. Readers will discover an iconic worldview that is simultaneously incarnational, sacramental, and transcendent. More than a book, it is an event that celebrates the universal and timeless relevance of Orthodox icons for the twenty-first-century church—East and West."

—Bradley Nassif, professor of biblical and theological studies, North Park University

culturalexegesis

William A. Dyrness
and Robert K. Johnston, series editors

The Cultural Exegesis series is designed to
complement the Engaging Culture series
by providing methodological and foundational studies that address the way to engage culture theologically. Each volume
works within a specific cultural discipline,
illustrating and embodying the theory behind cultural engagement. By providing
the appropriate tools, these books equip
the reader to engage and interpret the surrounding culture responsibly.

God in the Gallery

A Christian Embrace of Modern Art

Daniel A. Siedell

Baker Academic
a division of Baker Publishing Group
Grand Rapids, Michigan

© 2008 by Daniel A. Siedell

Published by Baker Academic
a division of Baker Publishing Group
P.O. Box 6287, Grand Rapids, MI 49516-6287
www.bakeracademic.com

Printed in the United States of America

Library of Congress Cataloging-in-Publication Data
Siedell, Daniel A., 1966–
    God in the gallery : a Christian embrace of modern art / Daniel A. Siedell.
        p.   cm. — (Cultural exegesis)
    Includes bibliographical references (p.   ) and index.
    ISBN 978-0-8010-3184-7 (pbk.)
    1. Christianity and art. 2. Modernism (Art) I. Title.
BR115.8S57 2008
    261.57—dc22   2008012698

Contents

Preface

This project has two beginnings a decade apart. As a doctoral student studying modern and contemporary art in 1994, I happened across my father's copy of Francis Schaeffer's booklet *Art and the Bible*. I was no stranger to Schaeffer. My father's library was well stocked with Schaeffer's books, as well as those of C. S. Lewis, Carl Henry, and many others who were instrumental in leading a generation of conservative Protestant Christians out of fundamentalist cultural separatism. Although I had read Schaeffer's *How Shall We Then Live?* as a teenager, it had been several years since I had read his observations on art, particularly modern art. And now, in the midst of my doctoral studies, it appeared very narrow and limited.

I had been living in and with modern and contemporary art, criticism, and theory for several intense years, having already written a master's thesis on the critics of abstract expressionist Willem de Kooning under the direction of an active and high-profile critic, Donald B. Kuspit at Stony Brook, and was in the process of developing the contours of my doctoral dissertation on abstract expressionism under the guidance of Stephen C. Foster at the University of Iowa. I felt that Schaeffer's observations and conclusions betrayed a lack of interest in the subject and a too-easy inclination to move from art to philosophy, from artifact to explanation, from complex work of art to simple worldview. For Schaeffer, modern art was merely a visual illustration of a secular worldview philosophy, be it existentialism, nihilism, or humanism.

My discovery of Reformed evangelical Christian scholarship, initiated through Mark Noll's *The Scandal of the Evangelical Mind* (1994), was seminal in my development of a response to Schaeffer. It caused me to rethink the implications of my faith and its relevance to my intellectual vocation, which I had not considered as seriously at that time as I could have. It started me on an intellectual (and spiritual) journey that I could not have foreseen and on which I now continue. This book is thus an end and a beginning. It marks my response to Schaeffer, not only about modern art but also about vocation and, ultimately, discipleship in the world of contemporary art. It is also a beginning, as this book sketches the contours of future scholarship.

The second beginning occurred in 2004 after I read William Dyrness's *Visual Faith*, a book in Baker Academic's Engaging Culture series that explores the role of visual art in the contemporary church. Having long since completed my doctoral dissertation and having developed a career as a curator of modern and contemporary art at a university art museum, I wrote a review essay that addressed what I felt to be Dyrness's lack of attention to the history and theory of modern and contemporary art.[1] After I sent him a copy of my review, Bill encouraged and challenged me to pursue my line of reasoning in a book. Meetings at CIVA (Christians in the Visual Arts) conferences, talks at Fuller, and participation in his Visual Art and the Practice of Christian Worship seminar at Calvin College in the summer of 2006 further developed this book and nourished our relationship, which is continuing with a collaborative project on an alternative history of modern art.

Visual Faith begins with a specific issue—"worship and the arts" in the church—and touches only slightly on modern and contemporary art. In fact, Dyrness admits that his book could have taken different directions: "one might spend more time focusing on the secular art world, discussing ways in which God is present and at work there."[2] This book is just such an attempt. It begins unapologetically in the world of contemporary art. Thus *Visual Faith* and the present study face each other, in dialogue. This book would not have been possible without *Visual Faith* and Bill's encouragement.

This book bears the imprint of my work as a curator at the Sheldon Art Gallery at the University of Nebraska–Lincoln for the past ten years, working with an impressive permanent collection of modern and contemporary American art, developing relationships with a vast array of contemporary artists on curatorial projects, and speaking about contemporary art to a variety of different—and sometimes skeptical—audiences. In addition, much of this material has been taught in various classroom contexts to undergraduate and graduate studio art students at the University of Nebraska–Lincoln and to art students in a course on spirituality and contemporary art at Concordia University in Seward, Nebraska.

This book is for those who want a different image of modern and contemporary art to contemplate. It does not displace existing books on the subject; it is intended to be read in conjunction with them, including Schaeffer's *Art and the Bible*. This book is for undergraduate or graduate art students who want to bring their faith into a deeper relationship with their own artistic practice and who have not found compelling voices in Christian literature; it is for philosophers or theologians who want a more nuanced treatment of modern and contemporary art to flesh out their understanding of cultural practice or those theologians for whom aesthetics play a preeminent role; it is for missional church leaders, emergent or otherwise, who are reflecting on the role of the visual arts in the postmodern church.

I am indebted to David Morgan, whose scholarship has been influential and who has been a stable source of encouragement. He is the scholar and teacher I aspire to be like. I hope this book begins to repay the time and effort he has invested in my work over the years.

This book also bears the influence of Enrique Martínez Celaya, whose art and life have had a decisive impact on my practice as a curator, critic, and Christian. Most art critics experience the landscape of contemporary art through the lens of an artist who amplifies and focuses attention. Martínez Celaya is my lens.

John Wilson, editor of *Books & Culture*, has long been an advocate and supporter of my work; James K. A. Smith has also served as a conversation partner; and R. R. Reno, who plies his trade as a theologian just up I-80 in Omaha, has been a constant source of encouragement, provocation, and good cheer. I am also appreciative of the support of Robert Hosack at Baker Academic, whose encouragement has been more important than he realizes.

I would like to thank the Hixson-Lied College of Fine and Performing Arts at the University of Nebraska–Lincoln and the College of Communication Fine Arts and Media at the University of Nebraska at Omaha for providing modest but consistent and helpful annual research funds that facilitated this and other of my forays into this line of work. The Calvin College Seminars in Christian Scholarship were also helpful, providing me an opportunity in the summer of 2006 to reflect on the relationship between visual art and the church. Over the years I have had the opportunity to speak in various contexts at Baylor University, Calvin College, Wheaton College, Dordt College,

Valparaiso University, Westmont College, Azusa Pacific University, and Biola University. I have benefited immensely from all of these experiences.

I also want to thank my teachers Donald B. Kuspit and Stephen C. Foster, whose work continues to inform my work.

Finally, my father has been a constant—if often silent—conversation partner with me about Christian faith and intellectual life, although he knew I ultimately had to go it alone and reach my own conclusions. With children of my own, I am only now beginning to grasp the depth of my parents' faith and the challenges they faced. I dedicate this book to them in gratitude.

Introduction

St. Paul was faced with a choice at the Areopagus on Mars Hill, when he came upon the altar to the unknown god. He could have ignored it or even condemned it as yet another example of the Athenians' spiritual immaturity and further evidence of their pagan worldview ways. But that is not what he did. He argued that what he knew and worshiped, they were already worshiping, although as "something unknown" (Acts 17:23). Furthermore, St. Paul quotes their own poets in support of the God of Abraham, Isaac, and Jacob, thereby baptizing pagan poetry in the Scriptures, enabling the Spirit to work through those very words (Acts 17:28). St. Paul, then, not only used the cultural artifacts at hand (altar and poetry) but in a radical move he also bent them toward the gospel, making them work for him and his audience as a means of apologetic grace.

Altars to the unknown god are strewn about the historical landscape of modern and contemporary art. They are often remarkably beautiful, compelling, and powerful. But they have been too often ignored or condemned out of hand. This book is the result of choosing the way of St. Paul: to take the cultural artifacts and to reveal and illuminate their insights into what they are only able to point to, not to name. But point they do, and they should be examined and celebrated as such.

As part of the new Cultural Exegesis series by Baker Academic, edited by William Dyrness and Robert Johnston, this book offers an in-depth critical engagement with contemporary art that is nourished by the Christian faith as embodied in the Nicene-Constantinopolitan Creed and preserved in the ecumenical councils, which embody a maximal Christology.[1] This book is, in an important sense, applied or participatory exegesis. It is also a form of art and cultural criticism. In order for the contemporary church to speak to culture, it is important to have a fuller and more nuanced historical, critical, theoretical, and aesthetic narrative of the development of modern art. This book suggests why a certain kind of extended dwelling in contemporary art is important for both church and culture. The rich complexity of the Christian faith unfolds over time as the church engages in cultural practices. It is my conviction that the Christian faith will yield new fruit through its participation in the life of modern and contemporary art. And likewise, it is also my conviction that the contemporary art world will benefit from such an engagement, that it in fact needs the robust contours and textures of the Christian faith to deepen its own practices.

What is distinctive about this book is my vocational location. Before assuming my current position of assistant professor of modern and contemporary art history, criticism, and theory at the University of Nebraska at Omaha, I was, for over ten years, curator of modern and contemporary art at a university art museum. I mounted nearly a dozen exhibitions per year, worked with many contemporary artists, and did a substantial amount of critical writing on contemporary art. I am also trained as a historian of modern art, and my particular area of specialization is art criticism since 1945. In addition to curatorial and scholarly projects, I have taught as an adjunct in a graduate studio art program, teaching art history seminars and working with art students who themselves are struggling with what it means to be an artist and what it means to make art, not to mention the spiritual questions that consequently emerge. Unlike most other commentators on modern and contemporary art in the church, I am neither a philosopher nor a theologian, and therefore my interest in art is not from the vantage point of aesthetics or "theology and the arts." Both perspectives, the former in philosophy departments and the latter in seminaries, have tended to over-determine or over-inflect discourse on modern and contemporary art as an annex of theology or philosophy. Modern and contemporary art is what I practice—as a teacher, curator, critic, and art historian. It is where, to quote the pagan poet in Acts 17:28, I "live and move and have [my] being." It is where and how I live out my vocation as a Christian. I do not need warrant from philosophy or theology to practice modern and contemporary art. And so the essays in this book, although they reflect philosophical and theological perspectives, are not a covert attempt to attain philosophical and theological justification or to practice philosophy and theology by other means. The question, then, that the essays in this book pursue is not *whether* but *how*.

My practice as a curator involves serving as a translator for many diverse and often mutually exclusive publics and audiences. This book is no different. I seek the impossible goal of addressing theologians and philosophers, average Christians interested in the arts and culture, art students studying at Christian colleges, art students of Christian faith studying in non-Christian educational contexts, arts ministry leaders and participants in the emergent movement, and perhaps even artists or critics outside the church who are interested in the explosion of things spiritual and religious in the contemporary art world or who might have grown bored with current ways of thinking about contemporary art and thus are eager for fresh directions.

This book refers to numerous artists and works of art that because of space and cost constraints cannot be reproduced. Therefore, it should be read in conjunction with a good art history textbook with plenty of high-quality illustrations, such as *Art Since 1900*, written by Hal Foster, Rosalind Krauss, Yves-Alain Bois, and Benjamin Buchloch, or *Modern Art*, by Sam Hunter, John Jacobus, and Daniel Wheeler. There are no shortcuts to understanding as complex a cultural practice as art, and therefore these essays are intended only to contribute to the reader's education whatever his or her stage.

Whether or not one agrees with my conclusions or my interpretations of specific artists and works of art as I bend them toward Christ, naming the unknown god of modern and contemporary art, my wager is that my critical approach is expansive enough to encourage and stimulate further and deeper reflection on and experience of one of the least understood but powerful mechanisms of modern (and postmodern) culture.

My primary argument is that since most Christian commentators have been theologians, philosophers, and "Christian artists," there has been a remarkable lack of interpretive charity granted to modern and contemporary art as a whole. This lack of charity, however, is remarkably ecumenical, cutting across lines that usually divide mainline Protestants, Catholics, evangelicals, and the Orthodox. However, this ecumenism is derived less from the Nicene faith of the church fathers than it is from contemporary (secular) cultural discourse, which is deeply suspicious of high art in general and modern art more specifically, and which has developed a shrill polemics in public discourse that has grown immune to subtleties, qualifications, nuances, and ambivalences. Subsequently, most Christian commentators rarely address modern art on its own terms, within its own framework of critical evaluation. Rather, those commentators produce theology, philosophy, apologetics, or politics that rely on—or even require—a superficial understanding of modern and contemporary art. They do not produce art criticism. This book is nothing if not criticism of modern and contemporary art, criticism, however, that is nourished by a Nicene Christianity that seeks to embrace all that is good, true, and beautiful and to reveal, quite possibly, that some artists are "not far from the kingdom" (Mark 12:34).[2]

But it is not enough merely to offer an alternative narrative of the history of modern and contemporary art. Art needs to be engaged and experienced. This book is an attempt to chart ways to do this, revealing the rewards and challenges involved in taking every thought captive and receiving contemporary art as a manifestation of God's gracious gifts, revealing contemporary art itself to be gift, albeit one that needs to be named as both a gift and a gift *from God.*

An important consequence of the church's approach to modern and contemporary art is that in its commentators' zeal to engage it through certain philosophical, theological, or political perspectives, they have tended to reduce art to visual illustrations of propositional truths better expressed in other forms, usually words. This kind of soft iconoclasm, which is distrustful of letting art be art, has led to an impoverished ability to experience both the aesthetic presence of much of modern and contemporary art and to write about it allusively, expansively, and suggestively, recognizing that art is a distinctive mode of cognition and knowledge about the world.[3] As George Steiner provocatively observed, art is a dangerous thing that can take over our inner house and transform us.[4]

For art to work, we need to be receptive to this "danger" of transformation, trusting that our Christian faith—which is more than a philosophy, worldview, political perspective, or a theory of culture—is strong enough to handle it and that our own appropriation of the faith can become stronger, more supple, and more nuanced in the process. In this way, we may "grasp how wide and long and high and deep is the love of Christ" (Eph. 3:18) and in the process discover for ourselves how much wider, longer, higher, and deeper is the faith that we claim to know. Too often commentators on modern and contemporary art have approached the subject with a rigidly stable "Christian perspective" that is then merely applied to art. Little, if any, commentary reflects a dialogical and dialectical relationship with modern and contemporary art, in which the art is able to exert some counterpressure, stretching and shaping this "perspective."

This has indeed been my experience, for both my understanding of modern and contemporary art and my participation in the Christian faith have undergone significant and, at times, unexpected and uncomfortable changes. My practice of the Christian faith has become, as a consequence, more premodern and more ancient.[5] My experience of certain currents in contemporary art has provoked me to attempt to retrieve the ancient fullness of the faith as a network of robust liturgical, sacramental, and ascetic practices. Far from being out of step with the art world, this ancient, robust faith and practice might in fact offer a provocative framework for understanding contemporary art.[6]

An important part of this study's critical framework is the recognition of a distinction between *contemplation* and *communication*. From secular and Christian contexts, art is too often assumed to be merely verbal communication pursued by other (and inferior) means, that the artist is trying to send "messages" that we as viewers must receive and understand linguistically. This is distinctly not the case with art. Art requires contemplation that focuses attention on the viewer developing a relationship with the work of art, not merely passively receiving a message. Starting with the Reformers of the sixteenth century, particularly the Lutheran polemicists, art has tended to be viewed as a form of communication that serves specific educational ends. A Christian faith, however, that is creedal and conciliar has the resources—the very mind of the church at its disposal—to recognize the importance of contemplation as a spiritual discipline that can underwrite and manifest itself in artistic practice. This study pursues that course.

But this expansive, receptive, and hermeneutically open way of experiencing modern and contemporary art, which privileges contemplation as a spiritual and aesthetic virtue, does not merely baptize all modern and contemporary art for Christ, equating the movement of the Holy Spirit with the movement of a particular aesthetic practice of high culture. It instead offers a basis to discern what is worth our effort to understand and for what reasons.

Structure of the Book

This book consists of seven essays that address separate subjects from quite different vantage points, yet taken as a whole they form a comprehensive though idiosyncratic critical engagement with modern and contemporary art. These essays speak to the importance of a distinctive, yet expansive, Christian critical reception of modern and contemporary art. A narrow, monolithic "Christian perspective" will not be prepared or even concerned to name the altars to the unknown god that populate the landscape of modern and contemporary art.

Chapter 1 lays the conceptual framework for the remainder of the essays by providing historical, philosophical, and theological considerations. First, I discuss what art is and its relationship to other forms of visual imagery. What historical practices and traditions do I mean when I refer to "modern and contemporary art"? Second, it offers an explanation of the philosophical and theoretical underpinnings of my approach to art as a curator and critic. What is my working definition of art? And third, it explores the theological implications of icons in the Eastern Church and their potential for aiding the experience of modern and contemporary art. The "economy" of the icon can provide an important foundation on which to rethink modern and contemporary art.[7]

The one holy catholic and apostolic church, embodied and preserved in the conciliar Christianity of the seven councils from Nicaea I in the fourth century to Nicaea II in the eighth century, offers significant and provocative resources for approaching modern and contemporary art. Protestant approaches are simply not expansive enough. Although this is merely my own conclusion, the fact that there are very few professionally trained historians of modern and contemporary art (i.e., with doctorates in modern and contemporary art) teaching at evangelical Christian colleges, and little Christian (evangelical or other) scholarship being produced by historians of modern and contemporary art, might offer empirical evidence that my view has some basis in truth.

Be that as it may, the vast majority of Protestant approaches to modern and contemporary art, particularly those of the Reformed and evangelical persuasion, have taught a generation of Christians to avoid the subject altogether. And despite the flourishing of Christian colleges and the explosion of evangelical approaches to visual culture and the arts as part of the revival of the evangelical mind, the lack of critics and historians of modern and contemporary art and the paucity of modern and contemporary art history classes taught at these colleges is ample evidence of the continued success of Protestant approaches to avoid in-depth confrontation with the subject.

The focus on icons is an effort to retrieve premodern Christianity for the contemporary situation. As James K. A. Smith argues in his book on postmodernism and the church, "a thoughtful engagement with postmodernism will encourage us to look backward. . . . Ancient and medieval sources provide a useful countervoice to modernity."[8] Therefore, if we take the history of Christianity and the church seriously, if we embrace the creeds of Nicaea-Constantinople, Chalcedon, and Ephesus (as evangelicals are rediscovering the dogmatic importance of the Mother of God), then we might likewise benefit from Nicaea II, from the ancient church's advocacy of the use of icons not merely as aesthetic teaching tools, but as dogmatic markers of Christology and witnesses to the kingdom to come.

Chapter 2 offers an alternative history and theory of the development of modern art, revealing that Christianity has always been present with modern art, nourishing as well as haunting it, and that modern art cannot be understood without understanding its religious and spiritual components and aspirations. These religious and spiritual components, even when Christians claim to reject them, remain distinctively Christian.

Originally published in *Religion and the Arts* in the spring of 2006, chapter 3 considers a single painting by Enrique Martínez Celaya, using it as a window through which to view his artistic practice as structured and shaped by a religious worldview, a practice that is best understood through the lens of Christian thought. It also explores and assesses the impact this painting has had on my own development as an art critic and as a Christian. This essay was the product of several years of research and reflection beginning in 2001 on Martínez Celaya's artistic practice and its implications for my developing thoughts on Christianity and contemporary art. It also marks my initial foray into this line of thinking. Therefore, it is reprinted here, with only slight modifications, to give a record of my development and to provide an in-depth exploration of an artist whose work has been instrumental to my own work. A reader with experience in modern and contemporary art might read this chapter first as a way to track the development of my thought.

Chapter 4 moves outward from a single artist and work of art to consider the theme of "embodied transcendence" in contemporary art and how this "material spirituality" is evidenced in the work of a number of contemporary artists, several of whom would eschew the spiritual or religious nature and connotations of their work. This chapter also charts the interest in things spiritual and religious in contemporary art of the last twenty years and relates that interest to the history of modern art.

Chapter 5 examines the role and function of art criticism in modern and contemporary art, which has been long misunderstood by Christian commentators. This chapter rehearses the narrative of criticism's emergence as a distinctly modern literary genre and explores its diverse purposes. Oscar Wilde once quipped that it is much more difficult to write about a thing than to do it. This chapter reflects on and draws out the serious implications of this instructive aphorism. In addition, this chapter addresses the relationship between the work of art and artistic intention, particularly as that intention is manifest in what the artist says about the meaning of his or her work of art. In addition, this chapter explores the role of the church as an engine for cultural critique.

Chapter 6 explores the relationship between modern and contemporary art and the church, particularly as it relates to the liturgy. It leans heavily on some of the insights of Radical Orthodoxy advocates, including John Milbank, Graham Ward, Catherine Pickstock, and James K. A. Smith.[9] When the visual arts and the church are discussed, it is most often in the context of using art to enhance the worship experience, which is often shaped by the tendency to conflate aesthetic practices with the spiritual disciplines. This chapter addresses this common problem in the contemporary church from a very different perspective, one that sets up this relationship quite differently, and draws some surprising conclusions.

And finally, the conclusion sharpens my point and adds considerably more torque to the implications of the previous essays by interrogating a mysterious creature, the "Christian artist," which, like Bigfoot, seems everywhere present but nowhere seen. Both Francis Schaeffer and H. R. Rookmaaker devoted a considerable amount of time to discussing this creature, and organizations such as Christians in the Visual Arts (CIVA) and the underlying art education philosophy of the Christian College Consortium assume its existence as an article of faith. This chapter examines this creature and whether it is a figment of our imagination that does more harm than good as we proceed in and through contemporary art.

Eastern Orthodox liturgical theologian Alexander Schmemann once observed that a Christian sees Christ everywhere.[10] This is especially relevant for this study, which is about seeing with the eyes of faith—as the defenders of the icons put it—which opens up the world in order not only to name those altars made to unknown gods but also to see the world the way it truly is, full of Jacob's ladders, with commerce from the angelic realms. The distance between the immanent and the transcendent, between the material and the spiritual, is wafer thin. A Christian, then, does not merely believe a certain dogma, but has a transformed vision, one that sees the world as it truly is, as Christ's footstool, as the sanctuary of God, that is, the world that icons depict. Ultimately, this is the lesson of the economy of the icon. In the words of the psalmist, with all the sacramental echoes of the Eucharistic liturgy, "taste and *see* that the Lord is good" (Ps. 34:8, emphasis added).

1

Overture

Some of the most deep-seated pleasures of our natural selves . . . involve appetites
that had to be educated. If these pleasures are rooted in crude instinct, they
nonetheless grow in depth and power as we acquire hierarchies of discrimina-
tion, until second nature is nowhere separable from the first. Yet visual art—and
abstract art most particularly—remains one of the last bastions of unashamed,
unrepentant ignorance, where educated experience can still be equated with
phony experience. . . . This syndrome becomes ever more acute as the tradition
gets fatter and the works get leaner.

Kirk Varnedoe, *Pictures of Nothing*

Art is a deceptive cultural practice. On one hand, it is ubiquitous in popular
culture. Art museums attract thousands of visitors, and local community arts
projects abound. And with the current interest in the "creative class" and the
"creative turn" in the corporate world, art, as a manifestation of creativity,
is good for business.[1] But it is rarely defined. We seem to know what art is
when we see it; or, perhaps more accurately, we know what it isn't. On the
other hand, there are few cultural practices that have such a wide disparity
and disconnection between the populace and the specialists, who are almost
universally assumed to be irrelevant to understanding and appreciating art.[2]

Any talk of art's complexity and difficulty seems to fly in the face of its accessible, fun, "child-friendly" nature, which is the message communicated by museums and local arts organizations. By and large, art's popularity is derived primarily from its instrumentality as an economic tool for the chamber of commerce.

Art might be popular, but it is poorly understood, in large part because its historical and philosophical conditions are believed to be unnecessary for its appreciation. At the risk of being considered an elitist, I argue that such conditions must be understood. This popular understanding of art also manifests an arrogance that restricts art's horizon, limiting it to a form of decoration, cultural symbolism, or the like. Viewing and understanding art, as much as practicing it, requires hard work and discipline. The common assumption that modern and contemporary artists ignore their audiences ignores this fact. Therefore, it is important to lay some initial groundwork before an exploration of modern and contemporary art can begin in earnest.

Modern Art as Museum Art

The arts are very much a part of the contemporary church. But when the arts are referred to or discussed, it is often in one of two ways. First is within the context of worship, that is, what kinds of art will be incorporated into a worship service. Most often, this has to do with artistic practices that have no direct resemblance to the subject of this book: music, banners, dance, film clips, film stills, graphic design, or clip art downloaded from the Internet. Outside the church, Christian attention to the arts has primarily to do with music and film, a concern, incidentally, that reflects their popularity and ubiquity in the larger culture. Although the kind of art I deal with influences these art forms, this book is not about them.

This book is about museum art.[3] It is "high" or "fine" art. It is art made, as Nicholas Wolterstorff observes in *Art in Action*, for "contemplation."[4] This has made Christian commentators, particularly of the evangelical persuasion, nervous. It appears elitist. Huge swaths of visual images are ignored and subjugated to some practice that is considered higher, finer, and part of a practice of high culture that is enjoyed by very few. It is therefore neither populist nor democratic, which also violates key tenants of American religious experience. Even Wolterstorff restricts high art's importance, emphasizing that it is just one of the many ways that art functions.

This reflects a societal bias as well. Absurd and scandalous works of art, inflated auction prices, public controversies such as the Sensations exhibition at the Brooklyn Museum of Art, and an idealized and mystified lost "Golden Age" of the (pre-Reformation) past when high art was sponsored by the church and was accessible to the "average person," conspire to reinforce a deeply negative and suspicious view of museum art produced since 1900. This need not be the case. It is perhaps worth mentioning that both Hitler and Stalin condemned modern art as "degenerate," a fact that should provoke us to reflect on the origins of and reasons for our negative views of modern art.

The history and development of the art museum is an inextricable part of the history and development of modern and contemporary art. The public art museum developed as part of the political and cultural imperialism of France, England, and Germany in the early nineteenth century, when cultural artifacts from around the world were brought to these institutions for public display. What emerged was a distinctive tradition of experiencing them aesthetically, which de-emphasized the particularities and distinctives of history and culture that laid the groundwork for the development of modern art.[5]

This development evolved with, and in opposition to, the academy. As Egyptian, Assyrian, and Greek antiquities along with medieval altarpieces, icons, and Renaissance portraiture came to be interpreted within an internationalist, transhistorical modern aesthetic, a living tradition was established that was so powerful that the French realist Gustave Courbet could encourage art students to study with the "old masters" in the museums rather than with the faculty at the academy.[6] This living tradition of museum art came to exert a shaping influence on emerging modern artists in the mid-nineteenth century, who self-consciously submitted to this living tradition as the interpretive framework for their artistic practice. Products of aesthetic work by artists participating in this living tradition are responses to and critiques of this tradition, extending it, deepening it. As T. S. Eliot remarked in his essay "Tradition and the Individual Talent" (1917), the individual artist achieves his identity as an individual by participating in a historical tradition.[7]

Museum art, then, is a profoundly historical practice with a developed tradition, a living tradition of the dead rather than a dead tradition of the living, to paraphrase Jaroslav Pelikan's famous description of the church's Holy Tradition. That much of modern art appears to many museum- and gallery-goers as strange and arbitrary has much to do with not knowing the living tradition out of which such work emerges and into which artists, curators, and critics are baptized. That most are not a part of this living tradition does not invalidate its integrity. For example, that T. S. Eliot's *The Wasteland* or James Joyce's *Ulysses* requires extensive notes to explain references and allusions does nothing to undermine the fact that Eliot and Joyce were working within a living tradition. It just so happens that this living tradition is not the one of most contemporary readers, neither in Eliot's or Joyce's time nor in our own.

Modern art's profoundly historical character has given rise to important philosophical reflection on the nature of art. Philosopher Jerrold Levinson argues that art's historicity is the defining and distinguishing characteristic of what art is and how it is identified.[8] In addition to this historical aspect, two different and, at times, competing, ways of thinking about art have informed my own work as a curator, critic, and art historian: philosophical considerations and theological reflections.

Philosophical Considerations

Art is not only a cultural practice, it is also an institutional practice. Therefore, any discussion of art must take into account its institutional framework. Modern art's primary institutional framework is the art museum. Modern art and its living tradition exists not only *invisibly* in the hearts and minds of its practitioners and participants but also embodied, mediated in and through its *visible* public institutions. And it is in fact this public or outward manifestation that produces the private and inward experience of art.[9] What art is, then, is defined through a public network and not merely by private assertion or opinion.

Moreover, what art is cannot be derived exclusively from what it looks like—what philosopher George Dickie calls its "exhibited qualities"—because many examples of modern art look very similar, if not identical, to objects and images that are not considered art. Examining art's institutional framework enables those qualities that are *unexhibited* to be more proactively constitutive of what art is. These unexhibited qualities are the attitudes, beliefs, intentions, assumptions, and practices that are absorbed in the very institutions that produce, shape, nourish, display, and interpret art. Moreover, it is these unexhibited qualities that connect artistic practice with other cultural practices. The Russian art historian, mathematician, Orthodox priest, and martyr Pavel Florensky observed that "for better or worse, the work of art is the center of an entire cluster of conditions, which alone make possible its existence as something artistic; outside of its constitutive conditions it simply does not exist as art."[10]

An influential, albeit much criticized, definition of art is the *institutional* definition, whose primary adherent is George Dickie. He was influenced by Arthur Danto's essay "The Artworld," published in 1964. Danto's essay was an attempt to reflect philosophically on a single problem: how could Andy Warhol's plywood *Brillo Box* be understood as a work of art since it is virtually (visually) identical in every way to a simple cardboard Brillo box? "To see something as art," Danto observes, "requires something the eye cannot decry—an atmosphere of artistic theory, a knowledge of the history of art: an art world."[11] The difference, for Danto and especially for Dickie, is that Warhol's reliance on the familiarity of the ordinary object provides the interpretive ground for his hand-painted copy of the mass-produced original and becomes art when it is placed in a museum/gallery space that invites and provokes certain responses on the part of the viewer. The viewer, in short, responds to it as a work of art by contemplating its union of form and content, which Warhol produced, in a particular way and by reflecting on this experience as a distinctively aesthetic experience. For Danto, it is the presence of interpretation and theory that enables an object to become a work of art. For Dickie it is the museum/gallery space that enables this transformation. It is this space, as a literal and conceptual space, that shapes both artistic practice and audience response.[12]

Although Danto's test cases were Robert Rauschenberg and Andy Warhol, for Dickie it is Marcel Duchamp who is the prototype artist who reveals that art is an institutional practice. It is important for the purposes of this book that Warhol and Duchamp are the lenses through which Dickie and Danto view contemporary art, since these two artists are perhaps the most vilified by Christian commentators of any twentieth-century artists. This has much to do with the philosophy of art that many of these commentators utilize as well as the historical narratives of modern art that view Warhol and Duchamp in decidedly uncharitable ways. A more empathetic interpretation of both Warhol and Duchamp will acknowledge the importance of a robust living tradition of high art within which both artists worked, even while they critiqued and undermined certain of its aspects.[13]

That high art—museum art—has for over two centuries developed a living tradition that functions institutionally has important ramifications for Christian reflection on contemporary art. Museum art developed only with the emergence of museums. Thus art is but one manifestation and embodiment of a certain kind of aesthetic practice. Although this subject will be discussed in greater detail in chapter 2, it is important that modern art is not regarded merely as an abrogation of its divinely appointed place in the church. Human institutions are neither purely good nor purely bad. They are means by which human persons work out the cultural mandate in community (Gen. 1:28).

Modern art as an institutional and historical practice, defined in and through the museum, is no different. Not all products of modernity are theologically and spiritually suspect. The development of modern art offered a particular opportunity to address certain distinctive features of aesthetic practice and visual representation that were not given preeminence in other institutional manifestations of aesthetic practice, including the church.

A distinctive characteristic of modern art is the preeminent role aesthetic practice plays in the development of the self and its relationship to the world. This aspect of our humanity is given sharp focus and attention in and through the institution of high art. This aesthetic or stylistic aspect of our humanity has received broad-based attention from the church fathers, who understood individual Christians to be shaping themselves into icons of Christ through spiritual formation, to Jean-Paul Sartre's belief that our lives, as products of our decisions, are works of art. This characteristic has also received considerable popular attention recently, in works such as Virginia Postrel's *The Substance of Style*, and is confirmed through Robert Wuthnow's sociological research on the role of the arts (very broadly speaking) as a practice that forms identity.[14] The modern institution of high art draws particular attention to the role of aesthetic practice in human development, and as such, it has become, under the conditions of modernity, a significant framework for such reflection.

Institutional theories of art account for the role of museums and galleries, interpreters, and other non-aesthetic aspects of art that participate in constituting what art is, so that, to quote Danto, "nothing the Brillo people can make will be art while Warhol can do nothing but make art."[15] But institutional theories do not offer sufficient analysis of the mechanics of producing and experiencing art. This is perhaps not surprising, since theories of art most often have emerged as means to accommodate the most recent of artistic developments that challenge established philosophical frameworks for understanding art.[16] Institutional theories emerged in an effort to comprehend and interpret the work of Warhol and Duchamp, two artists for whom it is said that art was often more interesting to think about than to look at.[17]

The institutional approach to art locates a break between the modern notion of high art as being true art and premodern visual representation—which functions within other institutional frameworks such as the church—as being something else. Given this, some will assume that the term "art" cannot be applied to premodern visual representation, that art is a modern, Western (i.e., Eurocentric) concept. Although such an institutional approach is helpful in clarifying and distinguishing important differences in visual practices, there is a certain intrinsic meaning in visual representation, or aesthetic embodiment, that a *hard* contextualism such as the institutional theory cannot recognize.

Philosopher Paul Crowther offers a complement to relativistic approaches to art, such as the institutional theory, that pay insufficient attention to what occurs cognitively in the process of producing and experiencing art. Influenced by the thoroughly embodied phenomenology of Maurice Merleau-Ponty, Crowther develops what he calls the "ecological theory of art," which involves the development of the self through creative and imaginative interaction with the environment. Crowther addresses the important role that art plays in the growth of self-consciousness as the embodied self interacts with the world aesthetically. For Crowther, art possesses "phenomenological depth" because it has a "cognitive richness" since "we comprehend the world aesthetically, in ways that cannot be derived from other forms of knowledge and artifice."[18] Crowther observes that "it is the integral fusion of the sensuous and the conceptual which enables art to express something of the depth and richness of body-hold in a way which eludes modes of abstract thought—such as philosophy."[19] What is important for Crowther is that visual representation, as made manifest by art, is not merely an institutional practice but fulfills basic human needs such as affirming bodily presence and bodily knowledge, what Crowther calls "body-hold." Art imaginatively projects a harmonious relationship between the subject and object of experience, which reconciles the self to the other in the preservation of human experience. Crowther thus locates art's significance in the practice of its making and its experiencing. It "brings rational and sensuous material into an inseparable and mutually enhancing relation."[20]

Significantly, Crowther also argues that this relationship is at its foundation a transcendent one. A work of art enables the self to move beyond and outside itself toward another object, and this process has a significant impact on the self's development toward a reconciled relationship with the world. This transcendent relationship makes love possible—which is nothing if not transcendent—by helping us move beyond ourselves toward our neighbor and toward God. Philosopher William Desmond affirms and extends Crowther's views. For

Desmond, it is the space between Self and Other, what he calls the "metaxu," the rich "between" in which art, religion, and philosophy dwell.[21]

Crowther's ecological approach to art offers what he calls a "transcultural" definition of visual representation, of which the Western institution of high art is but a particular manifestation. Crowther argues that all cultures believe something important takes place in visual representation. Most cultures recognize that this importance is distinctively powerful, magical, and religious. This is not because these cultures are primitive or unenlightened but simply because what makes visual representation significant—that it offers a unique and complex "hypostatic union" between sensuous material and rational ideas—is inexplicable and thus named "religious."

This mysterious, hypostatic union is the source of high art's power. Crowther argues that the institution of high art acknowledges this mysterious power, which has given rise to the close relationship between art and religion that has preoccupied artists and critics since the advent of modernism. But it has been named the "aesthetic," and the museum is the place where such inherently religious experience is called an "aesthetic experience." Still, the inherently religious—even magical or mystical—nature of aesthetic experience, as a distinct embodiment of the hypostatic union, remains.

Whether a pre-Columbian artifact, African statue, medieval altarpiece, or a Byzantine icon is "art" in the modern institutional sense of the term, all these are visual representations and thus bear a transhistorical and transcultural relationship not only to each other but also to the artifacts made in and for the modern institution of art, because of the common (universal) human practice of making and experiencing. This offers a foundation for a normative aesthetics that can better enable cross-cultural comparisons of visual representations without imposing a modern Western view of art onto them or exaggerating their differences.

What is important to consider in these theories of art is that there has been no discussion of what art is supposed to look like and whether art is supposed to be mimetic (that is, representational, which is the conventional assumption of art's significance—that it makes images of the world that look *real* or that correspond to what is empirically seen). Unfortunately, the assumption that art is supposed to be representational, that its images are representations of what is seen and experienced empirically in the world, is often given moral, ethical, and spiritual justification so that representational art is life- or creation-affirming while abstract art is nihilistic and creation-denying.

This is simply not the case. And it was not the case for the Classical Greeks, from whom we receive much information about the remarkable likenesses of their aesthetic creations, whether birds trying to nest in a painting of a tree or a young man falling in love with a sculpture of a woman.

> Your artists, then, like Phidias and Praxiteles, went up, I suppose, to heaven and took a copy of the forms of the gods, and then reproduced these by their art, or was there any other influence which presided over and guided their moulding? There was, said Apollonius. . . . Imagination wrought these works, a wiser and subtler artist by far than imitation; for imitation can only create as its handiwork what it has seen, but imagination equally what it has not seen; for it will conceive of its ideal with reference to the reality.[22]

Visual art was recognized, then, as being more than something that depicts outward, observable forms; it also consists of imaginative projection. The history and development of modern and contemporary art necessitate that we understand that representational art requires imaginative projection while abstract art requires representation of some kind; in other words, abstract art is representational in different ways from representational or figurative art.[23] This dialectic between abstraction and representation, between outward form and inner feeling or spirit or imagination, will be discussed in greater depth in chapter 2. Furthermore, this dialectic between representation and imagination or abstraction is fundamental for understanding the economy of the icon.[24]

My working definition of art is thus derived in part from both a moderate institutional theory that recognizes the important role that the museum space plays in determining meaning and mediating a history, tradition, and theory of what occurs in that space, and an ecological theory of art that affirms that in its making and viewing, art does something to and with the self, projecting an imaginative world of thought in aesthetic form that is necessary for human development. The transhistorical nature of visual representation offers a basis for reflecting on modern and contemporary art through the theory and practice of the icon because its primary goal is to seek communion with God. Its foundation is prayer.

Artistic practice, then, is utopian. It recognizes that the world is not as it should be. And it therefore projects alternative worlds. Russian filmmaker Andrei Tarkovsky once said, echoing Dostoyevsky and other Russian thinkers, that if the world were perfect there would be no need for art. Art is a witness to both our fallen world and hope for its redemption. In a bracing introduction to the work of Lithuanian poet Tomas Venclova, Russian-born poet Joseph Brodsky declares, "Art is a form of resistance to the imperfection of reality as well as an attempt to create an alternative reality, an alternative that one hopes will possess the hallmarks of a conceivable, if not an achievable, perfection."[25]

Theological Reflections

In *The Crossing of the Visible*, a provocative book about images, icons, and idols, the phenomenologist and Roman Catholic thinker Jean-Luc Marion observed, almost in passing, that

> the image-affirming doctrine of the Second Council of Nicaea concerns not only nor first of all a point in the history of ideas, nor even a decision of Christian dogma: it formulates above all an—perhaps the only—alternative to the contemporary disaster of the image. In the icon, the visible and the invisible embrace each other from a fire that no longer destroys but rather lights up the divine face for humanity.[26]

This study takes seriously Marion's observation that the theory of images articulated in the Second Council of Nicaea—which in AD 787 reestablished the orthodoxy of icons, the holy images of Christ, Mary the *Theotokos*, the angels, and the saints for use in church worship and private devotion, and reversed the iconoclastic council of 754—can make a significant contribution to the study of contemporary art.[27] The key principle of icon veneration is that the honor shown to the image is transferred to the prototype, and whoever honors an image honors the person represented by it. The icon (*eikon*, "image"), then, is a material means of grace, a pointer through which devotion, contemplation, and communion with God are enacted. It is the sacramental presence of a transcendent world.

St. John of Damascus, the foremost defender of icons in the eighth century, laid out the several different images. The first image, what John calls the "natural image," is the image of the Son. The second image is God's predetermined will, the images that he will bring about. The third image is humanity as the image of God. The fourth image is found in the Scriptures: the use of figures, forms, and shapes that depict "faint conceptions of God." The fifth kind of image is also found in the Scriptures: images that prefigure the incarnation of Christ. The sixth and last kind of image is made up of those that recall the memory of past events either in words (Scriptures) or images. John's conclusion is "receive each [form of image] in the reason and manner fitting to each."[28]

An exploration of the economy of the icon is not possible without the study of iconoclasm, which was an organized movement against images used in worship that began in earnest during the eighth century in Constantinople. Although it was ultimately defeated by the church in 847, it lingered, only to reemerge with a vengeance in the West during the Reformation in the mid-sixteenth century.[29] Significantly, both iconoclasm and iconophilia trace their roots to Neoplatonic thought, particularly as it is manifest in Origen.[30] They are therefore two sides of the same coin. Cultures, communities, and institutions are *simultaneously* iconoclastic and iconophiliac.

Nicene Christianity does not merely tolerate images in the church. It *requires* them. Icons are not an alien Eastern addition to Nicene Christianity, but its essence. The Council of 787 in Nicaea, the seventh and last ecumenical council of the church, was an affirmation of the Nicene faith as embodied in the economy of the icon. Religious imagery, particularly the holy icons, was considered to be dogma in paint, painted Scriptures. Canon 82 of the Council in Trullo (691–92) forbids a symbolic representation of Christ as a lamb because it was a "type" or "image" of the coming Christ who has already come and thus should be depicted as a man in "remembrance of His incarnation, passion and redeeming death, and of the universal redemption, thereby accomplished."[31] One need not be chrismated in the Eastern Orthodox Church or be a cradle Roman Catholic to draw from the riches of this too-often ignored history of the church. The Protestant practice of freely appropriating from church tradition, which has culminated in what the late Robert Webber called "ancient-future faith," certainly legitimates the appropriation and adaptation of the economy of the icon for Protestant use.[32]

This aesthetic economy rests first and foremost on the cosmic implications of the incarnation of Jesus Christ, which did not merely or only effect our salvation, it renewed all of creation, bringing the creation itself, to quote St. Athanasius, into the eternal triune relationship of Father, Son, and Holy Spirit.[33] St. John of Damascus argues for the importance of Christ's incarnation for the veneration of icons.

Of old, God the incorporeal and formless was never depicted, but now that God has been seen in the flesh and has associated among human kind, I depict what I have seen of God. I do not venerate matter but I venerate the fashioner of matter, who became matter for my sake and accepted to dwell in matter and through matter worked my salvation, and I will not cease from reverencing matter, through which my salvation was worked.[34]

A key aspect of the theory and practice of icon veneration is that the material world is not, as Greek philosophy assumed, a burden that must be abandoned or transcended in order to achieve communion with God or participate in his divine nature (2 Pet. 1:4).[35] The material immanence of the world is the very means by which divine transcendence is or can be experienced. It is precisely at this point that Christianity critiqued and transformed Hellenic thought. Since the Son, the divine Logos, has put on creation through the incarnation, this is especially the case in the new covenant. Mocking his iconoclastic opponents as super-spiritual, St. John admits that, "since I am a human being and wear a body, I long to have communion in a bodily way with what is holy and to see it. Condescend to my lowly understanding, O exalted one, that you may preserve your exaltedness."[36] St. John's affirmation of the material world as the means of God's grace is repeated seven centuries later when Martin Luther returned to Wittenberg from exile in 1525 to battle the iconoclastic Andreas Karlstadt and his cohorts, to whom he referred sneeringly as the "heavenly prophets."[37]

Reflection on the economy of the icon has much to recommend for a study of modern and contemporary art. From a historical point of view, the icon has never been far from the history of modern art. The development of an autonomous institution of art in the West resulted in painting that takes place on portable panels and later canvases, materials that approximated the mobility and discrete look of icon painting.[38] Modern painting could be said to be the Western equivalent of Eastern icon painting.[39]

More important is that a number of avant-garde painters during the first decades of the twentieth century, particularly the Russian painters Malevich and Kandinsky, found in icons the embodiment of spiritual power. And spiritual power—real presence—has been perhaps *the* driving force of the history and development of modern art. The avant-garde was eager to access this spiritual power and so they began to describe their paintings as iconic. In addition, they borrowed various formal compositional devices, use of color, greater self-consciousness about how they practiced their craft, even, as is evident in Malevich's exhibition practices, installing some of their paintings in the eastern corners of the gallery spaces, which followed traditional Byzantine practice. For these and many other avant-garde painters well into the twentieth century, including the Russian immigrants John Graham and Mark Rothko, modern painting functioned like an icon, creating a deeply spiritual, contemplative relationship between the object and viewer. Rothko once observed that if the viewer doesn't cry in front of his work then he or she isn't having the same experience that he had while painting it.

The historical relationship between icons and modern art is largely metaphorical. This is not to say that it is insignificant. It is a way to denote that a painting has a certain spiritual and contemplative power. In the mid-1970s critic Joseph Masheck explored the range of this metaphor, perhaps revealing the real power of the metaphor: "We apply certain notions from the earlier history of painting, especially religious painting, to present-day art, not to project meaning onto contentless forms, but to inquire into integral contents in art, at a time when early modern aspirations to a transcendental function for painting have revived."[40] Is the relationship between icon painting and Western modern painting more than metaphorical? Can "iconic" be used in a way that is more than merely allusive? Can a more concrete relationship be established between icon painting and modern and contemporary Western painting? This study takes up Marion's observation and stretches Masheck's important essay in order to find out.

Iconoclasm haunts the history of modern art just as it haunts the history of icon veneration in the church.[41] Reflection on modern artists' interests in icons provides productive insights into the religious and spiritual underpinnings of the development of modernism.

Not only are icons relevant to the study of modern art, they are relevant to the practice of contemporary Western Christianity. Eastern Orthodoxy and Eastern Christianity in general have received a considerable amount of interest, particularly among those of the emergent or "ancient-future" faith movements, for which interest in icons is part of a larger interest that includes ascetic practices, candles, incense, plain-song and chant, bowing, prostration, and other forms of ancient practice. From more mainline and seeker Protestant churches, the role of the arts in worship has become an increasingly important subject. Visual images are playing an increasingly prevalent role in Protestant churches.[42] As Protestant churches puzzle out the question of the arts in general and images more specifically in worship, the study of icons, their theory, and practice within the Eastern Church can offer significant assistance. The deep riches of dogmatic reflection on icons in the eighth and ninth centuries are not exclusively the possession of the Orthodox or Catholic traditions but part of the rich deposit of the Nicene Christian faith.

The economy of the icon operates in a worldview that is profoundly sacramental, in which the transcendent is mediated through the immanent and is recognized, experienced, and contemplated through material means. As Graham Ward observes, "To desire or to love God is to invest the world with significance, a significance which deepens the mysterious presence of things."[43] The vocation of humanity is not only as prophets who proclaim God's love and as kings who rule as God's royal representatives but also as priests who mediate between creation and Creator. Alexander Schmemann asserts:

> The first, the basic definition of man is that he is the priest. He stands in the center of the world and unifies it in his act of blessing God, of both receiving the world from God and offering it to God—and by filling the world with his eucharist, he transforms his life, the one that he receives from the world, into life in God, into communion with Him. The world was created as the "matter," the material of one all-embracing eucharist, and man was created as the priest of this cosmic sacrament.[44]

For St. John of Damascus, humanity is by its very nature a mediation of the Creator and the creation: "Man is a microcosm; for he possesses a soul and a body, and is placed between spirit and matter; he is the place in which the visible and invisible creations, the tangible and intangible creations, are linked together."[45]

Much modern and contemporary artistic practice manifests this priestly function, this yearning for a liturgical reality that reveals the world as gift and offering. Many works of modern and contemporary art manifest this reality. They are indeed poignant altars to the unknown god in aesthetic form. The challenge for the Christian art critic is to name them and testify to what they point toward, however haltingly, tentatively, and incompletely. As the psalmist Asaph observed:

> When I tried to understand all this,
> it was oppressive to me
> till I entered the sanctuary of God;
> then I understood their final destiny. (Ps. 73:16–17)

2

A History of Modern Art

There are days when [Frank] Stella goes to the Metropolitan Museum. And he sits for hours looking at the Velazquezes, utterly knocked out by them and then he goes back to his studio. What he would like more than anything else is to paint like Velazquez. But what he knows is that that is an option that is not open to him. So he paints stripes.

Michael Fried, quoted in Rosalind Krauss,
"A View of Modernism," *Artforum*

It takes years to look at a picture.

Thomas Hess, quoted
in Leo Steinberg, "The
Philosophical Brothel," *October*

Beginnings

Modern art first came to the attention of the American public in 1913. It came, as it has time and again since, through spectacle and scandal. It is a mistake to regard modern art as a development in art studios on the European continent that was foisted on an unsuspecting American public. Modern art is a product of modernism. And modernism is, as T. J. Clark observed, "our antiquity."[1] It is our legacy, part of the air we breathe. We recoil in horror or are scandalized and offended at modernity's aesthetic manifestations in high art. But we embrace, almost without reservation, modernity's aesthetic manifestations in other forms of visual culture, including advertising, film, design, and cosmetics, not to mention its presence in a multitude of other forms of social and cultural practices. We fail to realize that it is all of a piece. When the French artist Marcel Duchamp, who became the bête noire of the Armory Show in 1913, claimed that the greatest artistic achievements America had produced were plumbing and bridges, he was not simply critiquing a lack of culture. He was also observing how and in what ways the values of modernity were embodied in the United States.[2] The twentieth century shows that the American public likes its modernity everywhere but in its museum art, and this fact has been demonstrated in numerous art museum scandals and debates over eliminating federal funding for the National Endowment for the Arts.

The Armory Show was organized by artists Walt Kuhn and Arthur B. Davies, two students of Robert Henri, the leader of arguably the first modern art movement in the United States, the "Eight" or the "Ashcan school." The Armory Show, so called because it was held in the 69th Infantry Regiment Armory on Lexington Avenue and 25th Street in New York City, consisted of over one thousand works that represented nearly a century of European and American modern art, from single examples by Ingres, Delacroix, and Goya to the impressionists, postimpressionists, French symbolists such as Puvis de Chavannes and Odelin Redon, and cubists and fauvists.[3] Although not comprehensive by any means, the exhibition was organized to present independent and progressive currents in contemporary art over against the conservatism of the National Academy. It traveled to Chicago and then to Boston. The exhibition was heavily promoted in the media and elicited considerable criticism from critics and journalists jeering the "look" of the art works on display, accusing the artists of being anarchists, invading the country to wage artistic war on American values, and worse. Critic Royal Cortissoz of the *New York Tribune* condemned the Armory Show as "Ellis Island art," because the United States "is invaded by aliens, thousands of whom constitute so many acute perils to the health of the body politic. Modernism is of precisely the same heterogeneous alien origin and is imperiling the republic of art in the same way."[4]

Duchamp and his *Nude Descending a Staircase No. 2*, painted in 1912, emerged as the cause célèbre and the icon of all that was wrong with the

Armory Show. *Nude Descending a Staircase* was described by one critic as an "explosion in a shingle factory." In a manner uncannily similar to the way that both Andres Serrano's *Piss Christ* and Chris Ofili's depiction of the Holy Virgin Mary in *Prince Among Thieves* became media icons that embodied the blasphemous corruption of the contemporary art world, *Nude Descending a Staircase* became the symbol of modern art's hucksterism, degeneracy, and elitism. What is often forgotten about the Armory Show is that it included many American artists, some of whom, including Robert Henri and most of his fellow Ashcan painters, were not involved in abstraction.[5] But it also included a number who were already working within the visual idiom of modern art, such as Marsden Hartley, John Marin, Charles Sheeler, Joseph Stella, Stanton MacDonald-Wright, and Morgan Russell.

But while the Armory Show introduced the American public to modern art, a tiny yet strong foothold of modern art already existed in the New York art world years before through the work of photographer Alfred Stieglitz and his Gallery 291. Stieglitz influenced American artists and developed American collectors through his exhibition of important European modern artists, such as Auguste Rodin, Constantin Brancusi, Francis Picabia, and Henri Matisse, along with emerging American artists Georgia O'Keeffe, John Marin, Marsden Hartley, Alfred Mauer, and many others.[6] Stieglitz's mission was to initiate American artists into the living tradition of modern art.

In 1920 Marcel Duchamp, Man Ray, and Katherine S. Dreier established the Société Anonyme, Inc., an organization founded as America's first "experimental museum" for modern art.[7] Nine years later, Alfred H. Barr Jr. was selected as the founding director of the Museum of Modern Art. His first exhibition, derived primarily from the private collections of the board, focused on the postimpressionists Gauguin, Cézanne, Seurat, and Van Gogh.[8]

Alfred Barr was born into a family that valued the Reformed doctrine of creation. His father was a Presbyterian minister who had been trained and subsequently taught at Princeton Seminary, and most of his male relatives had also been trained there. Barr himself, however, was ambivalent about his own belief. What he was not ambivalent about, though, was identifying certain connections between art and Christianity. In a letter to a friend he observed, "How can you be pessimistic if you open the shutter of your soul to beauty. . . . My Christianity is intellectual and therefore feeble. Belief is emotional and I have never had an experience strong enough to require an emotional religion."[9]

It is tempting to assume that modern art fulfilled the experiential and emotional role that Barr had expected Christianity to fulfill. Despite his ambivalence, Barr was a member of the Brick Presbyterian Church. As early as 1941, he proposed an exhibition titled "The Religious Spirit in Contemporary Art." And beginning in 1954, Barr served as head of the Commission on Art formed under the auspices of the National Council of Churches' Department of Worship and the Arts, which sought to improve the quality of Christian art and serve as an "initial attack upon the banality and saccharine vulgarity of most Christian art, particularly protestant Christian art in this country."[10] Art historian Sally Promey observes that although Barr's contemporaries often commented on his involvement in and commitment to Christianity in this public manner, scholars have not explored its implications for understanding Barr's influence.[11]

During the 1927–28 school year, when he was teaching art history at Wellesley College, Barr spent a full year traveling abroad, meeting many modern artists and architects who would become important participants and subjects in the Museum of Modern Art's projects. His trip to the Soviet Union was particularly important and formative.[12] Barr was eager to see Russian icons, which he was studying for his doctoral thesis that tracked sources for modern art. As art historian Sybil Kantor observed, "Barr's diary has as many entries on viewing icons as on viewing modern art."[13] In 1931 Barr published an in-depth review of Russian icons on display at the Metropolitan Museum in New York. Although his Calvinist leanings manifest themselves in his critique of the Russian Church's "abuse" of icons by encouraging "superstition of the most primitive order," Barr lauded the genius of Andrei Rubelev's *Old Testament Trinity* with its incomparable "detached authority."[14] Byzantine icons were formative in Barr's developing aesthetic of modern art. After his path-breaking exhibitions, "Cubism and Abstract Art" (1936) and "Fantastic Art, Dada, and Surrealism" (1937), the stage was set for New York to become the capital of the modern art world by the 1950s.

But what is modern art? Robert Storr, former curator of the Museum of Modern Art, observed, "'Modernism' is a term on which no one can agree, but one to which everyone nods in tacit understanding."[15] Modernism in art has been and remains a cluster of debates, discussions, and arguments. What follows are some general definitions that can provide more nuance to the subject than often comes from Christian commentators. Given the current interest (or horror) of the contemporary church in the opportunities (or dangers) offered by the arrival of postmodernism, it is important to define the parameters of modernism. As art historian Irving Sandler once told me, "you define modernism in order to get the postmodernism you deserve."

Definitions

What makes a work of art modern?[16] Simply put, modern art is art that is produced in the modern era under the conditions of modernity, which are the social conditions and modes of experience that are seen as the effects of the process of modernization in the West: the range of technological, economic, and political processes associated with the industrial revolution. Many scholars regard the advent of the French Revolution in 1789 as ushering in modernity. Others have begun to push the seeds of modernity back to the Reformation. High art is one of the developments of modernity. The regionalist figurative painter Thomas Hart Benton, who reacted vociferously against abstract modern art, is a modern artist in the same way that Duchamp is. They disagree only about what modern art should be.

If modern art is art produced under the conditions of modernity, how does one distinguish between Benton and Duchamp? The means for doing so invoke the concept of modernist art. According to Storr, modernist art is art

> that takes itself—as compositional techniques, methods of image making, physical presence, and constructive or destructive relation to the traditions of art—as its primary subject. Before modernist art is about anything else—an image, a symbol, the communication of an experience—it is about the logic and structure of the thing that carries meaning, and about how that thing came into being. In this respect, *all modernist art is essentially abstract, even though only some modernist art looks it* [emphasis added].[17]

Modernist art, then, is art that addresses itself first and foremost to the formal (and other) means by which a painting functions as a painting. Art historian T. J. Clark affirms Storr's conclusion: "Time and again within modernism, making convincing pictures seemed to depend on an ability to lay hold again of the fact of flatness—the object's empirical limits and resistance—and have it be interesting, even in some sense true."[18] Flatness is revolutionary in the history of Western painting, which had been dominated by the notion developed by Florentine theorist Leon Batista Alberti in his treatise *On Painting* (1435) that the painting surface is a "picture window" through which one peers into a world created by the painter through the invention of perspective.[19] The concept that the flat pictorial surface is a window is not a natural conception. It is a cultural construct that coincides closely with the development of Renaissance humanism.[20] And because of its ideological origins, which privilege empirical observation, Eastern theologians have long criticized Western painting on theological grounds precisely at the point of its excessive naturalism. In a remarkable essay on perspective, Pavel Florensky even suggests: "If you allow yourself simply to forget the formal demands of perspectival rendering for a while, then direct artistic feeling will lead everyone to admit the superiority of icons that transgress the laws of perspective."[21]

That Eastern Christian commentators have been critical of precisely the characteristic of Western painting championed by many Christian commentators in the West should remind us that flatness is not by itself nihilistic, atheistic, or otherwise anti-Christian. (Nor should Western painting be dismissed simply for its naturalism, as unfortunately too many Orthodox theologians have done.) Modernist art is often dismissed by Christian commentators because it *looks* like it is doing violence to traditional figurative art and thus by (dubious) extension doing violence to traditional (Christian) concepts of humanity and divinity. Michael Fried's poignant description of the relationship between Stella's stripes and Velasquez's paintings quoted in the epigraph flatly contradicts such thinking.[22] Modernist painting as embodied by Stella recognizes that the history of Western painting is the history of artists applying paint to a flat surface, not necessarily the history of producing *images*. It is the tense union of form and content that gives the best modernist painting its aesthetic power. Storr thus concludes: "While it is fair to say that much art made in the twentieth century is intentionally anti-modernist, one cannot say that it is antimodern. No art made in modern times is antimodern, even when it strives, as a great deal does, to flee backward in time."[23]

Modern art, modernist art, and antimodernist art are much more difficult to ascertain and interpret than Christian commentators have often assumed. Self-described Christian artists, making self-consciously Christian art in their efforts to reject what they believe is modern art, have unknowingly and problematically perpetuated the very theories and practices they claim to reject.

Modernist art is saturated with intense and passionate belief. As Clark explains,

> Abstract art, right from the moment of its inception in and around 1914, was haunted by a dream of painting at last leaving the realm of convention behind, and attaining immediacy. . . . Abstract art was late-Romantic. It thought that painting, of all the artforms, was best equipped to move signification from the realm of the discursive into that of the symbol—where symbols would simply make or be meaning, with meaning inhering in them, as substance or essence.[24]

From where does this intense, even tragic, utopianism come? It comes from the avant-garde worldview.

The concept of the avant-garde adds ideological flesh and blood to modern art, and thus it is important to devote some attention to its origins and the way it functions.[25] In 1825, the Utopian Socialist pamphleteer and engineering student Henri de Saint-Simon (1760–1825) wrote an essay called "The Artist, the Scientist, and the Industrial: Dialogue," in which he argued for a "new priest class" to lead society into the future. (The explicit Christian language that Saint-Simon adopted cannot be overlooked and will be the subject of further discussion in the next section.) In this essay, he co-opted a military term, avant-garde, for cultural use, defining avant-garde as an advance team of elite cultural combatants who would lead society into the utopian future. Saint-Simon's artist claims: "What most beautiful destiny for the arts, that of exercising over society a positive power, a true priestly function, and of marching forcefully in the van of all the intellectual faculties, in the epoch of their greatest development! This is the duty of artists, this their mission."[26]

Painters, poets, philosophers, and other public intellectuals including en-trepreneurs (interestingly enough) formed this avant-garde that produced work that would critique the status quo in an effort to improve society. This could be done most powerfully and convincingly through art: "The power of the arts is in effect the most immediate and most rapid of all powers. We have all kinds of weapons. When we wish to spread new ideas among men, we inscribe them on marble or canvas."[27] For Saint-Simon art came to serve a prophetic function in modern society. This Saint-Simonian doctrine of the avant-garde was intoxicating for artists precisely because it expanded their social role and gave their aesthetic work a larger sociopolitical relevance akin to the Old Testament prophets, the ability to shape and guide the develop-ment of society.

Perhaps the most complete embodiment of the avant-garde worldview in painting is Gustave Courbet's gigantic painting, eleven by ten feet, called *The Studio of the Painter: A Real Allegory Summing Up Seven Years of My Artistic Life* (1854–55). In this work the painter sits in the middle of the por-trait group (in his studio) representing the avant-garde (behind him) as he paints for modern bourgeois society, which he faces. A homeless street urchin represents this society and stands with Courbet looking at the landscape he paints.[28] It is this transaction, this child's experience of the painting, that promises revolution and redemption. The painting Courbet is working on is not of the nude model standing next to him (or is she his muse?); it is of the rural Franche-Comté region in France, derived from his imagination. This painting is an intensely utopian projection saturated with belief and faith in the role of the artist and the power of the work of art to effect personal and social transformation. The circumstances surrounding this painting and the context in which it was presented and experienced are an important part of the avant-garde worldview and therefore deserve special attention.

Courbet had exhibited his large realist paintings *Burial at Ornans* and *The Stonebreakers* at the Salon of 1850–51 to much scandal, given their unapologetic and intense realism, lack of sentimentality and spirituality, and flouting of academic pictorial convention. (It is ironic that realism was an early manifestation of avant-gardism.) Courbet later submitted *Burial at Ornans* and his newly finished work, *The Studio of the Painter*, to the Universal Exposition in Paris in 1855. Both works were rejected by the jury. In response he pulled the eleven of his works that had already been selected for the exhibition and set up his own solo exhibition, which he called the Realist Pavilion, adjacent to the one at the University Exposition. His exhibition consisted of forty paintings and included a manifesto about his paintings. His primary critical advocate, the critic and essayist Champfleury, called the exhibition "an incredibly audacious act; it is the subversion of all institutions associated with the jury; it is a direct appeal to the public, it is liberty, say some."[29]

Courbet's Realist Pavilion exemplifies the avant-garde desire to critique established institutions, in this case the institutions associated with training artists (the academy) and the institutions associated with presenting and evaluating art (the annual salons and other juried competitions). It also manifests the avant-garde's proclaimed desire to speak directly to culture at large, to transcend and overcome the limitations of specialization, tradition, class, and custom, limitations that constrain freedom and prevent justice. This critical spirit is also necessary for distinguishing who is part of the avant-garde.

The history of avant-garde throughout the nineteenth and twentieth centuries is not only a debate between avant-garde and the larger culture, it also consists of intramural debates among rival avant-gardists and their communities over cultural authority. Moreover, the critique of larger culture yields two results necessary for the operation of the avant-garde. First, it requires rejection by society, which, significantly, justifies the validity of avant-gardist actions. Second, it is predicated on the existence of a small community of devoted followers, a "faithful remnant" as it were, of believers within which their work is intended to be received and interpreted. Rejection of its art and ideas by society is therefore regarded by the avant-garde as a badge of honor, as justification of the very need for the avant-garde as well as revealing the contours of an avant-garde community.

This characteristic is clearly evident in the dynamics involved in the performance of Alfred Jarry's scandalous play, *Ubu roi* (1896), which began with an actor taking the stage and yelling "Merde" (shit), which caused a riot among Parisian theatergoers on opening night that ultimately shut down the performance. What is often not recalled is that Jarry had already performed the play in its entirety to his friends—members of the avant-garde—the night before.[30] So, the audience for avant-garde remains an important concern: does avant-garde communicate with the larger culture or does it communicate with its own fellow participants? This tension between audiences gets played out again and again in the history of avant-garde. Moreover, in the avant-garde vision, art (visual arts, music, theater, etc.) becomes the means to enact cultural critique in an effort to change society.

The case of Courbet's Realist Pavilion also reveals the challenges and high stakes involved in liberating oneself from establishment institutions. (Neither Courbet, who had eleven pictures accepted by the jury of the Universal Exposition, nor any other avant-gardist can completely free himself or herself from establishment institutions. In fact, they must, in some way, rely on institutional existence and power to justify their own alternatives.)

Deprived of the interpretive context provided by the 1855 Universal Exposition, Courbet was forced to create an alternative interpretive context for the reception of his paintings. This situation cannot be overemphasized. Unlike the traditional painter—the one who paints and sculpts comfortably within the institutional framework of the establishment—the avant-gardist purchases liberty and freedom at a high price: he or she must continually create and maintain interpretive contexts for the reception of his or her work. The avant-garde is not an adolescent form of rebellion with irresponsible declarations of freedom in which artists can do "whatever they want and call it art" or ignore their audience for the sake of some mystical autonomy. Avant-gardists may indeed do anything they want, but in order to call it art, or even to reject the name "art" as a description of their activities, they must create and maintain the interpretive context that makes it meaningful as a particular cultural practice. Avant-gardists must not only make art, they must also make the context within which their art must be interpreted. Far from rejecting and ignoring audiences, the avant-gardist is obsessed with audience, with creating and maintaining an audience.

For both Courbet and Jarry, then, audience is a primary preoccupation. This is why the avant-garde is also responsible for the development of new literary genres, the manifesto and the artist statement, which are additional means by which the artist defines his or her interpretive framework. Ironically, the avant-garde artist who, like Courbet, champions direct access to the work of art and its transformative powers is compelled to produce words to go along with the images. So, alongside the history of the avant-garde and its modernist stylistic developments in visual art, there is a parallel development in literature.[31]

Courbet was thus forced to produce the "Realist Manifesto" that sketched out the interpretive contours of his art as an art that is direct, empirical, and individual. Courbet's created context would be the framework for experiencing and interpreting his work, not the framework of the academy (although he presumed his audience understood and had thoroughly assimilated the framework of the academy). Without this interpretive framework, Courbet's paintings become failures of academic painting; within this interpretive framework, his paintings are manifestations of revolutionary and potentially transformative ways of seeing, thinking, and acting in the modern world. To criticize modern and contemporary artists for ignoring their audience and trading in autonomy merely shuts down the possibility of understanding the complexities of modernist and avant-garde art.

This avant-garde interpretive framework also requires assistance. The artist cannot do it alone. He must have a community of writers who can expand and flesh out his interpretive framework. This is exactly what Champfleury, Jules-Antoine Castagnary, Pierre-Joseph Proudhon, and Théophile Thoré were able to accomplish.

But while Courbet claims to paint only what he sees and rejects invention ("painting is an essentially concrete art and can only consist of the representation of real and existing things"[32]), the painting the artist is working on in his *The Studio of the Painter* is not done from observation but from recollection, imaginative projection, and even invention. This fact reveals an important tension in the history of avant-garde between artistic intention (what the artist says about his or her work) and how that work is experienced, as artists participate in defining their interpretive contexts, while works of art have a life beyond the artist's intentions.

Saint-Simon's belief that the avant-garde would serve as a new "priest class" was not merely the cynical co-optation of religious language for decidedly nonreligious purposes. Shortly before his death, Saint-Simon wrote "New

Christianity: First Dialogue," in which the "innovator" and the "conservative" discuss the innovator's claims that the church must return to the "sublime principle" that "men should treat one another as brothers."[33] Saint-Simon praises the church fathers but criticizes the post-Reformation church for encouraging disunity between laity and clergy. He lauds the Lutheran Reformation for its concern for the laity but criticizes the paucity of its worship and the overemphasis on the study of the Bible. This "new" Christianity, which would become "Christian Socialism" and have a tremendous impact on intellectuals and artists in France and Great Britain, is the larger cultural context in which to understand Saint-Simon's notion of avant-garde.

In fact, Saint-Simon broke with his disciple and adopted son, Auguste Comte, because Comte attempted to develop a purely positivistic scientific and antireligious program of social progress. Saint-Simon criticized Comte precisely because he "had neglected the religious, or imaginative and sentimental, side of human nature in his desire to reorganize society on the basis of pure reason and scientific ability."[34]

The concept of avant-garde throughout the nineteenth and twentieth centuries continued to carry with it this larger, if ambivalent, often unorthodox or heterodox Christian context, a context that cannot easily be dismissed by the avant-garde and thus requires continual conscious rejection. And, of course, even in this rejection Christianity remains. Even as rejected, it lingers to haunt the avant-gardist, for it will not be rejected completely. Ultimately, it cannot.

Secularization

Auguste Comte, the founder of modern sociology, sought in his theory of positivism to abandon the need for the spiritual in modern society. Comte claimed that modernization meant secularization, in which science, not religion, would serve as the basis of moral judgments. Generations of sociologists and social scientists found in modernity what they believed (and perhaps hoped) to be there in the first place: as modernization increased, so did secularization, that is, the gradual elimination of the authority of both organized institutional religion and personal religious belief.

Recently, sociologist Peter Berger, one of the chief proponents in the last fifty years of the secularization theory, has for all intents and purposes changed his mind.[35] Modernization did not stamp out religious institutions and religious belief. In fact, the opposite occurred. Berger says, "The world today is massively religious, is *anything but* the secularized world that had been predicted (whether joyfully or despondently) by so many analysts of modernity."[36] This raises the important question: Has religion increased in the last thirty years or has religion, both organized religion and especially personal religious piety, never gone away?

The history of modern art suffered terribly from this secularization theory of modernity, at the hands of friend and foe alike. Following modernists of the nineteenth and early twentieth centuries, who claimed for modernism the defeat of religion, Christian commentators likewise viewed modern art as the manifestation of such a reality. One wonders whether such commentators wanted a modern art that was purely anti-Christian and nihilistic in order to promote their own cultural commitments. No doubt the entrepreneur Thomas Kinkade needs such a modern art world. Kinkade brands himself in contrast to the popular perception that modern art is anti-Christian and elitist. The theory of secularization provided culturally conservative and Christian commentators on art a lens through which to view the history of modern art, a history that inevitably culminates with the decadence of the contemporary art world. For those like Kinkade, the theory of secularization is good business.

Theologian Graham Ward argues that the very existence of the secular is predicated on a Christian worldview. "In the traditional world view the *saeculum* had no autonomous existence."[37] Moreover, the secular referred to those who were not part of a monastic order. Ward also argues that the very notion of religion is defined by Christian apologetics, first used in the sixteenth century (e.g., Calvin's *Institutes of the Christian Religion*). This view, which is characteristic of the so-called Radical Orthodox theologians, is that secular modernity is deeply religious and fundamentally theological. It is, in fact, a Christian heresy, a parody of the City of God.

In many respects the secularization theory of modernity served the needs of both secularist modernists and conservative fundamentalists. Both wanted Christianity out of the secular realm. Abandoning the secularization theory has important ramifications for this study. What separates Christians from non-Christians is not that the former have religious commitments and faith while the latter do not. Both have faith; both require belief. The difference is in the nature and kind of belief. Ward argues for a new "politics of believing" as a means to develop a "softer Christian ontology."[38] Rather than talk about what is more truthful, talk about what is more believable, what is more compelling for belief.

This has important implications for understanding the history of modern art. Histories can be (and have been) written that privilege the anti-Christian, antireligious, and profoundly secular statements of the artists and critics and that interpret the works of art as visual manifestations of those beliefs. These histories of modern art have been authoritative not only in the secular contemporary art world but also among Christian intellectual communities. This is where the secular modernist and conservative and fundamentalist Christian critics embrace: neither secular scholars nor conservative Christian critics want Christianity in the history of modern art. But a history of modern art can be written that reveals that Christianity in all its myriad cultural and material manifestations is never absent from the modern artist; even when he or she rejects Christianity or aspects of Christianity, the artist uses Christian language, types, and precedents. These traces should not be ignored or dismissed.

T. J. Clark suggests that "abstract art, right from the moment of its inception in and around 1914, was haunted by a dream of painting at last leaving the realm of convention behind, and attaining immediacy."[39] This kind of immediacy is not exclusively the province of abstraction but part of the larger modernist and avant-garde project. Amid the various sociological and institutional analyses of the avant-garde vision that Courbet's *The Studio of the Artist* embodies, it is easy to overlook the most important aspect of the painting: Courbet believes that the young boy looking at his landscape painting will be transformed, converted. A boy on the margins of society, who has no education and is homeless, is transfixed by a landscape painting by one of the most famous and infamous painters of his day. This is the epitome of *immediacy*, an immediacy that converts heart, soul, and mind. Despite Courbet's antireligious perspective, he retains—even relies on—religious belief and spiritual transformation to underwrite the experience of his painting.

Nearly a century later and across the Atlantic, a very different but hauntingly similar embodiment of this immediacy is found in Mark Rothko's project for the city of Houston (fig. 1). Rothko began his career in the early 1940s, painting objects and figures enacting various dramas in a surrealistic-inspired framework. But by 1949 Rothko had abandoned the figure and figurative elements, never to return to them, and began painting very large canvases that were essentially fields of rich color. Rothko is reported to have sat in front of these canvases for days, simply looking at them, deciding what to do next. Rothko famously claimed that it is a "risky business sending a painting out into the world." For Rothko, his work was both expansive and constrictive, ephemeral and material: "Maybe you have noticed two characteristics in my paintings; either their surfaces are expansive and push outward in all directions, or their surfaces contract and rush inward in all directions. Between these two poles you can find everything I want to say."[40]

It is possible that everything he wanted to say was summed up in the so-called Rothko Chapel, which was the last project that the remarkable collectors John and Dominique de Menil worked on together.[41] Dedicated in 1971, a year after Rothko's tragic suicide and shortly before John de Menil's death, the chapel was intended to rival other great religious works by modern artists such as the Chapel of the Rosary in Venice by Henri Matisse and the Chapel of Notre Dame du Haut in Ronchamp, France, by Le Corbusier.

As Barbara Novak and Brian O'Doherty recall, "One of Rothko's many subversive comments was that his art was not 'art'—a limiting category—but communication on an exalted level of experience."[42] This "communication on an exalted level" approaches the notion of contemplation and communion that regards participation, not merely the receiving of a message or meaning, to be the goal of experience. Rothko's desire to produce something *more* than mere art is parallel to the view that icons are not, and cannot be, experienced solely or primarily as art. Subsequently, Novak and O'Doherty observe: "The chapel paintings (1964–67) are a testament to Rothko's faith in the power of art—'imageless' art—to meet, create, and transform an audience one by one, to place each person in contact with a tragic idea made urgent by the contemplation of death."[43]

The Rothko Chapel was initially planned as a Roman Catholic chapel and now functions as an ecumenical chapel, museum, and forum. The chapel space provided Rothko with the context within which he could control the experience of viewers by moving them from the white cube of the museum or gallery space into an environment that was as material as it was spiritual, one in which the contemplation of the divine was not merely an intellectual or optical one but a bodily one. Viewers physically participate in these works that confront them bodily within a space that assumes the reality of spiritual presence.[44]

Novak and O'Doherty believe that the Rothko Chapel, far from being an outlet for the artist's marginalized interests in spiritual experience, is crucial for understanding the entire history of modern art.

> As the last great "abstract" ensemble of paintings set in a specially designed physical and spiritual site, the Rothko Chapel, at modernism's end, makes a claim stated differently but no less vigorously by Malevich at modernism's beginning:

that abstract painting—that is, painting with what Rothko paradoxically called "nothing but content"—is capable of communicating, through its means, matters deeply relevant to the human estate. Ultimately, the stakes for abstraction as a convincing genre rest in considerable part with the Rothko Chapel.[45]

The quest for aesthetic immediacy has haunted modernist and avant-garde art since the beginning, and this quest has been identified with a desire for spiritual immediacy.

This modern quest was influenced, in various ways and degrees, by the economy of the icon, a form of painting predicated on the reality of an "embodied transcendence" whose light is not the light of this world but the Uncreated Light of the Holy Trinity, in whose energies we are invited to participate. However, Rothko's paintings function ambivalently as icons; or rather, the content of their iconicity is undetermined. But this does not mean that they do not participate in some way in the reality of the icon.

As critic Donald B. Kuspit observed, Rothko's paintings "hover." He writes, "The hovering intends something, but nothing in particular; it is simply the muscle of consciousness."[46] This muscle makes a picture by Rothko "empty but not nothing; its flatness is activated and its emptiness pregnant."[47] Artist Robert Ryman's observations on Rothko are provocative: "I don't think he was thinking of an illusion of light or any kind of illusion at all. His paintings dealt with real light."[48] As Christians we can name this "real light" even if, tragically, neither Rothko nor his paintings could.

Conclusion

The history of modern art is not simply the history of sexual liberation and licentiousness, *l'épater les bourgeoisie*, and attacking traditional values and mores. It is the utopian projection of a new world, a better world, a perfect world, redeemed, perhaps saved. These aspirations presuppose a relationship between the aesthetic and the spiritual. Many artists saw in the icon a useful metaphor and model for the function of their own work. That many artists sought to deny Christianity, at least in its institutional forms, should not deter us from experiencing and interpreting their work through the lens of the fullness of the one, holy, catholic, and apostolic church. In fact, such interpretive strategies can often point the artist toward reflecting on the deeper, inherently Christian motivations, images, symbols, and meanings that underwrite his or her work.

The crucial aspect is how the work of art is received, experienced, and interpreted. Do we declare that the altar to the unknown god points to the God of Abraham, Isaac, and Jacob revealed by the Son? Or do we dismiss it out of hand as hopelessly pagan? Modern and contemporary art is not, to be sure, for the faint of Christian heart. It requires as expansive and as creative a critical reception as St. Paul's close reading of Greek poetry on Mars Hill.[49] It requires the courage to pour and sift through the "spoils of Egypt," as Origen and St. Augustine would suggest.[50]

The essays in this book do not claim to offer *the* Christian explanation of these works of art. There are many ways Christians can experience and interpret modern and contemporary art. Art at its best defies easy and monolithic interpretation and even encourages such diversity. It is not merely a form of communication but requires contemplation and communion—an active experiential relationship with the artifact.[51] This process is decidedly at odds with what is often encountered in public discourse, in which sound bites, branding, and labeling seem to be necessary in order to be heard in the cultural arena. Contemplation and communion imply a myriad of responses through prolonged engagement or relationship with the work of art. It thus exceeds any single explanation and even exceeds what its maker intends for it.

Therefore, the simple and final declaration that a work of art is "anti-Christian" or even "Christian" can never be made, even if the work was produced by a vehement atheist or a confessing Christian. Furthermore, the aesthetic product of an anti-Christian or non-Christian artist is not necessarily anti-Christian or non-Christian. Nor does it follow that a Christian artist produces works of art that are Christian or embody a Christian worldview. All things, St. Paul tells us, are good if received with gratitude. Let us likewise receive modern and contemporary art critically but with gratitude.

3

Enrique Martínez Celaya's
Thing and Deception
The Artistic Practice of Belief

Today, to claim any significance or meaning, even if only to ourselves, is to flirt with ridicule.

Enrique Martínez Celaya

Our cultural birthright is iconoclastic. The legacies of the Reformation and the Enlightenment, as well as the reactions they spawned, conspire to render images, traditions, and other "nonrationalistic" forms of knowledge (including belief itself) irrelevant or even dangerous. It is therefore not surprising that a constant focus of this iconoclastic urge is directed toward artistic and religious practice. But in profound ways, art and religion are intimately related to one

I presented a significantly modified version of this essay at the biennial conference of Christians in the Visual Arts (CIVA), hosted at Azusa Pacific University, Azusa, CA, June 18, 2005. The final form of this essay benefited greatly from the process of preparing my talk and subsequent conversations. This essay was originally published in *Religion and the Arts* 10/1 (Spring 2006): 59–88.

another, even though a consequence of this iconoclastic urge is to separate the two. This chapter explores religion and belief through art.

Art is often viewed as an inferior or even untrustworthy guide to Truth. This view assumes that the best art can do is serve as a visual illustration of some truth better expressed through science, philosophy, or religion. But as philosopher Michael Kelly quite convincingly argues, this view is a particularly subtle but powerful form of iconoclasm. Far from revealing the impotence and irrelevance of art, the persistent presence of iconoclasm might indeed prove otherwise. Historian Dario Gamboni even suggests that our iconoclasm "bear[s] witness to the substance and weight" of art.[1] This essay explores the "substance and weight" of one painting and how it can help us understand the nature of belief and disbelief, art and religion.

Thing and Deception as an Icon of Doubt

Enrique Martínez Celaya's entire body of work is an aesthetic meditation on iconoclasm, on the complex relationships between images and words, between visual art and its interpretation. This is particularly the case with *Thing and Deception* (1997; fig. 3), a large canvas that depicts a gigantic chocolate Easter bunny covered by a pink veil or cellophane wrapper that seems either to hover or emerge out of a messy, murky, roughly painted white background. The Easter bunny has been broken into several chunks and has been reassembled.

At the bottom of the painting is a hand-written inscription "Needed Proof" in pencil. The white ground has many hairline cracks and evidence of wear and tear. It also reveals a bluish under-image that has been over-painted. The back of the painting features a handwritten fragment of a poem by Charles Baudelaire in addition to another inscription.[2] The Sheldon Memorial Art Gallery at the University of Nebraska acquired the painting in 2001, and I featured the work in a major reinstallation of the permanent collection in March 2003.[3] It was on view throughout the year in the permanent collection, including an exhibition I organized with the artist that featured a series of twenty-two black paintings.[4]

The enigmatic power of *Thing and Deception* has to do in large part with the fact that the painting internalizes, works over, and re-presents the most fundamental of tensions in art and religion, frustrating easy solutions, all the while seeming to offer clues to its interpretation. It is and is not what appears on the surface; it affirms and negates interpretation; it invites yet frustrates free associations; it attracts and repels. It seems simultaneously banal *and* profound. This painting is an icon of doubt. But doubt is not outright skepticism, for doubt has belief as its constant companion. As the father of a boy with convulsions declares to Jesus, "I do believe; help me overcome my unbelief" (Mark 9:24)!

Reworking Memories to Nourish the Present

Enrique Martínez Celaya was born in Palos, Cuba, in 1964 but left with his family when he was seven years old, living in Spain and then Puerto Rico as his father pursued business interests. This exile had a deep impact on him; his painting, sculpture, and writing have explored the meaning and significance of this experience. A deeply intelligent and philosophical artist, Martínez Celaya was trained as an experimental physicist in quantum electronics, first as an undergraduate at Cornell University and then as a doctoral student at the University of California-Berkeley. He ultimately abandoned this work to pursue art because, in his words, science could not answer the questions he believed he could answer in art. He has produced and exhibited sculpture, drawings, photography, and what he calls "environments." In addition to this visual work, a crucial part of his creative efforts is writing—poetry, short fiction, and aphoristic writing—that engages, extends, and weaves its way throughout his visual art. Widely read in Spanish and American literature as well as German philosophy, poetry, and art, his keen intelligence has made him an ideal subject for interviews, and he is deeply committed to generating, extending, and shaping discourse about his work.

Working in the Los Angeles area since 1997, Martínez Celaya's Latin culture has been a constant source of tension. His Latin identity has been much ballyhooed by art critics, although he did not fit the Chicano "cult of the streets"-type art and has in fact often been dismissed by other Latin American artists and their network of curators, critics, and collectors. In addition, his own experience often did not jibe with what is commonly assumed about the "Latin American experience" in this country: the experience of the uneducated lower classes from Central and South America. Consequently, his most insightful critics and interpreters have been European and Caucasian American.[5]

Moreover, his philosophical sophistication and incorporation of fragments and traces of body parts in his paintings, sculpture, photography, and installation work have made it very easy for critics to interpret his work within the context of poststructuralist academic discourse. Save for the occasional poetic riff or rhetorical flourish by a poststructuralist critic, the religious and spiritual implications of Martínez Celaya's art have been ignored, nervously allegorized, or quickly contextualized. Despite the fact that his career has benefited greatly from postmodern perspectives, this subtly undermines and obscures the deeper structures of his work, particularly as he has matured. It is not unimportant that, despite the fact that he considers himself to be first and foremost a painter, commentators have devoted most of their critical energies to his sculpture and photography, two media that are more malleable and conducive to their poststructuralist approaches. But painting is the medium through which Martínez Celaya's aesthetic project can best be explained. Critic Donald B. Kuspit has argued that it has the "power to evoke and convey what is subjectively fundamental in human experience" and that at its best it "can become an expression of personhood and individuality."[6]

Although he is not religious, everything Martínez Celaya does seems nevertheless to be religious. His orientation brings to mind the perspective of Wittgenstein, who quipped, "I am not a religious man but I cannot help seeing every problem from a religious point of view."[7] *Thing and Deception* is an early transitional statement of this Wittgenstinian religious point of view. Despite the fact that he abandoned his family's Roman Catholicism as a boy, Martínez Celaya has nevertheless been shaped and influenced by the deeply religious atmosphere of his eclectic Caribbean culture.

> Myself and the people I knew growing up in the Caribbean had their feelings framed by kitsch and I had to start there. . . . I was inundated with images of the harlequin crying, the Caridad del Cobre as a water fountain, the movie of the dwarf who dies, the novel Maria, caravan of the Corolla Club de Bayamon following a wedding, the priest drinking the wine before everyone else, the whole congregation seeing him swallow, plastic flowers on the tombs of Loiza, beauty queens speaking through loudspeakers from the back of trucks, children holding hands as garden statues.[8]

This religious material culture informs (but does not define) Martínez Celaya's work in general and *Thing and Deception* in particular. It is a culture in which the profound and silly, elegant and grotesque, sacred and banal, all emerge from a carnivalistic cultural practice of presence that utilizes both Roman Catholicism and Caribbean folk religion, Santeria.[9] It is also a culture that exists as a foundational memory, a memory of the past that continues to be reexperienced anew and thus continues to shape his present experience. Art is a means for Martínez Celaya to rework memories of the past to nourish the present in an effort to shape the future.

Shaping the Future

Finished in 1997, *Thing and Deception* was first exhibited later that year as part of an installation at Galerie Douyon in Miami, Florida, entitled "Saint Catherine Watches Over Me." The exhibition consisted of a severed head cast from polyester resin with a rosary imbedded in its neck, sitting on a silk pillow; a painting titled *The Account*, a blood-red painted velvet surface with a large gash in the center; *The Only Truth is You*, a gigantic painting on polyester that depicts what appears to be one hand giving another a glowing item adorned with hand-stitched embroidery; and a large canvas painting that features the outlines of a bowed head painted in clay that seems to be either crying tears or dripping blood, titled *The Fountain (Lordship)*. This peculiar installation, which the artist himself arranged, presents the work less as an exhibition and more as a collection of artifacts in silent conversation with one another.

But these artifacts are unusual, uncommon, and untraditional appropriations of canonical Catholic icons and their uses. The exhibition title alludes to the traditional Catholic practice of asking saints to intercede on our behalf, but Martínez Celaya's chosen saint is a mysterious one. With a rosary imbedded in her neck, the head offers an unconventional and personal appropriation of the Catholic spiritual and meditative tradition. (Martínez Celaya subsequently produced a series of St. Catherine heads that feature other objects embedded in her neck, such as silk flowers and a hummingbird.) Church tradition teaches that Catherine was a fourth-century Alexandrian of royal descent who not only converted to Christianity and withstood the advances of a pagan Roman emperor but also disputed with fifty pagan philosophers enlisted by the emperor to convert her. Her responses so convinced the philosophers that they were converted and then martyred. She was ultimately beheaded after the intended means of her execution, a spiked wheel, blew apart and killed the executioners. Significantly, Catherine is a patron of young girls and students, particularly philosophers.

Martínez Celaya reiterates this philosophical connection as he titled his subsequent heads with keywords drawn from Hegel's *Phenomenology of Spirit*, such as "The Ethical Question," "Culture," and "Beautiful Soul," that are drawn from the movement toward "absolute knowledge." Interestingly, the connection between a Roman Catholic saint and one of the saints of Enlightenment philosophy through this series brings out the philosophical power of the Catholic faith, with its capacity to convert through disputation. It also brings out the Christian theological context that nourished the Lutheran Hegel's philosophy. "St. Catherine Watches Over Me" conflates the devotional mysticism of the religious and the intellectual rationalism of philosophy.

Martínez Celaya explores this conflation in a different manner in his photographic book project "Berlin: Photographs and Poems," completed a year or so after the Miami installation, where he uses Hegel's own tomb as a devotional and sacramental memorial shrine. That he used his soon-to-be wife as a model for this photograph might indeed identify her with St. Catherine. *The Account* in "St. Catherine Watches Over Me" refers to St. Thomas's famous doubt about the resurrected Christ and how his doubt was transformed into belief by being able to touch the very body and wounds of Christ (John 20:24–31), an event famously depicted by Carravaggio. Martínez Celaya focuses only on the open wound, a wound taken from its sacred context in the Scriptures and tradition and recontextualized in an installation of religious relics and fragments, in which the object of such faith and belief is less clear. This tear, however, differs radically from those of Lucio Fontana and the Arte Povera avant-garde, for which such violence was addressed toward art itself rather than toward Christ. The meaning and significance of the wound in *The Account* is unclear, in large part because the relationship between belief and skepticism is unclear. This is further complicated by the artist's use of velvet, a medium more conducive to kitsch and the trite rather than the profound through high art. It is in this display context that *Thing and Deception* was first exhibited.

An important aspect of this installation was its use of dangerously sentimental objects that referenced the kitsch culture of the Caribbean. But Martínez Celaya was not content merely to appropriate kitsch. "Instead of simplifying kitsch I wanted to have it hover, undefined. The flickering between charge-no charge and meaning-no meaning, is a strong one. That flickering of meaning is maybe the only way left for recharging the sentimental or the kitsch."[10] This "hovering" and "flickering of meaning" is characteristic of his attempt to resist or avoid easy references to stable meaning and significance. This aspect of Martínez Celaya's work is intensified in this exhibition, in which the kitschy and sentimental is combined with religious undertones. About *Thing and Deception*, Martínez Celaya observes,

I chose a seemingly banal image, a chocolate bunny rabbit with all its reference to childhood, treat and wish. It is magnified until it is larger than a human and then it is broken, with visible seams. The rabbit by itself is both sentimental and resistant to sentimentality. The red veil makes it both safe and threatening. The veil is delicate but suggestive—maybe blood. The veil reveals and hides and sets up a metaphor for the real. It is from there that the title *Thing and Deception* comes from. The rabbit and the veil exist in the whiteness of the canvas. Shadows of buried images can be seen. It is painted with a special mixture of paints to give it a powdery consistency. Over the years it has developed cracks that I find wonderful, the fragility and ageing of the object directly interacts with the image and the suggestions of memory and mortality that are invoked by the covered rabbit.[11]

Written four years after installation of this work in "St. Catherine Watches Over Me," this text de-emphasizes the religious connotations of the chocolate bunny as an *Easter* bunny, as a symbol—a kitschy and sentimental symbol—of the most important Christian holiday from this unlikely perspective. Despite the de-emphasis of explicit religious connotations, Martínez Celaya does focus on the painting as a "metaphor for the real," particularly in the relationship to the subject (the rabbit) and the veil that covers, obscures, protects, or reveals it. Moreover, it continues to function for him as an icon, relic, or object of devotion of sorts, as he responds positively to the cracks that show its use, and perhaps even its age, as a long-held and worked over and handled memory. Its identity as a devotional object of personal value is emphasized in the fact that the painting had been in the artist's own personal collection until it was made available to the Sheldon.

That Martínez Celaya de-emphasized the original display context for *Thing and Deception* is not surprising, given that his work continues to live, shaping his present work as well as being shaped by it. It continues to accumulate and expand its references, intensifying the potency of its "flickerings of meaning." The work becomes an object of contemplation again and again as the artist considers his own past through the objective means of his art. This is suggested when Martínez Celaya observes, "As I have thought more about this painting I have come to see it as a work about mortality. I originally thought it was more related to sentimentality and memory but now I see it as a work of passage. A work of premonition and of finality."[12] *Thing and Deception* seemingly acquires more meaning, since it becomes for the artist less about "sentimentality and memory" and more about "premonition and of finality," a passage from one state to another. But what are the objects of such memories and sentimentalities? From where is this painting understood as a passage?

It is my contention that *Thing and Deception* marks out a transition from an art dedicated to exhuming the past, an art preoccupied with memories and nostalgia, to an art that works over his past to shape the present and *project a future*. What the artist has developed in the five years between its making, initial display, and entrance into the Sheldon's collection is a telos that is less explicitly religious in its subject matter but more profoundly religious in its structure, a structure that not only pervades his subsequent work but underwrites his behavior as an artist and human being, guiding his thoughts, words, and deeds.

Dangerous Territory

Thing and Deception resurfaced for public viewing in a major retrospective exhibition organized by the Contemporary Museum, Honolulu, Hawaii, in 2001–02. The exhibition was a collaboration with the artist that featured over eighty works from 1992 to 2000, including sculpture, drawings, paintings, and photography. The works were divided into four categories, "Dialectic of Resistance (silence, kitsch, and the specific)"; "The Question of the Object (presence, staging, and authenticity)"; "A Language of Traces (time, memory, mortality)"; and "Self and Other (the algebra of identity)." *Thing and Deception* is placed in the category of "The Question of the Object." In the interpretive entry that accompanied a reproduction of this painting, the author writes,

> I find it hard to escape seeing this object in a religious context as a remainder perhaps of the old-fashioned altarpiece in a sanctuary (it might be an "Easter bunny"). Does it touch on an issue like resurrection, deal with the possibility of "new life"? Such dangerous territory for an artist working today! Can it be explored visually in the new *sanctitas* of the Modern art gallery?[13]

Indeed, the "dangerous territory" for a contemporary artist to be working in is the religious and the spiritual. This is particularly true for Martínez Celaya, whose work has been praised for its postmodern sophistication, for evoking in some sense a lost world of innocence, naïveté, and magic in which the world did make sense. One would then assume, given the focus of this major exhibition and publication, that such "magic" would recede further and further into the past, become less and less accessible and compelling for the artist. But this does not appear to be the case. The "dangerous territory" that Martínez Celaya walks around in his work up to 2000 becomes the arena in which he subsequently acts in his most recent work. *Thing and Deception* can help us understand this transition. It is important to keep in mind that this transition is not necessarily a radical one, nor is it a movement away from previous concerns and interests.

In fact, this religious turn does not negate but fulfills, extends, fleshes out, deepens, and completes in some important way the implications of his work before 2000. This is accomplished through a de-emphasis of explicitly recognizable religious objects and images but a more thorough assimilation of their deep structures. It is in the context of these deep structures that *Thing and Deception* emerges as a transitional piece, a liminal work, and perhaps this is why the artist refers to it as "a work of premonition and finality."

Words and Interpretation

While he was working with the Contemporary Museum in Honolulu on his traveling exhibition and publication, Martínez Celaya was also writing *Guide*, a fictional account of a conversation that the artist has with an old friend, Thomas, while he accompanies this man on a journey up the California coastline to buy a cow. Writing has always been an important part of Martínez Celaya's aesthetic work. Significantly, Thomas happens to be a former Franciscan friar and he prods and probes Martínez Celaya incessantly about the religious implications of his life and work.

Martínez Celaya appears to speak through both characters, offering an opportunity to embody the ambivalence and ambiguity of his views through two quite different characters. Thomas serves as the artist's Other, who forces him to confront issues he has too easily dismissed in the past and encourages him to follow farther the paths he has set for himself, drawing out their deeper implications. Religion is an intense focus for Thomas. At one point in their conversation, Thomas asserts, "For someone who claims not to be religious, you speak in a way that sounds very religious to me." Thomas serves to register doubt and tension in the artist's assumed beliefs. "Back then I thought that spirituality was oppressive. Now I think that what really bothered me was my community's superficial and insincere spirituality." Elsewhere, the artist asserts that, "I have tried to live and think without the aid of an ideology or a religion." Martínez Celaya is able to bounce ideas, assumptions, and arguments off each of his characters, which frees him to be both a skeptic and a believer at the same time, allowing him to explore the question of religion and spirituality from both the inside and the outside, as it were, without the pressures or conventions of traditional categories of "believer" and "unbeliever."[14]

Writing always seems to accompany Martínez Celaya's visual work, in some way. *Guide* was published on the occasion of the exhibition of a number of his paintings from *The October Cycle*, the first major series of work after his Honolulu retrospective. Painted between 2000 and 2002, these twenty-three paintings derive their genesis from the artist's poem entitled "October." The poem invokes the ominous arrival of autumn and the coming of winter, experienced through darkness, cold, and isolation. These aspects of winter came as a shock to the artist during his first winters in Madrid and then in the northeast United States as a young adult. Martínez Celaya's interest in both writing and publishing his writing as ancillaries and complements of his visual work (not necessarily explanations or definitions) also includes publishing the writing of others he finds of interest under his own publishing imprint, Whale and Star.

One important writer he has published is Charles Baudelaire. In 2001 Martínez Celaya published, for the first time in English, selections from Baudelaire's *Les Fleurs du mal*, which included the full portfolio of nine etchings from Odilon Redon's *Les Fleurs du mal*. Interestingly, the back of *Thing and Deception* has two stanzas in French from Baudelaire's "Danse macabre." The poem, with its metaphors of flesh, flowers, heat, and light to describe the unchildlike pleasures and anguish of passion, seems ill-fitted to the subject of the painting. But the poem marks the existence of previous versions of the painting, subsequently painted out by Martínez Celaya.

> The Baudelaire poem began with the previous incarnation of that painting. First it was a dark tulip—in my mind tulips are connected/related to human excess and death. I wrote the poem during that phase. The second phase (or finished painting) was a silk rose coated with paint, so that the whole work looked like a burial or more properly, like a tomb coated with white dust. The final incarnation is *Thing and Deception*. So, the painting has been three different paintings and each one contributed its discoveries to the last phase.[15]

These discoveries, buried beneath the canvas and available only to him through his recollection, are important parts of his painting process, which often consists of completely painting over images. In fact, the painting with a silk rose

God in the Gallery

coated with paint was exhibited as *Laberinto* in a group show entitled "Nature re(Contained)" at the Irvine Fine Arts Center in 1995. A photograph of the artist shows the painting with a tulip painted on top of a hand with the silk rose still on the canvas. But the romantic intoxication of Baudelaire's poem written in French on the back of the canvas is contrasted sharply with more of the artist's handwriting on the front of the painting, the analytic, objective notation in English: "Needed Proof." Scrawled on the bottom of the canvas, the two words function as a reminder to the artist that he does indeed need "proof," or needed it in the past.

Martínez Celaya will often employ handwriting directly on his paintings as a means to expand or complicate the meaning of the work. Moreover, it becomes a metaphor for immediacy, spontaneity, and directness that counters and contrasts with the seemingly painstaking and calculating paintings, in which each gesture and stroke is made and then laboriously critiqued, evaluated, and worked over. The handwriting offers, in contrast, an informal gloss, a seemingly offhand thought, quickly recorded to secure its immediacy. "Needed Proof" is an attempt to anchor the complex and complicating image of the Easter bunny with some kind of meaning, as the word might anchor the image in Protestant—particularly Lutheran—images.

This serves as a caption, a gloss, an explanation, but it does not clarify the work. These two words manifest not merely the artist's own skepticism as a scientist and a philosopher; the words are also ironic, for who "needs proof" when trading in the currency of chocolate Easter bunnies? Can an Easter bunny—or a painting, for that matter—serve as "proof" of anything?[16] Martínez Celaya's use of handwriting on his paintings also appears in one of his most recent works, which features an iconic portrait of Leon Golub, whom the artist has long admired, with an inscription: "Leon whom I miss so much." The work was painted during a residency at the University of Colorado at Boulder, when he learned of Golub's death.

Not long after the Sheldon acquired *Thing and Deception*, Martínez Celaya and I began to work together on an exhibition of twenty-two of his paintings from his *October Cycle*, which was on view at the Sheldon from November 2003 through January 2004 (fig. 4). The project featured only the paintings from this series and a publication that included a critical essay by me, a series of reflections on the project by Martínez Celaya, and the republication of his poem "October," which served as the impetus for the *Cycle*. Later, when the exhibition traveled to the Museum of Art, Fort Lauderdale, Florida, Martínez Celaya made a gigantic wall drawing on the occasion of the exhibition with pigment mixed from his own blood and birch ashes, which included hand-written notes and diagrams of the proper names of artists, philosophers, musicians, and other important influences on him. In addition, the following inscription appeared:

> You may read other things about the "October Cycle" but you shouldn't trust them including whatever I've said. The "October Cycle" is a failure, those of you who dislike this work already know that and those of you who like the work should see to quickly understand its futility.[17]

The artist's handwriting, which intensifies the personal and spontaneous aspect of his observations, can also serve to destabilize and "flicker" a meaning that has become too comfortable, too self-evident and obvious. Martínez Celaya's surprising inscription is not an example of Duchampian intellectual gamesmanship or a cynical intellectualism, but echoes Wittgenstein, particularly in his enigmatic *Tractatus Logico-Philosophicus*: "My propositions are elucidatory in this way: he who understands me finally recognizes them as senseless."[18] Following Wittgenstein, Martínez Celaya reminds us to throw away the ladder that got us where we are in front of the works, whether that ladder was his or others' words. The installation of the *October Cycle* at the Sheldon Art Gallery also made (selective) use of words. It featured almost no explanatory text, save for different fragments from the artist's writings that were placed in each of the three gallery spaces, fragments intended to extend rather than reduce the experiential range of the paintings.

The inscription also reveals another important aspect of Martínez Celaya's aesthetic project: his ambivalent relationship to words and interpretations, his own as well as others'. Again, faint echoes of Wittgenstein can be heard: "What can be said at all can be said clearly, and what we cannot talk about we must consign to silence."[19] Despite both his and his interpreters' many words, Martínez Celaya wonders whether his art might best be consigned to silence. This is further suggested in the self-doubt and self-criticism he levies at himself through the mouth of the former Franciscan friar, Thomas, in *Guide*. It also manifests itself in his statement that one should not trust what has been said about *The October Cycle*, even by the artist himself. He recognizes the emptiness of words even while his own art and life-project rely on them as he writes, lectures, gives interviews, and invites critical commentary.

In fact, Martínez Celaya's approach bears a resemblance to apophatic, or negative, theology, which understands knowledge about God to consist primarily about what we do not and cannot know, in order to preserve God's radical transcendence. The avant-garde of the twentieth century likewise approached the concept of "failure" in similar ways. Samuel Beckett states, "Ever tried. Ever failed. No matter. Try Again. Fail again. Fail better."[20] For the avant-garde, success is often explained as "failing better." This approach to knowledge thrives in the Eastern Orthodox tradition as well as other Eastern religious traditions, such as Zen Buddhism, a religious practice that exerted some influence on Martínez Celaya in the early nineties, particularly while he was teaching at Pomona College and the Claremont Graduate School.[21]

James 2:14 asks, "What good is it, my brothers, if a man claims to have faith but has no deeds? Can such faith save him?" It seems as if Martínez Celaya has come to understand the disjunction between "claims" and "deeds," between knowing philosophy and living it, or between reading a philosopher's work and learning about the philosopher's life. His admiration for such figures as Wittgenstein, Golub, and Beethoven, for example, has as much to do with the exemplary, extraordinary, yet flawed lives they led, as with the creative work they left behind.

Perhaps the most striking manifestation of this perspective is found in Martínez Celaya's studio, where he has hand-written directly onto the wall the following creed, "Keep Your Actions Faithful." He has inscribed this commandment or exhortation on the wall of every studio he has ever worked in. The concept of "faithful actions," or the fact that actions can and must embody "faith" of some kind, is a remarkably astute perception of the world's major religions made by a self-described secular person, of the common goal and teaching; the religious believer is exhorted to be not merely a hearer but a doer. And of course, it is the chasm between the two he recalls as a child that turned him away from the Catholic faith.

Relationships: Art, Religion, and the Spiritual

Like the 1997 Miami exhibition that offered a religious context within which to experience and understand *Thing and Deception* as part of a small group of religious relics, Martínez Celaya's inscription in his studio contextualizes his working space as a sacred space. He marks it off, as it were, as a place where faith is worked out in actions and where even the most banal of actions and gestures achieves profound meaning and significance. These actions and gestures are aesthetic gestures of an ethical worldview. This gives art an intense spiritual and religious significance for Martínez Celaya, a significance that transcends his identity as an artist and incorporates his entire life as he makes sense of his childhood past and charts his future as an adult. Art is the aesthetic constitution of his selfhood, and it is the means by which he reconciles himself with himself and the world. It is therefore intensely ethical as well; making art must make him a better person.

There is a common assumption that there exists a sharp distinction between "religion" and "spirituality": the former is rule-governed and public and thus conformist, the latter is related to the heart and private and thus more authentic and sincere. Although this perception has deep roots in the history of modern art, it goes back to the radical, pietistic movements of the Protestant Reformation in Germany. It is not inconsequential that most of the German thinkers who have influenced Martínez Celaya have been profoundly shaped by this German pietism of the "inward spirit." Whether it is Martin Luther, Søren Kierkegaard, Karl Barth, or Dietrich Bonhoeffer, a "religionless" religion based on authentic spirituality has been a powerful influence in Western religious thought.

However, as Tom Boyd argues, and Robert Wuthnow's recent sociological research confirms, the relationship between spirituality and religion cannot ultimately be severed.[22] Wuthnow's research, for example, demonstrates that an increased interest in spirituality, manifest in art, music, new-age forms of prayer, contemplation, etc., has not driven people from traditional religions but toward them.

Martínez Celaya's spirituality is not merely a private, psychological orientation or one confined to a view of his studio as sacred. In the midst of finishing his *October Cycle* series in the fall of 2002, he presented several of the paintings at Griffin Contemporary in Venice, California. At the opening reception, which also featured the publication of *Guide*, Martínez Celaya asked Margo Timmins, lead vocalist of the contemporary music group Cowboy Junkies, to sing an impromptu a cappella version of "Mining for Gold," a spiritual her band included on their album *The Trinity Session*, which was recorded in a Toronto church in 1988. The song served a liturgical function by sacralizing the space, imbuing it with a spirituality that was embodied in the very performance of the song. The effect was to recontextualize the opening.[23] Martínez Celaya's choice of singer was related to his personal enthusiasm for the group and the effect it had on him as he listened to their music while he worked in the studio. The installation of the *October Cycle* exhibition at the Sheldon intensified this aura of the sacred and liturgical, not through music but by relying on and intensifying the quasi-religious and sacred space created by the museum's architect, Philip Johnson. By eliminating interpretive text in the three-high modernist gallery spaces, he emphasized an aesthetic experience of the work over its explanation.

The dark tar-painted canvases that depict outlines of figures standing, bowing, embracing, and sitting function as icons of contemplation of Truth. But what is Truth? Martínez Celaya leaves this question unanswered. The exhibition parallels his experience of the paintings of the mystical artist from Stockholm, Hilma Af Klint, in which he had the feeling that he was in the presence of a cosmos that was right, profound, and true.[24] But the specific meanings of the paintings themselves remained obscure, as does the nature and identity of Truth that his paintings embody. These paintings seem to hit the bedrock that Wittgenstein observes: "If I have exhausted the justifications, I have reached bedrock, and my spade is turned. Then I am inclined to say: 'This is simply what I do.'"[25]

Can one experience Truth aesthetically without knowing Truth cognitively? Perhaps. Martínez Celaya's paintings embody his "doing," which is why I often felt as I entered the *October Cycle* exhibition at the Sheldon that I was walking into a liturgical service of some kind, as figures sat, stood, bowed, and gestured, inviting me either to watch or to participate. To say that Martínez Celaya pursues art with a religious zeal is not merely to offer a well-worn figure of speech but to describe his seriousness. It is to acknowledge that the formal, public, rule-governed institution of art is the space within which he works out his spiritual (not just his artistic) life. This is evidenced through his use of events from his childhood and adult past that involve his family, events that are deeply personal and remain so even while they become objectively embodied in the public sphere through art. Martínez Celaya understands the relationship between the heart and the mind, words and deeds, the inward state and how it gets worked out and embodied in faithful actions. Art is a religion for Martínez Celaya because it does what religion does: provides the institutional framework within which, and the material means through which, a person's spiritual life is developed as he relates to himself, others, and the divine. As the transcendent and the immanent find their embodiment in religion, so they find their embodiment in art for Martínez Celaya. But it is not so simple that he has abandoned religion for art, for the former informs and sustains the latter.

In his introduction to Erich Auerbach's influential book *Mimesis: The Representation of Reality in Western Literature* (1947), the late critic Edward W. Said observed that the Christian doctrine of the incarnation played an important role in the development of Western intellectual history: "Auerbach, I believe, is bringing us back to what is an essentially Christian doctrine for believers but also a crucial element of *human* intellectual power and will."[26] That a secular Jew writing in exile in Istanbul during World War II and a secular Palestinian could both argue that the incarnation of Jesus Christ, if only as a metaphor, could serve as a catalyst for creative thought and action in the West is remarkable and underwrites the relationship between art and religion.

High Art as the Incarnation of Belief

Thing and Deception incarnates art. The power of art relies on the belief that smelly oils, rough canvas, graphite, and other banal materials can provide a profound aesthetic experience. Martínez Celaya intensifies this belief in art, particularly in painting, as a vehicle for the profound by using these banal materials to paint a banal image, a chocolate Easter bunny. Can this image be a vehicle for a profound aesthetic experience? Can a painting of an Easter bunny be a religious or a spiritual painting? From its first incarnations as a dark tulip and then a silk rose, both common visual metaphors for life, love, and death, came forth this banal, idiosyncratic kitsch image of a chocolate Easter bunny.

The painting is not only iconic but also eucharistic. Both require the eyes of faith to see what is truly present. In both cases, what is seen and experienced is more than pigment on a piece of canvas or a wafer and wine; they are material means by which a window of the world as it truly is, as a spiritual and divinely charged reality, is thrown open. Moreover, as classic Christian teaching emphasizes, the icon and the sacrament of the Eucharist do not only *require* faith, they also *generate* and *sustain* it. That the subject of the painting is a delightful treat only deepens its eucharistic associations. The liturgy of the church interprets Psalm 34:8 in a eucharistic manner: "Taste and see that the Lord is good."

Both mechanisms—tasting and seeing—are operative, at least metaphorically, in *Thing and Deception*. I imagine Martínez Celaya as a young child with his own symbol of heaven, a chocolate Easter bunny, broken and wrapped in a veil, simultaneously obscuring and revealing, perhaps even preserving the broken pieces together. Perhaps he tried to eat the bunny before Easter morning. Perhaps the artist views religious belief through the chocolate Easter bunny: simultaneously arbitrary and slightly silly but strangely powerful and compelling nonetheless. And of course, this can be applied to the conventions of high art.

Thing and Deception draws on the risk one takes as a religious believer to suggest that the art believer likewise risks, that both the religious believer and the viewer must have belief. Both risk ridicule for devoting so much effort and investing so much meaning in seemingly irrelevant and inefficient superstitions and conventions in the face of American materialism, practicality, and efficiency. *Thing and Deception* also generates and incarnates belief. This was particularly so when the painting was featured in the Sheldon's permanent collection from March 2003 through June 2004. This context differs significantly from its two previous public exhibitions.

In the Sheldon's permanent collection, *Thing and Deception* hangs near such works as a large photograph by Vic Muniz, a large-scale painting by Enrique Chagoya, and works by Shimon Attie, Carrie Mae Weems, and Robert Gober, in a gallery devoted to contemporary art adjacent to five other galleries that survey late-nineteenth- and twentieth-century American art. That *Thing and Deception* hangs in a contemporary gallery with other works that deal in one way or another with memory and loss and the past reinforces that reading of the painting. Rather than showing it within the original context in which Martínez Celaya intended the painting to be exhibited or within the larger context of the artist's oeuvre, this installation places *Thing and Deception* within the larger and more diverse context of American art. The painting served as the focal point of the entire six-gallery installation, the first painting viewers saw after entering the gallery spaces.

For well over one year I viewed this painting in these galleries, while I walked in the galleries alone, talked to tour groups of all kinds, and lectured to my students. The gallery spaces reverberate with the profundity and banality, seriousness and silliness of the painting. Looking at this work almost daily for sixteen months reminded me of the belief required of all artists, the risk and wager that out of banal materials, something of meaning and significance will emerge. And so *Thing and Deception* glosses the Sheldon's entire permanent collection, causes all the works on display—whether works by Edward Hopper, Marsden Hartley, Albert Pinkham Ryder, and Philip Guston, or nineteenth-century still-life and impressionist paintings—to "flicker" just slightly, like a temporary electrical short, and cuts the lights for a split second, thereby charging these works with the power surge of belief *and* skepticism. It shows belief working alongside skepticism, laboring right next to unbelief.

Religious and artistic belief do not get nourished and strengthened by reading theology and aesthetics, they get strengthened by doing them: by participating in religious services, by shaping one's life around its habits and practices, by making and looking at art, talking about art, and practicing it. For a child, the Great Lent that leads to the Paschal celebration of the Easter feast could plausibly be represented by the Easter bunny, an image of child-like faith or "childhood, treat and wish," as Martínez Celaya describes his childhood experience. Art and religion are not diametrically opposed to one another.

Perhaps, following the leads of Auerbach and Said, the Christian doctrine of the incarnation has indeed made possible the aspirations that high art has set for itself. So in a very real way, high art is incarnational at its core. The example of how Enrique Martínez Celaya conceives of his aesthetic project can offer important insights for religious believers, particularly as he conceives of art not merely as an object but as a practice that shapes belief. Belief is not merely the sum total of cognitive acts, a bias from our disembodied rationalistic and iconoclastic "information society," but consists of the received traditions, customs, habits, and disciplines that sustain and shape belief.

Thing and Deception confirms aesthetically what historians and sociologists of religion have recently shown: religion is not simply (or even primarily) the sum total of theological teachings, abstract catechisms, or other doxological statements. It is lived in the daily lives of the faithful, whose lives are imbedded in a material culture of portraits of Jesus, figurines, and even chocolate bunnies. The distinction between belief and unbelief is much less clear than is usually acknowledged or admitted by commentators (believers or unbelievers). Art (both the making and experiencing) offers a means to clarify and shape the nature of this relationship. Believers and unbelievers alike usually live simultaneously in an ambiguous and ambivalent state of belief and unbelief, faith and skepticism, whether they are within or outside a religious tradition.

Two Sides of the Same Coin

The ancient church father St. John of Damascus, the great defender of icons against the iconoclasts in the eighth century, observed, "Man is a microcosm; for he possesses a soul and a body, and is placed between spirit and matter; he is the place in which the visible and invisible creations, the tangible and intelligible creations, are linked together."[27] The human person is the place where the visible and invisible, tangible and intelligible are linked together. And it is through the human person's actions—in Martínez Celaya's case, through the practice of art—that they are revealed, often through glimpses and "flickerings."

More than fifty years ago, French cultural critic René Char observed, "It will be a bad night when, lacking truth itself, man suppresses the superstition of truth."[28] No doubt religious and aesthetic faith hover suspended between truth and superstition. The latter often can preserve the space for the former, like the Jewish practice of setting out a plate of food for Elijah during the Passover in anticipation of his coming. *Thing and Deception* narrows the gap between belief and unbelief, banal and profound, art and religion, sacred and secular, truth and superstition, revealing each to be two sides of the same precious coin.

4

Embodying Transcendence
Material Spirituality in Contemporary Art

You have made us for yourself, and our hearts are restless until they rest in you.

St. Augustine, Confessions

And I still haven't found what I'm looking for.

U2

Religion and Spirituality in Contemporary Culture

The last twenty-five years have witnessed a resurgence of religion and spirituality in American cultural, social, and political life. As sociologist Rodney Stark's research emphasizes, although religion has never been as marginalized as public intellectuals, critics, and other inheritors of the Enlightenment have claimed, there is most definitely an increase in public discourse in, around, and about religion and spirituality.[1] While the assumption exists that interest in private "spirituality" is rising at the expense of public, organized "religion," there seems to be ample evidence that this is not the case. From the rise of Islam and Roman Catholicism, particularly among the younger generations, to the emergence of evangelicalism as a powerful sociopolitical group, to a host of other indicators, it appears that both private spirituality and public religion are on the ascension. Some observers credit the impact of postmodernism, which provided more diversity of viewpoints and embraced pluralism and inclusiveness as twin pillars of the faith, as opening the way for religious discourse. John Caputo suggests that the postmodern critique of the Enlightenment embodied by Nietzsche has wrought surprising results. Caputo observes that "what no one saw coming was the way the Nietzschean critique undoes the modernist critique of religion and opens the doors to another way of thinking about faith and reason."[2]

While "religion" has often been pitted, favorably by conservatives and negatively by progressives, against "spirituality," the relationship between the two grows more complex and interrelated. Spirituality is individualistic, private, and thus capable of being shaped, changed, and modified by the individual, while religion is defined publicly and historically and prescribes a set of practices and beliefs to which the individual must, to some degree, submit. The separation between religion and spirituality has been a powerful one in the United States, shaped as it has been by the antiauthoritarian and progressive ethos of Protestantism, the private faith of the heart, and the authority of the conscience pitted against the "empty" practices of ritual and suffocating habits of tradition. But it is toward these rituals, including ancient Christian spiritual practices, that many seekers both within and outside the church have been drawn.

This situation, as countless scholars and critics have observed, offers unique opportunities and challenges for those guided by the Nicene Christian faith. As theologian Graham Ward warns,

> Religion is, once more, haunting the imagination of the West. The various attempts to exorcise its presence . . . have failed, for the secularism upon which they were each founded is imploding. A new remythologizing of the real—media-driven, market-led—is emerging. But what does the appearance of this spectre at the end of the twentieth and the beginning of the twenty-first centuries portend?[3]

Ward and his colleagues John Millbank, Catherine Pickstock, and James K. A. Smith, among other thinkers associated with Radical Orthodoxy, offer a critique of both skepticism that regards any interest in religion and spirituality as a hindrance to the purity of the gospel, and optimism that cheers the advent of post-Christian culture and radical pluralism. Ward cautions, "What we are witnessing in Western culture today is the liquidation of 'religion' through its commodification."[4] The rise in discourse about religion and spirituality in the public sphere has done much to facilitate this "commodification," which now makes it possible for religion and spirituality to function as marketable brands for music, film, books, and even art. Postmodernity, which has done much to undermine the antireligious rationalism and scientism of the Enlightenment, thus giving religion and spirituality a seat at the table of public practice and discourse, also easily flattens it out into just another "perspective" among "perspectives," just another brand among other consumable brands.

Contemporary art plays a prominent role in working through the opportunities and challenges related to the rise of things spiritual and religious. As Robert Wuthnow's data suggest, the arts have played an important role in what he calls the "revitalization" of American religion.[5] Although Wuthnow's study focuses on the arts, including the visual arts, he remains largely silent on the issue of contemporary fine art except for certain observations about the museum-going habits of various representatives from different denominations. Wuthnow instead focuses attention on the practice of doing the visual arts as a means to access or develop deeper spiritual awareness. Wuthnow's surprising discovery is that the interest in spirituality and, in particular, the practice of the arts do not lead people away from organized religion but toward it, as individuals rejoin the congregations of their youth, become more active in the ones they are already a part of, or seek out religious congregations.

Although the contemporary art world does indeed reflect the larger culture's interest in things religious and spiritual, it does so only tentatively and ambivalently. Conservatives often interpret this caution as outright resistance or cynical toleration while progressives tend to interpret it as outright acceptance and evidence that the contemporary art world has made its peace with religion and spirituality. The so-called culture wars, with the conservative insistence that "family values" be the lens through which art and culture are viewed, distort the contemporary art world and ignore those quiet and tentative spiritual murmurings by redirecting attention to form and content that might "offend" the average sixth-grader or soccer mom. Far from offering a sensitive means of experiencing and interpreting contemporary art, the cultural warriors offer means by which it can be dismissed and avoided, a practice that would have horrified Hans Rookmaaker and Francis Schaeffer, critics whom many cultural warriors believe they have been following.

Thierry de Duve has explored the relationship between religion and modern and contemporary art, with similar results. In *Look, One Hundred Years of Contemporary Art*, de Duve claims, "the best modern art . . . has endeavored to redefine the essentially religious terms of humanism on *belief-less* bases."[6] For de Duve, modern art is concerned with exorcising the religious impulse. But de Duve suggests that it is only in the "beholder's gaze" that painting's religious meaning can be restored, a restoration to which de Duve is himself only ambivalently committed. De Duve puts his finger on the important role that art criticism must play in restoring a religious and spiritual sense to modern and contemporary art. His approach at least acknowledges the presence of religion in artistic practice, if only as a sustained attempt to fend it off.[7]

Although de Duve's motivation for exploring religion and spirituality in modern and contemporary art is ultimately to dismiss it, James Elkins offers a much more provocative and useful approach. An internationally respected art historian of broad interests, catholic tastes, and considerable intellectual integrity, Elkins offers an honest query into the role that religion and spirituality play in contemporary art through his own experience as a teacher. The core of Elkins's book is five responses to the problem of art and religion, embodied by five different students who represent different attitudes about art and religion. Although he comes to the conclusion that art and religion do not mix, Elkins argues that it is "irresponsible not to keep trying."[8]

A chief virtue of Elkins's book is that he seems dissatisfied with the conclusions he offers as to why they do not mix. Unlike de Duve, Elkins cannot dismiss religion. We must continue to reflect on both of these cultural practices, together. Elkins's winsome and irenic project will be immensely helpful in working through the nuances of spirituality and religion as they are embodied in artistic practice, which will fundamentally change the shape and texture of further conversations about art and religion.

Why, as Christians, should we be content to see Christ only where we expect to see him? Perhaps we should follow the lead of the Gospels themselves and to look for him where we least expect him to be, even in the contemporary art world. Elkins's project, by offering honest reflection on religion's "strange place" in contemporary art, will help point the way.

Religion, Spirituality, and Art Historical Scholarship

Recent art historical scholarship has helped provide some tools to critics and scholars in order to hear the religious and spiritual echoes in the contemporary art world and interpret them in ways that resist the antagonistic art versus religion framework that remains the dominant paradigm even for those, such as Elkins and de Duve, who show a serious interest in exploring art's unavoidable relationship with religion and spirituality. The research done by art historians David Morgan, Sally Promey, and Erika Doss interrogates the complex relationship between art and religion and offers rich resources for extending and adjusting Elkins's and de Duve's perspectives.

An example is Sally Promey's research on Alfred H. Barr Jr., the founding director of the Museum of Modern Art in New York.[9] As previously noted, both Barr's father and his grandfather were Presbyterian ministers who received divinity degrees from Princeton, and Barr himself was a member of Brick Presbyterian Church in New York. As early as 1941 Barr proposed an exhibition on art and religion at the Museum of Modern Art, called "The Religious Spirit in Contemporary Art." Barr was deeply influenced by Russian icons on his trip to the Soviet Union and even published a long essay on them. Barr headed the Commission on Art formed under the auspices of the National Council of Churches' Department of Worship and the Arts, and he was, throughout his life, deeply concerned about the low aesthetic standards of Protestant Christianity. Christianity played virtually no role in scholarly accounts of Barr's activities. But Promey's research revealed that it played a definitive role in his work as the most influential apologist for modern art in the United States in the twentieth century.

Moreover, for such scholars as David Morgan, the very concepts of art and religion are not clearly demarcated with their own autonomous essence, as seemingly assumed by Elkins and de Duve, but are forged over time and often in relationship to one another. Neither art nor religion is merely the product of beliefs and dogma but is constituted through practices and, as Mircea Eliade calls them, "hard things."[10] David Morgan observes, "Visual practices help fabricate the worlds in which people live and therefore present a promising way of deepening our understanding of how religions work."[11] In the process, this also deepens our understanding of how art works and the roles religion and spirituality play in it. Morgan's approach is important because it considers both art and religion to be linguistic-cultural practices, practices that not merely give form to inward experience but actually are responsible for producing it. Moreover, Morgan's research reveals that artistic practice and religious practice are inextricably related. Furthermore, they are in fact similar in structure. Morgan's approach enables the subtle but profound spiritual and religious echoes and murmurings of much contemporary artistic practice to be heard, echoes and murmurings that get easily overlooked by critics who are predisposed not to see religious and spiritual implications in serious high art, to see art and religion as autonomous and mutually exclusive.

Religion, Spirituality, and Exhibitions of Modern and Contemporary Art

The contemporary art world's interest in the relationship between art and religion and/or spirituality is suggested by a number of significant museum exhibitions. They reveal that, at the very least, the art world is growing increasingly uncomfortable with its collective unbelief. And so there appears to be openness toward contemporary art's participation in things spiritual and religious. A survey of recent exhibitions will sketch out a context within which a critical approach to contemporary art, nourished by the Nicene faith, can have a significant impact on the contemporary art world beyond merely providing a "Christian perspective" that claims to sort out the aesthetic sheep from the goats.

The first and most comprehensive exhibition was the Los Angeles County Museum of Art's groundbreaking "The Spiritual in Art: Abstract Painting 1890–1985" (1986).[12] This exhibition explored the historical relationship between abstract painting and the quest for the spiritual. It argued that the development of abstract painting operates within a larger modern search for transcendence. Art historian and curator Kirk Varnedoe observed that early European abstraction is largely idealistic, neoplatonic, and mystical in its desire to attain an unmediated experience of the divine, truth, or Spirit.[13] Far from attempting to deny belief, as Elkins and de Duve suggest, modern art is itself a form of belief, which, through the cultural-linguistic forms it takes, both complements and competes with religious belief. The Museum of Contemporary Art in Chicago organized "Negotiating Rapture" (1996), an exhibition that explored the relationship between aesthetic and spiritual experience, which itself has been a chief feature of modernity's transcendence.[14] The Aldrich Museum of Contemporary Art in Ridgefield, Connecticut, presented an ambitious exhibition, entitled "Faith: The Impact of Judeo-Christian Religion on Art at the Millennium" (2000), which demonstrated the continued viability and potency of institutional religious imagery for contemporary artists, even in a post-Christian culture.[15] John Ravenal curated an exhibition at the Virginia Museum of Fine Arts entitled "Vanitas: Meditations on Life and Death in Contemporary Art" (2000), which showed many of the most important contemporary artists working with a theme that has preoccupied artists for centuries. Jeff Fleming curated "Magic Markers: Objects of Transformation" at the Des Moines Art Center (2003), which presents contemporary artists who recognize the power of "hard things" in general and art in particular.[16] "The Inward Eye: Transcendence in Contemporary Art," organized by the Contemporary Arts Museum in Houston (2001), presented specific works by contemporary artists that elicited an intense spiritual response from the curator, Lynn Herbert.[17]

And finally, artists Meg Cranston and John Baldessari organized "100 Artists See God" (2004), an exhibition organized under the auspices of Independent Curators International, which revealed the diverse ways artists make reference to "God," as a cultural or linguistic trope or metaphor, in their work.[18] In his essay in the catalog, however, critic Thomas McEvilley suggests that even these ways of "seeing" God are, in fact, insufficient: "It seems to many that art, in partially shaking off its ancient connection with religion, has begun at last to emerge from the Dark Ages. It seems best to acknowledge only with irony, then, that the ancient connection still somewhat hiddenly exists."[19] McEvilley offers a subtle rebuke to the approach of many of the artists included in this exhibition who used irony and satire to shield themselves from the reality that the connection with religion still obtains. And David Morgan observed this in the exhibition: "Most work in the present exhibition tends to reinforce a traditional aesthetic of distance."[20] This distance, wrought from the Enlightenment through the Kantian notion of "disinterestedness," and a purely secular interpretation of the history of modern art, presupposes, like Elkins and de Duve, that religion can (should?) be "examined" and "scrutinized" by art only at a critical distance.

Another significant project is "Awake: Art, Buddhism, and the Dimensions of Consciousness," a collaboration organized by Jacqueline Bass and Mary Jane Jacob, from 1999–2005, which brought together artists, curators, critics, and other arts professionals to explore the relationship between the "meditative, creative, and perceiving mind and the implications of Buddhist perspectives for artistic and museum practices in the United States."[21] A significant aspect of the contemporary art world's interest in things religious and spiritual finds expression in Buddhism. No doubt this interest is reflective of an Enlightenment-based distaste for institutionalized religion in favor of an unfettered individualistic spirituality of the heart. But this is not a sufficient explanation. It can also reflect a significant interest in practices, habits, and rituals that recognize the importance of contemplation and communion as spiritual disciplines that produce experience, which can be considered significant points of contact for a Christian approach to contemporary art that embraces the fullness of the Nicene expression. Moreover, from an apologetic perspective, the Nicene faith is as Eastern as it is Western, and can therefore be an effective and productive conversation partner with other Eastern religious practices, such as Buddhism, Hinduism, and Taoism, that avoid making Christianity captive to American cultural politics.

These are just a few projects that through their engagement with religion and spirituality, no matter how ambivalently and insufficiently, still provide significant opportunities to reflect further on the religious and spiritual dimension of contemporary art nourished by the Nicene Christian faith. Most of these projects have interpreted the work of these artists (some of them modern, others postmodern) largely through the lens of a modern understanding of the transcendent. They have not considered that transcendence itself is in transition, that the purely intellectual or optical experience of the spiritual that transcends the limits of history, culture, tradition, and embodiment, has lost its authority. What remains to be done is reflection on the very nature of what constitutes the religious or spiritual identity of contemporary art in light of the idea of transcendence in transition, a transition from modernity's disembodied purity to one that is sought in and through embodiment, tradition, cultural practice, and the material world itself, in which art and religion are of a piece, not mutually exclusive. The *spiritual* is thus revealed to cut through both artistic and religious practice, demonstrating that these practices are not merely reflective of but constitutive of personal identity and experience.[22]

New York–based critic and independent curator Klaus Ottmann has made the exploration and preservation of the distinctiveness of aesthetic experience his primary curatorial and critical project. Ottmann's work as a critic and curator offers fertile ground for critical engagement from the perspective of Nicene Christianity. In fact, Ottmann's approach shares many features and values with a Christian perspective, most especially in the context of his focus on experience, contemplation, and communion.[23] In an early essay, "The New Spiritual" (1989), Ottmann observes,

> There is a need for an art of silence, an art that leaves, in Kierkegaard's words, "the ironic nothingness" for a "mystical nothingness" rooted in terrains of silence

that make us listen to the innerness of our being, relate the myths of creation, and place us within the original purity and sincerity of the beginning of all things. A silence that restores art to the world by restoring its meaning.[24]

For Ottmann the contemporary art world has lost sight of the primacy and power of the fullness of aesthetic experience. "Perhaps what is needed," Ottmann suggests in an introductory essay in a recent exhibition catalogue, "are exhibitions that present art again primarily as 'experience,' with minimal curatorial and didactic intervention."[25] Ottmann continues, "But while art should not be complacent within our fast-paced, media-driven world, it also should not provide solace *without* critical reflection or perceptual discomfort."[26] Ottmann is adamant that art requires sustained contemplation, even communion, not "interpretation," "explanation," and "decoding."

An important part of artistic practice for Ottmann is what he calls the "genius decision." He writes,

> I describe the creative act as an active-passive leap that the artist is impelled to make and the viewer is challenged to repeat. Genius is traditionally understood as a passive quality, while decision is borne out of an act of free will. Genius decision expresses a paradox that, in my view, is essential to the creation and viewing of art. It asserts the artist's autonomy *precisely* by abolishing it; in a way, the decision is made *after* the extraordinary act has already been accomplished.[27]

Ottmann's "genius decision" is influenced by his reflection on Kierkegaard's "leap of faith," St. Augustine's reflections on time, and negative theology.[28] For Ottmann the work of art embodies its process, not merely the material means by which it has come into existence but also the decisions the artist made along the way. The process of making, of shaping materials, is a constitutive element of its spirituality. And the process is precisely what philosopher Paul Crowther argues is the transcendent nature of art.

Ottmann's project as a critic and curator, then, is to draw the viewer's attention to the multitude of decisions that artists make in their studio practice. It is this experience that Ottmann calls "spiritual" and "transcendent." In "The New Spiritual," Ottmann argues that the artists he discusses

> do not represent a new trend in art. Rather, they suggest a paradigm shift from a formalistic, self-referential, cynical art towards a more ecological, more feminist, more bodily, more process-oriented art that reinvents humanity within these terms. Their art carries glimpses of abandoned meaning, of the silence, that "mystical nothingness," in which the voices of meaning can still be heard.[29]

The still small voice of meaning is, for Ottmann, preserved in artistic practice that takes the human being as a process, a product of context, surroundings, and effort. Ottmann goes on to argue: "Only a new, ecological spirituality that abandons anthropocentrism and is in reverence of our environment and all its inhabitants can bridge the gap between religion and science, a gap that has tragic consequences for the well-being of our planet."[30]

In a more recent essay, Ottmann refines his understanding of the new spiritual:

> Much of contemporary sculpture has been newly engaged in a materialist formalism, one that is based in part on a structuralist analysis of the world that attributes ideological meaning to the materials themselves or inscribes linguistic codes onto them, and in part on a participatory humanism—a renewed involvement in the question of being, transcendence, and the social by way of its materiality—a new variant, which I have chosen to name "spiritual materiality."[31]

For Ottmann this "spiritual materiality" manifests at once an aesthetic and ethical moment by which aesthetic form embodies or shows forth the artistic decisions that brought it into existence, artistic decisions in which the viewer vicariously participates in the life of the Other through the work of art. Ottmann's views are shaped by French phenomenologist Emmanuel Levinas, whose understanding of the primacy of the Other has deep roots in traditional Jewish sources.[32] Ottmann himself is deeply interested in Jewish mysticism. As editor in chief of Spring Publications in Putnam, Connecticut, Ottmann has translated two works by Gershom Scholem, a leading scholar on Jewish mysticism. He is also in the process of translating F. W. J. Schelling's *Philosophy and Religion* (1804).

Ottmann's distinctive critical approach has found its embodiment in two recent exhibitions, the SITE Santa Fe Sixth International Biennial Exhibition (2006), entitled "Still Points in a Turning World," and OPEN ev+a 2007, Ireland's preeminent annual exhibition of contemporary art, entitled "A Sense of Place." Concerned with the context within which art is presented, Ottmann refuses to exhibit any artist's work next to the work of others, which he argues mutes the artist's distinctive voices while drawing too much attention to the curator's choices, selections, and placement. Rather, he prefers to create separate spaces for each to be experienced on its own terms, under its own ideal conditions. In both exhibitions, Ottmann presents distinctive aesthetic moments that open up onto a vista of experience that transcends the merely aesthetic or, perhaps better, reveals the aesthetic to be more encompassing than most critics would admit. Ottmann states, "This Biennial [SITE Santa Fe] attempts to insert a temporary still point between Presence and Presentation, between unmediated experience and interpretation."[33] With A Sense of Place, Ottmann chose numerous traditional and nontraditional sites in Limerick, Ireland, for the exhibition of thirty-two artists from Ireland, Continental Europe, and the United States, among them St. Mary's Cathedral, which included a sculpture figure by Enrique Martínez Celaya of a young boy raising his arm ever so slightly.

A shift in the very concept of transcendence has and is occurring throughout social and cultural practices, of which contemporary art is but one important part. Ottmann argues, "Transcendence is not a modality of essence—not a question of being or not-being—but rather an ethical imperative."[34] Following Ottmann, transcendence is in transition. The massive paradigm shifts of the last twenty-five years have brought with them a reevaluation and reconstitution of the concepts that underwrite our experience of the world. Transcendence is one such concept that, far from being limited to religious institutions, gives meaning and significance to a wide range of cultural practices, including the visual arts.

Modernity sought to distill a pure, optical, and even disembodied essence from myriad social, cultural, and political practices, including separating art from religion, or regarding them as competitors in their capacity to give form to personal experience. This understanding of transcendence privileged intellection, self-reflection, and the dislocation of mind from body, which are the particular legacy of Cartesian and Kantian thought as well as Protestant cultural practice. Moreover, as premodern discourses privileged religious institutions as the framework within which or the foundation upon which transcendence was understood in and through social, cultural, and political practice, modernity increasingly privileged the experience of the arts, particularly the visual arts, as the purest expression of transcendence for the modern world. Modernity's transcendence, whether it is embodied in art, politics, or religion, became predominantly and autonomously limited to the aesthetic. Contemporary artistic practice, however, as Ottmann has observed, opens the aesthetic back up in an expansive way to spiritual, ethical, and social meaning that draws art closer to religion, as a complex set of practices that produce experience, that constitute belief, rather than merely giving shape to preexistent experience and belief.[35]

This embodied, materialistic, even cultural-linguistic understanding of transcendence in which, as Edith Wyschogrod observes about Levinas, "transcendence is compressed into the sphere of intersubjective existence," offers important implications for remapping the discursive coordinates of cultural analysis and critique.[36] Transcendence is material as well as spiritual; engaged and not escapist; collaborative and communal, and not individualistic and private; ethical and not merely aesthetic. It is precisely at this place that a critical perspective nourished and funded by a Nicene Christian faith can offer a full-bodied critical approach to contemporary art that acknowledges the depth and breadth of the aesthetic and its experience that extends and clarifies work that is already being done by critics and curators who are sensitive to the relationship of the spiritual to the material, the aesthetic to the ethical and religious.[37] Given this new framework of embodied transcendence, it is perhaps appropriate to revisit the economy of the icon from another perspective, before initiating a discussion of contemporary art.

Icons and Contemporary Art

The Second Council of Nicaea in 787 was not simply an affirmation of a traditional practice, or even the legitimization of art, so-called, in the life of the church. It has significant christological ramifications for aesthetics, for the relationship of the immanent to the transcendent, and for contemporary artistic practice. It is worth quoting again the provocative statement by Jean-Luc Marion:

> The image-affirming doctrine of the Second Council of Nicaea concerns not only nor first of all a point in the history of ideas, nor even a decision of Christian dogma: it formulates above all an—perhaps the only—alternative to the contemporary disaster of the image. In the icon, the visible and the invisible embrace each other from a fire that no longer destroys but rather lights up the divine face for humanity.[38]

The Second Council of Nicaea declared that the veneration of icons was not merely to be tolerated but was the necessary practice of orthodox christological dogma. The council also clarified the implications of the incarnation of the Word for all image-making and aesthetic form, of which icons were simply the most fundamental or explicit part, given their role in private devotion and the divine liturgy, which ultimately is the church's aesthetics and poetics and is thus the ground of *all* aesthetics and poetics.

Nicaea II rejected the notion that icons were merely of educational value, which was the preferred emphasis of the Latin Church (and which was further intensified in the Reformation), in favor of the idea that the icon projects presence. Icons are a window through which the spiritual can be experienced in matter. They discipline sight as we look at the world through the eyes of faith. And although they never contradict revelation in the Scriptures or tradition, the icon is not merely a picture or an illustration of revelation. The implications of the icon in the Orthodox tradition are clear: since God deified matter through the incarnation of the Son, not only has all humanity subsequently been changed, so too has all visual imagery and aesthetic form. Herein lies the important difference between *veneration* in the new covenant and *idolatry* in the old covenant, which had not enjoyed the blessings of the incarnation.

An icon is not simply a tool of *communication*, an apparatus for education and edification in which a preformed thought, message, or meaning is wrapped in form and content and sent out to a viewer. An icon is thus not a visual illustration of a thought, message, or doctrine. It is alive in the sense that its meaning cannot be explained linguistically. It is overdetermined. One does not passively receive the communication, but enters into it contemplatively. It is a means of communion, a way to partake of the divine nature. The icon can work on us in different ways, perhaps toward different ends. There is thus not a single "meaning" communicated by the image to every viewer in the same way, even though it produces, as well as shapes and defines, our experience.

This idea of communion was something the Latin Church in the West was somewhat uncomfortable with, preferring to stress the icon's educational function, which is why the Eastern practice of bodily, physical veneration by touching and kissing was prohibited in the West, where the images were placed out of reach of the laity. This discomfort became even more pronounced with the Reformers, as Luther's own somewhat positive attitude toward icons and imagery in worship was predicated only on their educational value, which consequently had a profound effect on the work of Lucas Cranach. The Calvinist and Anabaptist communities took Luther's ambivalence to the extreme and prohibited all imagery. But recent generations have witnessed a serious effort on the part of Protestant denominations to restore the visual arts to their worship, including, and perhaps most provocatively, in the emergent conversation.

But these attempts often follow the Western view that the visual arts are illustrations or some kind of value added to a worship service, not a means of communion and contemplation, not reflective of an expansive aesthetic that is a window into the spiritual, but decoration or, in the case of more savvy and progressive communities, a brand. It is important to recognize—and the economy of the icon makes this abundantly clear—that an icon is not merely the sum total of what it depicts; it is not only an image, it is also an object, a piece of wood panel with paint applied to it. But it is also more than its physical properties. Its making, too, is what gives it power.

This view of icons has important implications as we look at the history of art since 1945. It is there that we find an aesthetic that draws significantly, albeit unconsciously, on the economy of the icon. About Frank Stella's influential *Die Fahne hoch!* (1959), Rosalind Krauss suggested that "the painting is not so much an icon as a meditation on the logic of the icon, on how such a form might have come into being as a vehicle of cultural meaning."[39] Krauss's modernism keeps her at a critical distance from meditating on the icon, but she allows herself to reflect on how Stella might have "meditated" on its "logic" as a sign system. The icon, and the spiritual presence it embodies and projects, continues to haunt the metaphors of even the most self-conscious secular art writers. Even the so-called logic of the icon embodies a spiritual reality.

The logic of the icon also consists of more than the artifact itself. It consists of its context to provide the ideal conditions for its experience. In a brilliant essay, "The Church Ritual as a Synthesis of the Arts" (1922), Pavel Florensky declares, "A work of art is a living entity and requires special conditions in which to live and particularly in which to flourish."[40] Florensky's observation falls in line with Georgie Dickie's institutional theory of art, George A. Lindbeck's "cultural-linguistic" approach to religion, and Klaus Ottmann's sensitivity to the context in which contemporary art is presented. In the same essay, Florensky describes in great detail the context in which the icon is intended to be experienced, which includes flickering candlelight illuminating the darkness of the sanctuary, the blue haze of incense, and the sounds of chanted prayer, a whole spatial apparatus that provides the framework for experiencing the icon in all its intended potential.[41] This is how reflection on the economy of the icon can be helpful in understanding other installation, conceptual, and performance art, art forms in which Ottmann is particularly interested.

Thus Nicaea II does much more than simply underwrite painting: it incorporates objects, practices, and environments into an expansive and comprehensive aesthetic framework. Christoph Cardinal Schönborn puts it well when he states:

> What is needed is a new way of seeing and hearing, a new sensitivity to the mystery. It is not by way of ingratiating herself or by trying to be "modern" at any cost that the Church can once again become a space for the arts, but rather by cultivating an awareness of the mystery of the One who is both God and man. A Church that in her liturgy, in her very life, draws vitality from the sense of awe in facing the mystery, will provide breathing space for any art whose primary purpose is not a breathless pursuit of outward success.[42]

Modern and contemporary art deserves the breathing space provided by the richness of the Nicene Christian faith.

Art since 1945: Precursors

Before a discussion of contemporary artistic practice can take place, it is important to discuss very briefly the development of American art after 1945, for it is this period (the 1940s and 1950s) and the following decades that set the stage for the present context. The most influential artists of this period are Jackson Pollock and Marcel Duchamp. They produced work that was so unusual and unexpected, and that undermined traditional notions of what constitutes art, that they were accused of destroying art. Critic Robert Storr, former curator of contemporary art at the Museum of Modern Art, observed, "Jackson Pollock's work is a reef on which theories crack."[43] Through their reconceptualization of objects, practices, and environments, the work Pollock and Duchamp created served as both a powerful stimulation and a challenge for aesthetic innovation for subsequent generations of artists.

Jackson Pollock was the first "star artist" in the United States. He was featured in a *Life* magazine story in 1949 titled "Is He the Greatest Living Painter in the United States?"[44] There were two reasons for his star status. First, he was a ruggedly handsome, Wyoming-born, California-reared American, who liked fast cars and denim jeans (his tragic death in an auto accident in 1956 at the age of 44 only intensified this James Dean-like persona). Second, he was at that time producing paintings that seemed to destroy every preconception of what painting was believed to be.

Pollock had already enjoyed early critical success when he and his wife, artist Lee Krasner, moved to The Springs in the Hamptons in 1947, where he took over an old barn for his studio. (By 1946 critic Clement Greenberg was already calling Pollock one of the most important painters working.) It was there that he enacted his complete break from conventional painting, which rendered even the most radical paintings in the early modernist tradition, Kasimir Malevich's white paintings and black squares, or Picasso's cubist canvases, conventional by comparison.

In his cramped barn, Pollock rolled out unstretched and uncut canvas on the floor. With sticks and the back ends of brushes, he began to drip skeins of enamel paint onto the surface, covering every square inch of canvas with a tangled web of strands and drips of paint. Pollock produced these remarkable canvases, called "poured" or "drip" or "all-over" paintings, from 1947–50. These works were unusual for two reasons. First, and most obviously, was the means by which they were produced—by pouring and dripping paint while walking about the canvas laid on the floor, not applying paint slowly and deliberately on a stretched canvas propped on an easel. Second was that the paintings had no subject matter and so it was—and is—nearly impossible to interpret them, to ascertain whether they have any meaning at all.[45] Critic Donald B. Kuspit suggests that the power of Pollock's all-over pictures is that they "embrace generality, evoke totality. . . . They have concretized totality by overcoming traditional pictorial dichotomies."[46]

The "traditional pictorial dichotomies" to which Kuspit refers consist first and foremost of the tension between form and content—between the "how" and the "what" of the painting. Another pictorial dichotomy is the relationship between a painting's surface as consisting of the illusion of a foreground and a background and its identity as simply a flat surface on which pigment is applied. It is these dichotomies, these tensions, that create the vibration of painting as high art. Florensky himself declares, "True art is a unity of content and the means of expressing that content."[47]

It is this "unity," or "dichotomy," that Pollock's paintings appear to transcend, or destroy. Such classic dripped or poured paintings as *One: Number 31, 1950* (fig. 7) do not provide the viewer with a conventional way of experiencing them; that is, they seem not to include content or a subject, but instead to be *all* content or *all* subject. In addition, the surfaces of these paintings refuse to allow the viewer to read a foreground and a background, further complicating and frustrating the habit inherited from the Renaissance of viewing a painting as offering the illusion of a perspective on an object that is depicted. This makes it difficult for the viewer to both enter into and exit from the painting; that is, these paintings do not seem to invite the viewer into the picture at a specific point, lead the viewer through the composition, and lead him or her out. Instead, the viewer is presented with a totality that defies such nuanced optical movement on the viewer's part.

The experience is strangely akin to theologian R. R. Reno's provocative description of Origen's writing as being like standing under a waterfall.[48] One seems to take it in, as much as one can, in one gulp. This is not to say that the surface is unnuanced, undifferentiated, and chaotic. Rather, these pictures offer a vertiginous variety of foreground and background shifts and changes, so much so that such relationships, such dichotomies, seem to dissolve. Perhaps this is what an early critic, Emily Genauer, experienced and was trying to suggest when she wrote that Pollock's paintings were a "mop of tangled hair I have an irresistible urge to comb out."[49]

These remarkable paintings transcend the dichotomy between form and content; they can be read as either all form or all content. They affirm in shocking ways the materiality of painting and its identity as a physical artifact. According to Kirk Varnedoe, who curated the important retrospective of Pollock's work at the Museum of Modern Art in 1998–99, "Pollock reinforced this material quality by stepping on the canvas where it lay on the floor, by stubbing out his cigarettes on it, by pushing his hand against the surface of it. He affirmed that the painting was an option in the world, an extension of the physicality of the world, not a window onto anything else."[50] Pollock's dripped paintings forcefully reasserted the status of painting as an object, first and foremost, which influenced artists such as Donald Judd, Robert Morris, and Carl Andre, all of whom would become associated with minimalism, a movement that sought to draw aesthetic attention to the work of art as an object in the world.

Pollock's canvases also drew unprecedented attention to the process of their making. Pollock's drip paintings affirmed painting's identity as a process. In his famous essay, "The American Action Painters" (1952), critic Harold Rosenberg wrote: "At a certain moment the canvas began to appear to one American painter after another as an arena in which to act—rather than as a space in which to reproduce, re-design, analyze or 'express' an object, actual or imagined. What was to go on the canvas was not a picture but an event."[51]

Rosenberg's highly influential essay sought to articulate a broad interpretive framework that included such painters as Franz Kline, Willem de Kooning, and Hans Hoffmann in addition to Pollock. Rosenberg's concept of "action painting" was an attempt to deal critically with process as a primary part of painting's meaning. Rosenberg's concept was strengthened by the film stills published in 1950 by photographer Hans Namuth of Pollock painting in his Long Island studio. Namuth recorded Pollock's athletic movements and graceful gestures as he spilled, slapped, and dripped paint onto his canvases, drawing even more attention to the physicality and materiality of the paintings as well as offering empirical proof of Pollock's working method. These photographs, Rosenberg's essay, and the paintings themselves had a powerful influence on performance artists such as Allan Kaprow and George Maciunias who found the weight of Pollock's aesthetic meaning in his performance of them. This offered a foundation and legitimization of their own work, which was even less object-based and more ephemeral.

Pollock's work, then, could simultaneously affirm that painting is an object in the world *and* the record of a performance, a performance of a priest who could by his gestures and actions enact transformation in an almost sacramental manner. Pollock's barn thus became the sacred space within which the priest Pollock worked and the context within which his actions had meaning.[52] The paintings were the by-product, the residue, the aftermath of certain sacred actions at a particular moment in time in a particular context. It is no wonder that Pollock was often loathe to allow his paintings to leave the barn, since they were the product of an intricate set of practices in a particular space. At a certain level Pollock clearly understood that the space, the paintings, and his actions were all of a piece.

In addition to, or perhaps because of, the impact of Pollock's work, Marcel Duchamp experienced a revival in the mid-1950s. His revival was part of an attempt on the part of critics to find a historical precedent for the object-based work seasoned with ironic humor of such artists as Robert Rauschenberg and Jasper Johns, who were learning the lessons of Pollock and the other action painters and interpreting them through their own distinctive aesthetic preoccupations. After his scandal at the Armory Show in 1913 and the infamous urinal episode in 1917, Duchamp receded from public view, "quitting" art to concentrate on playing chess for the French National Team and splitting time between New York and Buenos Aires. But this was to change in the early fifties. Art historian Hal Foster even suggests that Duchamp only became "Duchampian" in the late fifties and early sixties.[53]

The rediscovery of Duchamp's readymades in the late fifties and early sixties helped facilitate the exploration of the aesthetic potential of all objects and the object status of all works of art and helped drive the minimalist aesthetic. Duchamp became "Duchampian" through his practice of presenting as art ordinary objects such as shovels, urinals, bicycle wheels on stools, combs, and other ordinary "found" objects that he called "readymades." It is therefore worth rehearsing the original context of Duchamp's most famous readymade, *Fountain* (1917; fig. 8).

There is probably no object that expresses more perfectly the various responses to modernist art than the urinal Marcel Duchamp submitted to the jury of the Society of Independent Artists in New York in 1917. For Christians and cultural conservatives, this work, which Duchamp humorously entitled *Fountain*, confirms all the suspicions that modern art is a joke that has been pawned off on an innocent and unsuspecting public.[54] Duchamp scholar William Camfield assesses the situation quite accurately when he observes that "some deny that *Fountain* is art but believe it is significant for the history of art and aesthetics. Others accept it grudgingly as art but deny that it is significant. To complete the circle, some insist that *Fountain* is neither art nor an object of historical consequence, while a few assert that it is both art and significant—though for utterly incompatible reasons."[55]

Duchamp had been living in New York City since the Armory Show and was instrumental in developing the Society of Independent Artists, which sought to provide an open, free venue for the expansion of modern art and the education of the public. Duchamp's *Fountain* was intended to test those principles. Under the pseudonym "R. Mutt," Duchamp submitted a urinal for presentation in the society's open exhibition. It was denied acceptance and, in response, Duchamp, defending the "artistic freedom" of R. Mutt, resigned his position on the board. In further defense of Mutt, Duchamp published (anonymously) a critical apologetic of *Fountain* in *The Blind Man*, a periodical established as an educational outreach of the society. The apologetic claims that "he took an ordinary article of life, placed it so that its useful significance disappeared under the new title and point of view—created a new thought for that object."[56]

The significance of the *Fountain* episode is important on several levels. Duchamp's readymades affirm that art is not merely an object, it is an institutionalized way of making, looking, experiencing, and interpreting. It is a confluence of specific circumstances that include the artist, viewer, object, and the way that object is presented and displayed. As Florensky's remarks suggest, this is as true for Rublev's *Holy Trinity* as it is for Duchamp's *Fountain*.

Duchamp considered *Fountain* and his other readymades to be more than a detached, analytical exploration of art's philosophical basis. Duchamp believed them to be works of art, and therefore they were not only deeply aesthetic but also saturated with carnal and spiritual desire that was mediated through and embodied by the complexity of the aesthetic. "Art cannot be understood through the intellect, but is felt through an emotion presenting some analogy with a religious faith or a sexual attraction—an esthetic echo. The important point here is to differentiate taste from the esthetic echo."[57] Despite the fact that Duchamp did not make *Fountain*, but found it, it still possesses an "esthetic echo," which is a complex harmony of sounds derived both from the object itself and its circumstances of presentation. Duchamp's objects are not dead, static, or neutral. They are alive, imbued with belief and desire, in large part because they were first part of Duchamp's lived environment before becoming a readymade work of art. The object's previous life outside the world of art, whether a urinal, bicycle wheel, shovel, or comb, remains in some way to inform the experience of the work.

This belief and desire come to the fore in the role that the photographer Alfred Stieglitz's photograph of *Fountain* came to play in twentieth century art. First, it documented an object that was lost almost immediately after its rejection from the exhibition. Second, the aesthetic beauty of Stieglitz's image brought out the aesthetic aspect of the object, which even invited commentary that likened the work to the forms of the Buddha and, perhaps more surprisingly, the Madonna and Child group.[58] Duchamp was not primarily or simply a joker but was fascinated with the complexity of his and our attachment to objects, and this fascination underwrote his interest in hermeticism, Gnosticism, alchemy, the erotic, and spirituality. His creative work is an aesthetic and creative reflection on the nature of knowledge and spirituality, which is overlooked by most commentators.[59] More recently, however, attention has also been paid to Duchamp's abiding but often overlooked interest in Buddhist thought and practice.[60]

Pollock and Duchamp shared an interest in the erotic aspect of art. The sensuality and materiality of Pollock's dripped paintings were often likened to sexual activity. The erotic and its embodiment in objects, environments, and practices characterizes an important direction in contemporary art that reveals the contours of a world saturated with desire. This offers productive space for critical exploration and elaboration from Nicene Christianity. This kind of exploration and elaboration is particularly evident in the metaphysical and mystical speculations of the Russian philosopher-theologians Sergei Bulgakov, Pavel Florensky, and Vladimir Soloviev. Art criticism can benefit from such an aggressively creative approach to contemporary art.

What is required is a renewed sensitivity to a world saturated with sacramental and liturgical meaning and significance that can emerge most fully through an analogical worldview. The premodern approach mediates the immanent and the transcendent because God is viewed as the cause of all things; all things are symbols and signs of other things, all of which have their being in and through God, which connects them. The premodern approach is reflected in St. Augustine's famous prayer in *Confessions*: "You have made us for yourself, and our hearts are restless until they rest in you." Desire plays an important role in the analogical worldview, for it is desire that leads one toward the other, and ultimately toward God. And it is this movement toward the other that is the ground of transcendence, a transcendence of one's own limitations, one's own lack. Graham Ward argues, "I desire not because I lack the other, but because the other is closer to me than I am to myself (and makes me aware that what I lack is, in part, myself)."[61]

The analogical worldview affirms that all desire, even erotic desire, manifests an ultimate desire for communion with God, to partake in the energies of his divine nature (2 Pet. 1:4). This desire for transcendence is at the same time a process of self-exploration, for St. Augustine's question, who is God? is inextricable from the question of who St. Augustine is.[62] There are many contemporary artists who are producing work that embodies this transcendent, analogical worldview.

Embodied Transcendence in Contemporary Art

Contemporary artistic practice reflects an interest in exploring the potential of objects, practices, and environments in relationship that suggest meaning and significance are contingent, relational, and transcendent. This practice builds on the legacy of Jackson Pollock and Marcel Duchamp. Moreover, this manner of artistic practice offers a way of thinking about and experiencing transcendence that is profoundly embodied, one that does not find escape in the deepest recesses of mind or spirit but in and through the body, often in community. This manner of artistic practice is related to what C. S. Lewis calls "amphibious existence," the seamless relationship between the material and the spiritual.[63] Much contemporary artistic practice embodies this amphibious existence, thus transcending even the limited intentions of the artist. It also recognizes that objects, practices, and environments produce personal experience, selfhood, and identity.

St. Paul says "honor God with your body" (1 Cor. 6:20). According to modern tastes and habits (including modern Christian tastes and habits), Nicene Christianity is disturbingly embodied. But it is this analogical paradigm, in which the sacramental and liturgical life of the church saturates every fiber of life, that offers deeply powerful and suggestive ways of experiencing and understanding this trend in contemporary artistic practice.

What follows are brief—admittedly too brief—discussions of six works of art that suggest this contingent relationship between objects, practices, and environments. The artists and works of art discussed below are highly idiosyncratic, representing only a small sample of artists that interest me. Many more artists and works of art could be, and should be, discussed in this context. Each aspect will be illustrated by two works of art. Each work is inflected, in some way, by the achievements of Pollock and Duchamp and each one, in some way, embodies in aesthetic form the "amphibious existence" of the Nicene Christian worldview.

Objects

That a work of art is an object in the world like other objects was an important rediscovery by artists influenced by Duchamp through his readymades and Pollock through his dripped and poured canvases. Duchamp rejected the notion that his readymades destroyed the power of art or the aesthetic.

> The curious thing about the Ready-Made is that I've never been able to arrive at a definition or explanation that fully satisfies me. . . . There's still magic in the idea, so I'd rather keep it that way than try to be exoteric about it. . . . Let's say you use a tube of paint; you didn't make it. You bought it and used it as a ready-made. Even if you mix two vermilions together, it's still a mixing of two ready-mades. So man can never expect to start from scratch; he must start from ready-made things like even his mother and father.[64]

Duchamp is reflecting here on the contingency of his readymades, that they are not easily explained and categorized, in large part because they are analogical: their meaning emerges in and through their connection to other objects, practices, and environments. This is similar to the way objects function in the church, whether the wood panels of icons, the bones of saints and martyrs and other materials that function as sacred relics, or liturgical furniture that participates in and projects the sacramental and liturgical life of the church.

Janine Antoni's *Gnaw*, 1992 (fig. 9), which is in the collection of the Museum of Modern Art in New York, is a nightmare for art museum curators and collections managers. It is also a nightmare for critics and commentators who worry that modern art is a joke played on the innocent, unsuspecting "average person" by ultra-elites. She can't really be serious about this, can she?[65] *Gnaw* consists of two large (600 lb., 24 x 24 x 24 in.) minimalist cubes, one made of chocolate and the other of lard. But she has altered them by biting and eating them, hence the work's title. In addition, the piece also includes a mirror-and-glass case displaying lipstick forms made from the bitten-off lard mixed with wax and pigment, and heart-shaped versions of chocolate candy containers made from the bitten-off chocolate.

> Through her choice of materials and method, this female artist has taken abstract geometric forms identified with the largely male realm of minimalism and shaped a work that speaks both viscerally and quite specifically to our associations with the materials. These are not simply substances that can be consumed, but ones that carry anxious connections between body image and the pleasure that can turn into disgust with the over-consumption.[66]

Another important part of this work is its entropy—that both the chocolate and the lard are not stable materials. They are contingent. Their death is imminent. The difference, however, is one of time. The chocolate cube is decaying, showing the brittleness and the change of color that comes with aged chocolate. The lard, when it ages, loses its shape and falls apart. And it does so very rapidly. Therefore, each time *Gnaw* is presented, a new cube of lard is fabricated. What is presented, then, are two different forms of degeneration, one barely noticeable, one quite obvious. As art museum professionals know, all works of art are in the process of deteriorization. Some might take millennia, others two months. Therefore the goal of conservation is merely to slow that process. No object is autonomous, stable, or inert, and Antoni makes this fact a primary aspect of her work.

The cubes are relics of Antoni's ritualized physical presence as she bites the chocolate and lard away from the cube. Antoni knelt in front of the cubes and touched them only with her mouth, similar, she says, to "receiving the host from the priest in the old-fashioned way."[67] *Gnaw* suggests that making and experiencing art is much more than an optical—and thus disembodied—experience. Likewise, worship is profoundly corporeal, bodily. "Honor God with your body," St. Paul tells the Corinthians. The practices of fasting and feasting emphasize the fact that you are what you eat (bitterness of lard and sweetness of chocolate), and what you eat does indeed have spiritual significance.

This is similar to the way icons are experienced in the Eastern Church: they are touched, kissed, bowed in front of, not merely looked at or used as teaching tools. The psalmist says, "Taste and see that the Lord is good" (Ps. 34:8). The effect of *Gnaw* relies on the fact that tasting and seeing are closely related: so close, in fact, that the relationship can be expressed outside the divine liturgy only through the aesthetic complexities of art. Antoni's work shows us the relationship of tasting and seeing and its function within the context of time, its loss as well as its recovery through imaginative recollection. It is up to the sensitive viewer to discern that this relationship is contingent on the goodness of the Lord, and that it is worth contemplating because of it.

The German artist Wolfgang Laib's artistic practice, like Antoni's, makes use of nontraditional artistic materials with their own nonartistic histories to create aesthetic experiences that affirm the inextricable relationship between the spiritual and the material. His work is characterized by what critic Klaus Ottmann observes as "the desire to participate in the beauty of nature. . . . Laib considers the attempt to create beauty the tragic failure of most art. For him, art is an act of participation and sharing—'participating in nature and sharing that experience with others.'"[68] Unlike Antoni's work, Laib's artistic practice does not emerge from his understanding and subsequent development of form. Instead, Laib's work is described as follows: "A pursuit of simplicity as a means of order, it relates to cultural practices and religions around the world: Japanese Zen Buddhism, Chinese Buddhism, the teachings of Saint Francis of Assisi, American Quakerism."[69]

Laib's father, a doctor born in Metzingen, Germany, developed an abiding interest in India, where they traveled often and where Laib's father developed a passion to help ease the poverty of several communities. In 1972 Laib spent six months in India working on his medical thesis, which is devoted to analyzing the drinking water in the rural areas of Southern India. Laib returned to Germany a changed man. As Ottmann explains,

> After returning to Germany, Laib decided to take time off from his medical studies. Discovering a large black rock, about three feet in length, in the countryside near where he lived, he brought it home and set to work on carving it into a perfect ovoid. During the three months he took to do this, it became clear to him that he was dissatisfied with medical science, which he felt addressed human needs only imperfectly, and that he wanted to turn to art instead. He eventually finished his dissertation, but he has never practiced medicine. The

black oval stone has remained in his home ever since, the only artwork of his own creation that he has chosen to live with on a daily basis.[70]

Laib's aesthetic practice thus emerged slowly from this original experience of finding and laboriously shaping this stone. The materials he most often chooses to work with are milk, marble, pollen, beeswax, and rice. The forms that usually emerge are houses, cones, white and yellow rectangles, corridors and chambers, ships, and ziggurats.[71]

The best known of Laib's works are his pollen installations and milk stones, both of which he began in the 1970s. The pollen pieces consist of painstakingly collecting pollen from the fields near his home and, following the seasons, collecting pollen as it comes into season from hazelnut, dandelion, buttercup, and ending with pine. He stores the different pollens in jars, which he often exhibits, and then uses the pollen to create large mounds of vibrant color that seem to float off the floor and have a rich, dense, yet strangely ephemeral character.

In his milk stone works, Laib takes a rectangular slab of polished marble and sands a barely perceptible depression in it (fig. 5). He then pours milk onto the slab in order to fill this slight void, which creates the perception of a solid whitish object while at the same time generating the experience of solidity and instability. Another important aspect of these pieces is the subtle contrast between the visual textures of the marble and milk. In both the milk stone and pollen pieces, organic and natural materials are meticulously worked over and crafted to create an aesthetic manifestation of contemplation. Both works require a labor-intensive process, not only in their production—as Laib separates the pollen and sands the marble—but also in the very act of displaying the work. Laib installs each pollen work himself, spooning out jar after jar of pollen onto the floor. The milk stone pieces are slightly but importantly different. For Laib performs the milk pouring only once for each object. Those who install and exhibit the work are responsible for all subsequent pourings: the milk must be removed from the marble slab *each day* and poured again at the beginning of the next day. Thus we participate in Laib's ritual processes and practices. There are opportunities for such participation, which, not unlike Antoni's works, suggest the temporality of nature's materials, the daily gift of natural experience that quickly disappears but then returns anew. The simplicity of Antoni's and Laib's works succeeds in revealing the rich complexity of aesthetic experience.

Practices

Despite the fact that Antoni's and Laib's works are presentations of "things," they bring to the surface the importance of process as a liturgical practice, whether of biting chocolate and lard or of sanding marble and pouring milk. For many artists the "practice" of art plays an increasingly important part in their work and cannot be separated from the work. The "art" of art is not to be located only in the object, as Harold Rosenberg's notion of action painting revealed, but in the events that lead up to it. This is nowhere clearer than in the practice of icon writing, in which the iconographers, before working on any icon, devote themselves to fasting, Scripture reading, and prayer. The icon is thus the result of those practices, as well as its correct presentation in a worship situation, and is in fact *sustained by them.* This can be seen in Andrei Tarkovsky's film on Andrei Rublev, in which Rublev is never seen working on a single icon as he struggles with disbelief and his passions. Just as the Christian faith is not to be found solely in the doctrine of the creeds, art is not found solely in the object. Christianity is not merely a doctrine, nor is art merely an object. Both are expansive practices that generate objects and doctrines but cannot exclusively be defined by them.

Born in Detroit, James Lee Byars studied art, psychology, and philosophy at Wayne State University. In the late 1950s he moved to Kyoto, Japan, where he lived on and off for the next ten years. After leaving Japan, he lived in New York, Venice, Florence, Bern, and Santa Fe. While in Japan, Byars learned the importance of the ceremonial in communicating meaning and significance, and he incorporated this into his artistic practice. Ceremony plays such an important role in Byars's practice that his work is largely performative, relating closely to the work of the German Joseph Beuys. Max Hollein suggests that

> his performative approach to his own art went so far that in 1994 he donated *The Perfect Smile*, the brief flickering of a smile, to the Gesellschaft für Moderne Kunst at the Museum Ludwig in Cologne. Thanks to this conceptual stroke of genius, it was the first performance to become part of a collection. At the same time this explicitly articulated Byars's desire that it be possible to exhibit the smile for the future even beyond its connection to his person.[72]

Byars's work consisted of exhibitions, actions, and various performances that during the 1960s and 1970s established a lasting presence in Germany. His work is a distinctive blend of minimalism, conceptualism, and Fluxus that sought to transcend the chasm between art and life, to meld

1. Installation view of the Rothko Chapel showing the northwest, north triptych, and northeast wall paintings by Mark Rothko. Photo by Hickey-Robertson. The Rothko Chapel, Houston.

2. Installation view, Robert Gober, Matthew Marks Gallery, New York, 2005. Photographer: Russell Kaye. Copyright Robert Gober, courtesy Matthew Marks Gallery, New York.

3. Enrique Martínez Celaya, *Thing and Deception*, 1997, oil on canvas, 78 x 88 in., Sheldon Memorial Art Gallery, University of Nebraska–Lincoln. Gift of Mr. and Mrs. Arthur Goldberg by exchange.

4. Enrique Martínez Celaya, *The October Cycle*. Installation view, Sheldon Memorial Art Gallery, University of Nebraska–Lincoln, November 2003–January 2004.

5. Wolfgang Laib, milk stone piece, Museum of Contemporary Art, San Diego, 2002. Photograph courtesy Klaus Ottmann.

6. Gabriel Orozco, *Island within an Island*, 1993, Cibachrome, 16 x 20 in. Courtesy Marian Goodman Gallery, New York.

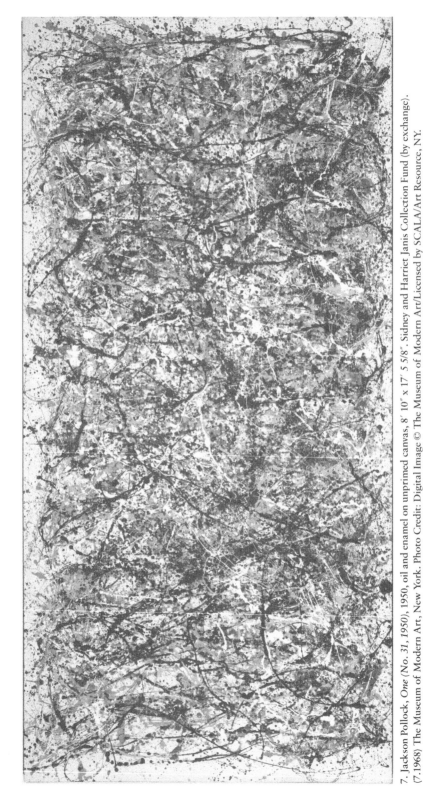

7. Jackson Pollock, *One (No. 31, 1950)*, 1950, oil and enamel on unprimed canvas, 8′ 10″ x 17′ 5 5/8″. Sidney and Harriet Janis Collection Fund (by exchange). (7.1968) The Museum of Modern Art, New York. Photo Credit: Digital Image © The Museum of Modern Art/Licensed by SCALA/Art Resource, NY.

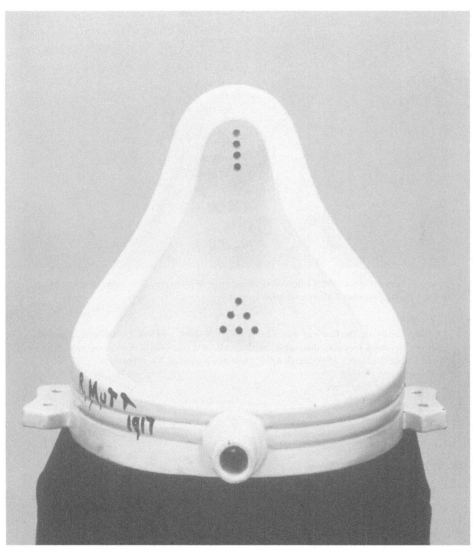

8. Marcel Duchamp, *Fountain*, 1917/1964. Third version, replicated under the direction of the artist in 1964 by the Galarie Schwarz, Milan. Photo: Philippe Migeat. Musee National d'Art Moderne, Centre Georges Pompidou, Paris. Photo Credit: CNAC/MNAM/Dist. Réunion des Musées Nationaux/Art Resource, NY.

9. Janine Antoni, *Gnaw*, 1992. Collection of Museum of Modern Art, New York. Courtesy of the artist, Luhring Augustine Gallery, and Brian Forrest.

10. James Lee Byars, *The Death of James Lee Byars*, 1994–2004, gold leaf, five artificial diamonds (Swarovsy crystals), Plexiglas, dimensions variable. Musée d'art moderne et contemporain, Strasbourg, France (December 2004–March 2005). Photograph courtesy Klaus Ottmann.

11. Enrique Martínez Celaya, *Schneebett*. Installation view, Berliner Philharmonie, Berlin, Germany, November 2004–January 2005.

12. Enrique Martínez Celaya, *Coming Home*. Installation view, Sheldon Memorial Art Gallery, University of Nebraska–Lincoln, August–October 2006.

13. Franz Kline, *Chief*, 1950, oil on canvas, 58 3/8" x 6' 1 ½". Gift of Mr. and Mrs. David M. Solinger. (2.1952) The Museum of Modern Art, New York. Photo Credit: Digital Image © The Museum of Modern Art/ Licensed by SCALA/Art Resource, NY.

the former into the latter, infusing it with the aesthetic self-consciousness of the former.

Byars's work in the late fifties, which caught the eye of curator Dorothy Miller at the Museum of Modern Art, consisted of large-scale minimal black ink drawings and sculptures made from hundreds of sheets of hinged traditional Japanese flax or *kozo* (mulberry) paper that he folded into solid geometric shapes. This laborious process echoes Shinto, an ancient Japanese philosophical practice, in which folding paper is an important part.[73] Byars's interest in elaborate costuming reflects another Japanese influence, Noh theater.

Byars's artistic project is also influenced by his admiration of T. S. Eliot. He believed Eliot's personal life was completely, perfectly identified or submerged with his work. The objectivity of Eliot's approach to his poetry and its relationship to the poet finds an unusual companion in Byars's very subjective performance-based art, in which he plays such an important role that he once mused, "I cancel all my works at death." Byars's goal was to make himself disappear or dissolve into his work in order to focus on the experience of the present, which his artworks and performances were to celebrate. In the early sixties he donated works to the Carnegie Museum of Art in Pittsburgh and the Museum of Modern Art in New York with the stipulation that the artist be listed as "anonymous" and the titles as "untitled."[74] Byars absorbed the Japanese penchant for ceremony, particularly as it manifests itself in Shinto, as a means to imbue ordinary gestures with highly specific meaning and significance. Byars's art is an attempt to use his presence to draw attention to the many overlooked but profoundly important aspects of everyday life. In this way, Byars's work bears important affinities to Fluxus and the American neo-Dada art movement, which first came to critical attention in Berlin in the late 1950s.[75]

Participation becomes an important aesthetic category in much of Byars's work. In the 1960s Byars created a number of garments (another Shinto influence) that would incorporate more than one person, such as *Four in a Dress*, *Three in a Pants*, *Two in a Hat*, and *Dress for 500*. These works brought people into intimate relationship with one another, unifying them rather than distinguishing them, as clothing usually does. Byars's desire for perfection, for creating and bracketing that moment of perfection, wherever he could find it, manifests itself not only in the "perfect smile" performance but also in performances such as the "perfect kiss," which he orchestrated with two others.

Perfection, however, is elusive, and Byars, as a philosophical artist, understood that death haunted the world. Death was closely related to Byars's interest in disappearance, anonymity, and removing his presence from the work of art or aesthetic situation. Moreover, the ephemeral and transitory nature of his work acknowledges that life is a preparation for death. (The church fathers often speak of the life of the church as a sacrament of our death.) And therefore it is not surprising that he devoted a considerable amount of time staging performances that dealt not only with death in general, but with his own death.

In 1983 Byars performed *The Perfect Death of James Lee Byars* in front of the Philadelphia Museum of Art. Wearing a gold-lamé suit, he lay on the ground, which was also painted gold. Byars was made "invisible." He performed this ritual disappearing, called *The Death of James Lee Byars* (fig. 10), in Brussels at the Galerie Marie-Puck Broodthaers, in 1994. Byars's performance of this death ritual took on additional meaning and significance since he was dying of cancer. In 2004, Klaus Ottmann curated a small exhibition of Byars's work at the Whitney Museum of American Art, which featured this piece, without Byars, of course, but with a gold-painted box qua casket and a gallery space painted completely gold, the affect of Byars's absence was profound.

Byars's work suggests an abiding concern with the relationship between absence and presence. Many of his "art works" were seemingly insignificant gestures, actions, or "plays," as he called them, that only existed in documentation, vestiges of an action long gone that survive only in memory or recollection. Ottmann suggests that Byars was a "conjurer who bet the fate of his art on random events supervised by carefully orchestrated rituals."[76]

Ottmann sees in Byars a manifestation of Kierkegaard's distinction between the "genius" and the "apostle," one standing for knowledge, the other for faith. Ottmann observes: "Byars managed to wear both hats (in fact, he would literally alternate between a red hat and a black hat), at times playing the role of analytical philosopher and founder of the World Question Center and, at other times, the spiritual artist/apostle, who rejoiced in the paradoxes of faith."[77] For Byars the "paradoxes of faith" were embodied in the fact that chance was not random. His work presupposes not merely the meaning and significance of random events but that these random events are contingent: their meaning and significance depend on a loving designer, a gifting lover who creates the opportunity for such "chances" to occur.

Like many artists associated with Fluxus, Byars's work is predicated on the gift, freely given. Many, if not most, of Byars's works that are in museum collections are there because he offered them as gifts. And this is not merely Byars's strategy for getting into museum collections without the museum having to pay for the work but an extension of his artistic project, his desire to offer gifts of his presence and absence. Byars's work cannot ultimately be separated from his life. His was a life lived as a work of art, shaped and formed to produce something of beauty in preparation for death. Despite the fact that Byars's primary influences are Japanese, his practice is similar to the goals of the early church fathers, for which there exists no distinction between a person and his works nor a distinction between important and unimportant in one's life. Ultimately for Byars, the world was a matter of interpretation. It could be received as a gift or experienced as a curse and burden. Faith was a way of seeing the world, of noticing. Byars's artistic practice, without question, regarded all the world had to offer as a gift. And he considered his performances as gifts to his audience.

Similar to Byars, process and practice play an important role for Mexican artist Gabriel Orozco, whose work consists of sculpture, photography, painting, and installations in which he intentionally conflates and dissolves the boundaries between them. Orozco, who lives and works in Mexico City and New York, considers himself a "post studio" artist, that is, an artist whose work does not occur sequestered alone in a studio, but out in the world, roaming about, taking notice of things that are often overlooked. In fact, much of Orozco's work is the product of walks with his dog, and this reflects the limits of his own bodily presence in the world; his work is produced through the limits of his bodily presence in a specific geographical location.

Orozco creates and collects objects, documents them through photography, and then displays them as artifacts in his museum and gallery installations, revealing their histories in relationship to him. He considers his artistic practice an "intervention," a way to engage the everyday world through a certain sensibility. This distinctive sensibility has taken the form of such works as *Black Kites* (1997), in which Orozco covered a human skull with diamond, or kite-shaped, forms in graphite pencil. For an exhibition on installation art at the Museum of Contemporary Art in San Diego in 1996, Orozco took an ordinary yellow garden hose and spread it out throughout the museum's campus, tracking his own walk through space. Both works reveal a desire to use art and the aesthetic to celebrate nature. *Black Kites* reveals Orozco's process of studying, appreciating, and celebrating the nuances of the human skull through the simple act of drawing, while his *Yellow Hose* installation does nothing but trace his path through the museum's beautiful grounds. Both works suggest the importance of his own presence: "My body is very important," Orozco observes, "not just in the act of making the intervention in reality, but also in the act of taking an image with a human scale contact."[78]

Orozco's photography serves to document his experience in the world. An important part of his practice is creating what he calls "sculpture on the spot," which are installations made on site in urban environments, such as his *Penske Project*. Art historian Molly Nesbit explains that "each piece in the set was made quickly on the street, the result of a fishing expedition in a dumpster. The work had to be finished there on the spot; it had to be light enough so that one person could lift it. Its scale would be personal, its initial reference the city, though as the work came back into the gallery its elements gave more pause."[79] After he photographs them, documenting their presence, Orozco loads the objects into his rented Penske moving truck, which serves as his temporary studio space. These objects are subsequently used in his gallery and museum installations as relics, documents, and artifacts of personal experiences (fig. 6).

Mia Fineman suggests that these documentary photographs are "quietly beautiful works [that] offer themselves as ephemeral documents of a profoundly personal encounter with the everyday. What carries these photographs above and beyond the anecdotal register of personal documents . . . is Orozco's unfailing eye for the exquisite interplay of color and form."[80] *Island within an Island* (1993) is an excellent example from Orozco's *Penske Project*. Orozco collects debris and creates an installation of debris that mimics the form of lower Manhattan, which is seen in the background (including the World Trade Center), creating a composition that not only blends the junk and trash produced by an economy whose engine is in lower Manhattan but offers a subtle yet powerful contrast in forms and scale.

Environments

Given its development outside of the common institutional framework of the church or the state, a distinctive feature of modern art is its obsession with context as a constitutive part of artistic meaning and as something that must be created and maintained. From Gustave Courbet to Marcel Duchamp, artists have focused as much attention on *how* their work will be experienced

God in the Gallery

as on the work itself. And for many, there is no distinction. This has become an increasingly important part of contemporary artistic practice, as museums and galleries offer opportunities for artists to conceive of exhibition spaces as a total space to be shaped, and their exhibitions to function as installations. This trend reflects, to some degree, the influence of Duchamp and the impact of the readymade on installing and experiencing art. Artists thus seek to create personal aesthetic environments, in which discrete parts of their work, such as sculpture, photographs, drawings, and paintings, fit together in relationship with one another, providing a comprehensive environment in which an overarching idea is embodied throughout. Without the cosmological environment of the church and state to provide that meaning and significance, the modern artist is obliged to create this environment for himself or herself. This is what can give the best installation work theological substance, if not in content, in form; that is, a created world in which every object and the space between them is connected to another. Installation art is the embodiment of an analogical worldview. It acknowledges that meaning is contingent and that it is contextual. Installation art regards each object as a part, a fragment, of the larger context.

What follows are two different approaches to installation art: one explores the form of the diorama, the other explicitly rejects it. Both, however, explore religion, religious experience, and religious forms through the creation of an aesthetic environment, one through public, contemporary cultural forms and the other through a quest to transcend the specificity of such forms.

Robert Gober describes his installations as "natural history dioramas about contemporary human beings."[81] Gober creates objects that appear to be merely readymade but are in fact meticulously handcrafted, from newspapers and sink drains, to briefcases, trash cans, and urinals. Gober's two primary interests are to explore the symbolic power of water and the human body as metaphors and cultural inscriptions, zones of meaning, which evoke the experience of generation and destruction. His project has been called a "highly personal, deeply idiosyncratic archaeology of contemporary life."[82]

Gober's work is deeply influenced by Marcel Duchamp, through the faux-readymade appearance of his sculptured objects and his own use of the urinal as a subject. Gober works primarily through the installation, creating a single, unified environment of drawings, objects, and prints. Gober represented the United States in 2001 at the forty-ninth Venice Biennale, which was co-organized by the Art Institute of Chicago and the Hirshhorn Museum and Sculpture Garden, Smithsonian Institution. In it Gober chose to pursue in greater depth his longtime interest in the symbolic and metaphorical power of water, which Venice, a city on water, offered him.

In a similar manner, Gober chose to explore the religious themes provoked through the cultural artifacts generated from the 9/11 tragedy in the city on which it was inflicted with his installation at the Matthew Marks Gallery, March 5 through April 23, 2005 (fig. 2). The installation, which took up the entire gallery space, consisted of a trash can with a priest's collared shirt folded with a newspaper clipping that introduces the viewer to two aisles made up of various objects, including diapers and bowls of fruit, placed on what appear to be Styrofoam planks, but are actually bronze castes of a Styrofoam piece he found on a Long Island beach. These aisles culminate at the altar, as it were, with a large headless crucifix, with water pouring out of Christ's breasts into a roughly cut hole in the concrete floor, which circulates to two bathrooms that flank Christ. With doors cracked only enough for the viewer to glimpse a fragment of the interior, one bathroom consists of a man soaking in the tub and in the other, a woman doing the same, as water circulates in and out, as a fountain.

Art historian Hal Foster observes: "The presentation of these things was at once forensic, like evidence laid out in a police warehouse or morgue, and ritualistic."[83] He continues, "As is usual with Gober, the installation is a broken allegory that both elicits and resists our interpretation; that, materially, nothing is quite as it seems adds to our anxious curiosity."[84] The iconography of the installation is made up of cultural detritus, including references to 9/11, disrupted suburban isolation, and religious justifications of the war on Iraq. "In this way different levels of allegorical reading are set up, from the anagogic to the literal, but they are fragmentary, and the real disrupts the symbolic (the tacky elements around the crucifix) just as the symbolic haunts the real (the amorous bodies over the 9/11 reports)."[85] As Foster observes, an important part of Gober's installation, as it is with much of his work, is the newspaper, particularly *The New York Times*, which he uses to declare "truth" and "documentation," through which he crafts his narratives. The newspaper articles are the "real," or the supposedly real, against or with which his symbols interact.

Perhaps the most notorious and recognizable of Gober's sculptures are his leg fragments, painstakingly and realistically rendered, with leg hair, pant, sock, and shoe included, which protrude from the wall. This surrealistic fragmented image emerges in part from childhood images of amputation that have continued to function in Gober's visual imagination as a marker for masculinity,

God in the Gallery

truncated and fragmented, and in process. Furthermore, these legs have come to be born from a woman; the idea of *adult birth* and *rebirth* (and perhaps even being *born again* and its possibility/impossibility) is a preoccupation for Gober.

The most shocking but important of the eleven sculptures in the installation is the headless crucified Christ with water flowing from his breasts. On a superficial level, the crucifix marks the use of religion by fundamentalists in the 9/11 attacks and the subsequent war on terror. But more than that, the mysterious and surreal crucifix is the focal point of the entire installation, casting it in an undeniably religious, even sacred, form beyond even its religious content. About his intentions for the installation, Gober observed simply, "I want to make a sacred space."[86] Although Gober left the Roman Catholic Church as an adolescent, it remains a powerful force in his work. Brenda Richardson suggests, "The imprint of the Church is not easily effaced from the hearts of the once pious."[87] The installation functions as a sanctuary filled with relics. The space includes an aisle that leads toward the Crucifix. Mysterious relics, such as diapers in a milk create, a bowl of fruit, and "molded" wood planks, all of which sit on Styrofoam bases, flank both sides of the aisle. (All of the relics and bases are painted bronze.)

It might at first blush appear that this crucified Christ, without a head and with water streaming from his nipples, is blasphemous and clearly an example of contemporary art mocking Christianity, since it is easy to assume that Christ has been decapitated. But this is to jump too quickly to a conclusion. The headless figure resulted in part from a two-part decision in the studio. First, the head was removed to facilitate the modeling process. Then, for weeks, Gober lived with the crucifix model without the head and, over time, it began to seem more appropriate or natural to keep it headless.[88] Therefore, it can be experienced also as evocatively headless, which can allude to the broken yet beautiful sculptures from classical antiquity, such as the Elgin Marbles, which evoke a melancholic aesthetic beauty that emerges from the ravages of time on the artifact, rather than violence perpetuated against the *belief.*[89]

The water flowing from Christ's nipples relates to a vessel Gober saw on view at the Metropolitan Museum of Art, New York, which consisted of a Diana goddess figure with her nipples as spouts for pouring wine. This conflated nicely with Gober's own interest in sinks with holes where faucets should be, which, un-utilized, begin to seem like eyes peering back at the viewer. In addition, the flowing water, far from desecrating the crucifix, enlivens it, since fountains are *alive*, that is, the water is moving; it is not stagnant. Moreover, flowing water alludes to baptismal rebirth, a sacramental practice with allusions Gober was well aware of. The flow of water from the body of Christ also repeats the elegant trajectory of the flow of water and blood from Christ's side in the Christian iconographical tradition.

The American robin that perches on the driftwood crucifix is a deeply personal adaptation of his own grandmother's crucifix, which was given to him after her death and which hangs over the mantel in his Long Island home. Gober found a cast bird fragment from some discarded debris found outside his home and placed it on his mantel, creating the association between Christ and the bird, whose crimson breast acquires symbolic associations with the crucifixion, which he—coincidently—re-creates in this installation. The bird might also suggest hope and transcendence, perhaps even the Holy Spirit.

Gober is preoccupied with faith. When he was asked to curate an exhibition of his work with work from the Menil Collection, Gober was fascinated with John de Menil's religious faith, and particularly his relationship to the Catholic priest Father Marie-Alain Couturier, who served as an adviser to John and Dominique de Menil in establishing their collection.

[This relationship] stood in such counter-distinction to America's current obsession with using religion where, in my opinion, loud, public expressions of a supposedly private faith are often used to bully and exclude and raise money for so many dubious adventures, whereas Father Couturier's mission was to reconnect the Catholic Church with great living artists.[90]

The iconographical associations embodied in Gober's installation are staggering and, for many viewers and critics, overwhelming. How can a work embody and provoke such diverse—even contradictory—meanings simultaneously? These multiple associations are the very crux of the experience and contemplation of art, which separates it from mere communication, in which a single and stable meaning is sent from the sender to the receiver. The mistake that is often made with art is the assumption that the artist has indeed a single meaning in mind that he or she intends to communicate to the receiver. This is not how art is experienced, nor is this how icons are experienced. The meaning and significance of Gober's installation is expansive rather than restrictive, layered and complex. It invites the viewer to enter into a contemplative relationship with the installation, to allow the world Gober has created to work over time on the viewer's own expectations, desires, or "horizon of expectation," as the reception theorist H. R. Jauss calls it.

God in the Gallery

Just as Gober grew into the appropriateness of a headless crucifix over time or got used to the robin placed near his crucifix at home, we too are called upon to grow into his installations. Gober's installations embody an analogical worldview in which all objects are symbols. Indeed Gober's worldview requires the existence of a world saturated and even over-determined with meaning and significance that connect all objects, processes, and environments. How they are connected, how they relate, is the subject of Gober's aesthetic explorations.

Schneebett ("Snowbed") is Enrique Martínez Celaya's most ambitious project to date (fig. 11). The title comes from a poem by Paul Celan, whose stark yet powerful language has been an important catalyst for Martínez Celaya's visual work and poetry.[91] This complex two-room environment, created for the Berliner Philharmonie, offers an aesthetic reflection on Beethoven's long and painful process of death in Vienna that culminated in his death in 1835. From a Heideggerian perspective that recognizes the importance of one's death to the authenticity of being, this work scrutinizes the existential question of what can be learned about death from the demise of another, and thus, by extension, learned about Being *at a distance*. *Schneebett* is the third and final part of what he calls the *Beethoven Cycle*. It examines what Camus calls the only philosophical question: suicide. From the perspective of the deathbed, this question becomes retrospective: was life—this life, my life—worth living?

Schneebett challenges Martínez Celaya's skills as an artist, forcing him to start, as he says, "from a disadvantage," that is, from the very real possibility of failure, whether technical or conceptual. The focal point is the bed, a life-size bed cast in bronze, which, through the complex workings of an elaborate (and even absurdly complicated) generator, is frozen. A painting of a birch forest, made of tar and feathers, serves as the room's "window," out of which Beethoven peers and reflects on his life. Also included is a stack of birch branches and a poem by Martínez Celaya, written by hand in German on the wall, and, finally, a chair.

This chair is for us. It is here that, in contemplating the now cold and empty bed of snow and ice, we contemplate our own bed of death, as Heidegger called it. Despite its theatricality, "This work is not a diorama; it is not a recreation of the room, but an exorcism of the spirit of the room as it was." *Schneebett* is a place of silence, of contemplation, deep in the recesses of a performance hall where the faint echo of music, perhaps Beethoven's, is heard. It "is one embodiment of a possible final moment. It's the memory of a room as the room remembers the demand of being."[92] This aspect of the room possessing a memory brings *Schneebett* into surprisingly close relationship to Gober's Matthew Marks installation. Both environments share the interest in memory as it is embodied through and worked out in aesthetic form.

"To the pensive wood I am driven" is the yearning of Beethoven's deeply introspective song cycle, "An die ferne Geliebte" (1816). The painting of the birch forest, as well as the birch branches that block the transition between the two rooms in *Schneebett*, transforms the bed of death into that "pensive wood" that stimulates contemplation and reflection. Martínez Celaya's recollection of the opening in Berlin is instructive. He remembered that "when the *Schneebett* opened at the Philharmonie, I saw the public waiting in line to see it and the orchestra playing Beethoven's late concertos in the lobby. I was humbled by the futility of *Schneebett*, and I love it more for it. That day my mind was filled with thoughts of Beethoven as a boy."[93] It would be two years later, however, after *Schneebett* was re-presented at the Museum der bildenden Künste, Leipzig, that this boy returned to Martínez Celaya's thoughts.

He returned via *Coming Home*, another installation that Martínez Celaya created first at GRIFFIN in Venice, California, in 2000. Berlin collector Dieter Rosenkranz donated the sculptural components (a boy and an elk) of *Coming Home* to the Sheldon Memorial Art Gallery at the University of Nebraska–Lincoln in 2005, and it was recently re-presented, with photographs that were part of the project, at the Sheldon. Exhibited four years before *Schneebett*, *Coming Home* anticipates its major themes. Now *Schneebett* seems to have anticipated the reinstallation of *Coming Home* (fig. 12).[94]

Both installations function as comprehensive, all-encompassing contexts in which one is intended to enter into a contemplative aesthetic environment maintained by a sacred, liturgical dimension. Moreover, the environment as a space provides the world within which our experience of these objects and images is guided. There is not merely a faux Styrofoam altar on which a faux bowl of fruit sits or a boy made of tar and feathers, they exist and function in a sanctuary format for the former, and a womb-like forest environment in the latter. There, meaning is embodied in their function in that space.

These installations are thus more than the objects in them, they encompass and transverse the spaces between them, calling us to experience them on their terms, that is, over time as we develop our own relationships with their projected world of experience and memory as we make it our own. And this

God in the Gallery

is possible only if we believe, as do all of the artists discussed in this chapter, that the world is profoundly and mysteriously meaningful, one that can be mediated in and through objects, practices, and contexts. It is our responsibility to follow the lead of the apostle and walk around and look carefully at these objects of worship (Acts 17:23).

5

Art Criticism

For everything God created is good, and nothing is to be rejected if it is received with thanksgiving, because it is consecrated by the word of God and prayer.

St. Paul, 1 Timothy 4:4–5

Test everything. Hold on to the good.

St. Paul, 1 Thessalonians 5:21

More difficult to do a thing than to talk about it? Not at all. That is a gross popular error. It is very much more difficult to talk about a thing than to do it.

Oscar Wilde, *The Critic As Artist*

Perhaps the only thing more confusing to the intelligent observer than modern and contemporary art is modern and contemporary art criticism. It is the disparity between the art and what is written about it—how it is interpreted—that is off-putting to many otherwise earnest art viewers. My interest in modern and contemporary art was initiated by fascination with the limits of what one could say or write about a work of art. Thus what follows here is an attempt to offer an explanatory framework for how the criticism of modern and contemporary art functions and, perhaps more importantly, how a critical perspective nourished by the Nicene Christian faith can contribute to the understanding of contemporary art.

In his memoir, critic and art historian Irving Sandler recalled a formative experience he had with art.

> In 1952, while walking through the galleries of the Museum of Modern Art, I was dumbstruck by a black-and-white picture. The label informed me that the canvas was titled *Chief* and painted by a Franz Kline in 1950. It was the first work of art I really saw, and it changed my life. . . . The painting did not provide any particular pleasure or delight. Nor did I "understand" it. I responded in another way—with my "gut," as it were. The painting had a sense of urgency that gripped me. I sensed Kline's need to create something deeply felt. That spoke to my own need. Moreover, *Chief* had a disturbing edge, a certain rawness, disorientation, lack of balance that reflected my predicament (and later, I would think that of humankind). It was at once surprising, familiar, and imposing. And it challenged me to find out more about it and my experience of it.[1]

Art criticism is an attempt to understand and articulate a particular experience with art in a particular way. Sandler's experience of Franz Kline's *Chief* (fig. 13) is reminiscent of George Steiner's eloquent statement that art makes a claim on us, does something to us, shakes us up, "gain[ing] the freedom of our 'inner city.'"[2] Art criticism is one by-product of this experience. Others include philosophical discourse, art history, and even new art forms. In fact, some have argued that the best art criticism is another work of art produced in response.

Although many experiences with art may not be as dramatic and powerful as Sandler's, all art criticism is in some way the result of a personal experience with art. It is important to observe that Sandler's recollection of his experience in 1952 is embodied in and through the literary genre of art criticism. Art critics write about art because they love art, desire it, need it, and it is through writing that they can articulate this love, desire, and need. As will become clear below, it is the writer's experience of the art that is the subject of art criticism. However art criticism functions, it remains a deeply personal and subjective literary genre, despite its pretenses to the contrary. This is why art criticism tends to be not only idiosyncratic but also obscure, difficult, and as complicated as the art it addresses. Whether art critics focus on philosophy, history, formal description, political ideology, Reformed Christian worldview, or the like, they are using their intellectual framework to understand and clarify their response to the art about which they are writing with the intellectual tools at their disposal.

It is precisely the robust depth and expansive breadth of the Nicene Christian faith's preservation of the relationship between the immanent and transcendent, the material and spiritual, the aesthetic and ethical implications of consubstantiality and the hypostatic union, and the inextricable relationship between dogma and practice as an intellectual framework, that offer the potential to make a significant contribution to contemporary art criticism. However, before we can pursue in greater depth a Christian contribution to contemporary art criticism, it is important to do some historical and theoretical preparatory work.

Preliminary Considerations

The emergence of abstract expressionism in the 1940s and 1950s—with Jackson Pollock, Willem de Kooning, Franz Kline, Mark Rothko, and Barnett Newman among others—as a distinctive American contribution to the history of modern art was simultaneously accompanied by the emergence of American art criticism by Clement Greenberg, Harold Rosenberg, Meyer Schapiro, Thomas Hess, and a number of other critics who wrote passionately and eloquently about this new art in New York at mid-century. Pollock and de Kooning's success was due in part to the success of Greenberg and Rosenberg in offering compelling interpretations of their canvases. So, just as American art came into its own with the abstract expressionists in the 1940s and 1950s, so too did American art criticism. It is therefore important to examine how abstract-expressionist art criticism functioned at mid-century in order to have a historical foundation on which to build our analysis of contemporary art criticism.

As it has functioned in the history of modernism since Denis Diderot wrote reviews of the annual salons for a readership that would never see the exhibitions, art criticism is its own creative and imaginary practice. It is a literary genre that has attracted the most talented writers of modernity—novelists, poets, musicians, philosophers, sociologists, painters, art historians, and, in Clement Greenberg's case, even customs clerks. It is also a form of cultural critique. Modern art and art criticism are part of this distinctively modern—and avant-garde—project of molding and shaping society, primarily through molding and shaping culture, and perhaps even more specifically, molding and shaping aesthetic taste.[3]

Art criticism is also unregulated. Anyone can do it; there are no degree programs, exams, or other credentials or vetting processes that are required for one to be an art critic.[4] The only requirement is that one achieves a venue for practicing it and maintains an audience. Therefore, art criticism is a competitive business. There are limited numbers of venues for art critics to ply their trade, and there is a limited audience from which to attract a following. These are important aspects to keep in mind as we attempt to grasp what art critics actually do, how art criticism functions in relation to art, and how we are to understand and use art criticism ourselves.

Given the unregulated, competitive aspect of art criticism, art critics are first and foremost concerned about themselves, not the art they are writing about. This cannot be overemphasized. Like the modern artist, who has to pay attention to crafting and maintaining a stable interpretive framework within which his or her art can be experienced as meaningful and significant, the art critic must do the same. And just as the artist, like Courbet, used other avant-garde art critics to help him, so too do art critics use artists. The relationship between modern artists and art critics is mutually inextricable.

Since, like art, *art criticism* is an open and contested concept with no stable definition, the art critic (like the artist) practices the craft with his or her own philosophy of art criticism, with an individual understanding of what criticism is and what it should be. So as readers we do not merely read a *review* of a Jackson Pollock exhibition, we are, perhaps more importantly, reading the art critic's philosophy of art and philosophy of art criticism—the critic's distinct aesthetic worldview. And if we find this critic or that critic compelling, we do so primarily because of the definitions of art and criticism that are deployed, whether or not we agree with a critic's assessment of or even interpretation of the art. Therefore, it is important to be sensitive to what the art critic says about art and art criticism in general and not simply focus on whether this critic likes or dislikes this or that particular artist.

It is perhaps important, in the context of discussing what art criticism is, to mention briefly what it is not. Art criticism is not a "thumbs-up" or "thumbs-down" practice; it does not function as a consumer's guide to art. It also does not function as an explanation or a *CliffsNotes* version of an artist's work and its meaning. A student interested in understanding the meaning and significance of a contemporary artist's work who assumes that reading a five-hundred-word review in the back pages of *Artforum* will give her or him the gist of what the work is all about will be frustrated. This experience is too often interpreted as a failure of the reviewer, adding further evidence to the irrelevance and obscurity of most writing about art. But this misconstrues what the critic is trying to do when she or he writes art criticism.

The history of art criticism suggests that the ultimate goal of the art critic is to achieve and then sustain authority as an art critic. In other words, the ultimate subject of art criticism is not, surprisingly enough, the art it interprets but art criticism itself. It is self-reflective, in part because both art criticism and the role of the art critic are always under contestation, their definition and function are constantly in the process of being worked out and argued over. Art criticism is a creative practice, parallel to, not derivative of, the art it addresses.

This can be observed in the critical debate between Harold Rosenberg and Clement Greenberg, which began in the 1940s and, for all intents and purposes, ended only with Greenberg's death in 1994, even though Rosenberg had died two decades earlier. Both critics are synonymous with abstract expressionism. However, the debate between these two critics, and the lines that were subsequently drawn by others who felt obliged to take sides (usually pro-Greenberg and/or anti-Rosenberg), throws into higher relief the perspective on art criticism explored here. An analysis of the debate between these two influential critics will provide an important frame of reference for evaluating the contemporary crisis in art criticism and provide options for new, more productive directions for its practice.

The Greenberg-Rosenberg debate had little to do with what many regard as the function of art criticism. The critical debate between Harold Rosenberg and Clement Greenberg must be interpreted around the authority of criticism, not promoting abstract expressionist art. Subsequent commentators have gone wrong by presupposing that this debate was about which abstract expressionist artist to champion or who offered a more accurate interpretation of this or that artist's work. What was at stake was the capacity of art criticism as a literary genre to offer a compelling account of abstract expressionism's form and content.

Clement Greenberg versus Harold Rosenberg

It would not be too simplistic to claim that in the scholarly community, Harold Rosenberg has fared poorly in comparison with his rival critic Clement Greenberg. Rosenberg's existentialist, poetic, and rhetorically rich essays, which rarely focused on the *meaning* of particular works of art (or even artists) is compared negatively with Clement Greenberg's pared-down literary style and ability to analyze a specific work of art. Moreover, there is an assumption that Rosenberg's existentialism dates his writing while Greenberg's sparse prose has remained relevant. This view of Rosenberg and Greenberg is largely inaccurate and has distorted the development of subsequent art criticism. The debate is not merely a question of historical meaning and significance but has important ramifications for the practice of art criticism in the wake of the demise of the "public intellectual."[5] In order to chart a direction for Christian participation in contemporary art criticism, therefore, this crucial debate must be reexamined.[6] The Greenberg-Rosenberg debate, then, must be understood not as an art argument but as an argument about art criticism within which certain art was mobilized in its service.

Both critics, whose Jewish identity was foundational, began their professional careers as poets and cultural essayists with strong Marxist beliefs, gravitated toward the so-called New York Intellectuals, and wrote for *Partisan Review*, a progressive left-wing journal of culture and politics. Both were drawn to writing about art as a means to advance their theories of culture and criticism as they defined their own roles as public intellectuals. Throughout the thirties and forties, both wrote art, literary, cultural, and even political criticism.[7]

But while Rosenberg's criticism remained broadly cultural, even while addressing more specific art world subjects, Greenberg's narrowed. While Rosenberg remained a critical *essayist* and *aphorist* in the tradition of the great nineteenth-century critics, Greenberg became more narrowly an *art critic*. By the late fifties, Greenberg's criticism was neither easily accessible nor particularly influential.[8] While Greenberg's reputation waned, Rosenberg's was on the ascension. The revival of Greenberg's reputation, in large measure through the efforts of a group of art history graduate students at Harvard and Columbia, was predicated on a reactionary effort to beat back the surging influence of Rosenberg, whose publication of a selection of essays under the title, *The Tradition of the New* (1959), was highly influential and capped a decade of prominence and influence. This influence came predominantly from Rosenberg's concept of "action painting," which signaled an aesthetic and cultural shift from the collective myths of modernism to private myths of individual transactional experience.

Rosenberg's criticism was intended for a broad readership and found a receptive home in *Art News*, which in 1952 published the critic's most radical and evocative essay, "The American Action Painters." Rosenberg's criticism continued the nineteenth-century tradition of art and cultural criticism as rhetoric and polemic. But it was precisely the popularity and self-consciously literary character of Rosenberg's criticism that Greenberg and his followers reacted against. Rosenberg's essay received a wide readership, which stretched from artists such as Allan Kaprow to the humanist scholar Jacques Barzun.[9] Rosenberg's influences, references, and affinities—including Melville, Camus, Merleau-Ponty, and Sartre—tapped into this wider readership's interest in existentialism. Moreover, during the fifties *Art News* was a platform for such writing, given editor Thomas Hess's own proclivities toward the rhetorical flourishes of *poetic-criticism*.[10]

It was against this writing and the institutional apparatus that supported it that Greenberg published *Art and Culture*, a selection of reviews and essays, and launched a diatribe against Rosenberg entitled "How Artwriting Earns Its Bad Name."[11] But Greenberg's desire to recapture the critical limelight from his onetime friend and now bitter rival was supported and facilitated institutionally through the establishment of a new art magazine, *Artforum*, which was started in 1962 in San Francisco as an explicitly anti-Rosenberg and pro-Greenberg venue. Art historian and critic Michael Fried was one of those young graduate students who admired Greenberg in the early sixties and had the following to say about this critical debate some forty years later.

> What there was was *Art News*. And it absolutely dominated the discourse—we're talking 1958. That's three years before the publication of *Art and Culture*. Clem Greenberg wasn't writing regular art criticism anymore anywhere. If you wanted to read him you had to get back issues of *The Nation* or *Partisan Review* or you might pick up the odd article as it appeared. But what was filling the space was all that Faustian writing—Hess and others. And it was actually useful to have that to react against—to discover that one really hated the sound of writing like that was I think very productive. In fact, the generation that you can say Frank Stella started—part of what was shaping it was a violent distaste for that kind of bullshit and a craving for something real.[12]

An important mission for *Artforum* was to revive and promote interest in Greenberg, whose writing was, by Fried's own account, buried in the back pages of cultural periodicals until the publication of *Art and Culture*. Barbara Rose recalled: "I had been nauseated by what was passing for art writing, it was obviously total garbage: mental doodling by poets and Harold Rosenberg's sociology. It had no solid grounding, it was not intellectual, it was not respectable."[13] This "solid grounding" and a "craving for something real" that Rose,

Fried, and others sought was tied to the connoisseurship tradition—the curriculum taught in graduate schools—and not the tradition of polemical cultural criticism that transcended disciplinary boundaries and engaged a public whose interests were not defined by academic scholarship. Rosenberg's concept of action painting was often erroneously taken (by friend and foe alike) to be a *theory* about interpreting works of art. But its ramifications were much wider. "At a certain moment the canvas began to appear to one American painter after another as an arena in which to act—rather than as a space in which to reproduce, re-design, analyze or 'express' an object, actual or imagined. What was to go on the canvas was not a picture but an event."[14]

Thus Rosenberg initiates his presentation of action painting in "The American Action Painters." But Rosenberg's interest in this new American painting was not exclusively aesthetic. Consequently, it did not function as a theory to use in order to produce art interpretations. In an article responding to his critics after the publication of Greenberg's *Art and Culture*, Rosenberg reiterated: "Action Painting solved no problems. On the contrary, at its best it remained faithful to the conviction in which it had originated that the worst thing about the continuing crisis of art and society were the proposals for solving it."[15]

In fact, Rosenberg introduced action painting in an essay that did not mention a single work of art or artist by name, hence the common refrain that his criticism "let rhetoric do the work of analysis."[16] But in such essays as "Tenth Street: A Geography of Modern Art" (1959), "Twilight of the Intellectuals" (1958), and "The Herd of Independent Minds" (1948), Rosenberg sketches the contours of a crisis of modernism that consisted of a systematic collapse of the myths that had sustained cultural activity for one hundred years, and that included the myths that had sustained not only art but also art criticism and the role of the intellectual.[17] For Rosenberg, any discourse that had to do with *action* was relevant to action painting, that is, "anything but art criticism."[18] Rosenberg's art criticism was deeply aware of the problems and challenges implicit in art criticism, including the very possibility of writing about art. In fact, Rosenberg's refusal to mention specific names and discuss specific works of art in his famous essay was an apophatic gesture, an attempt to preserve the integrity and *mystery* of the distinct aesthetic experience by talking *around* the art. How to negotiate this situation, to continue to write art criticism in its wake, was Rosenberg's project.

Greenberg, by contrast, has been lauded as a critic who analyzed works of art *sans* the "mental doodlings" of more popular writers, such as Rosenberg and Hess. Greenberg's reputation as the preeminent art critic of the twentieth century is attributable primarily to the revival of his reputation and his transformation through *Art and Culture*, which was published in 1961. This book consisted of heavily edited and even completely rewritten essays that, far from providing an accurate record of the critic's initial experience with the work of art, were reworked literary texts with over a decade of hindsight behind them and with an eye toward using them to reposition his role as a critic in a shifting cultural arena. It offered a comprehensive and highly refined critical worldview to an emerging postwar art world audience increasingly made up of "professionals" and "experts" eager to make use of a stable cosmology of modern and contemporary art that could be studied with the same scholarly rigor as medieval, Renaissance, or other traditional art historical subjects.[19] In the preface to the book Greenberg admits, "This book is not intended as a completely faithful record of my activity as a critic. Not only has much been altered, but much more has been left out than put in."

This statement is ironic given Greenberg's constant assertion that art criticism is *only* about the "experience" of art, the "direct encounter," or, in Donald Kuspit's words, that "the critic makes the first and presumably freshest response to the work of art, grasps it when it is still new and strange, and gives us a preliminary hold on its meaning."[20] Greenberg's slight—but important— revisions to his review of Franz Kline's second solo show in 1952 is indicative of how *Art and Culture* relates to his initial experience with the art.[21]

> Another important new painter is Franz Kline, who has just had his second show at Egan's. He at least got a better reception from his fellow-artists than Newman did, even if the official and collecting art world is still wary of him (and it would speak little for him if it were not). Kline's large canvases, with their blurtings of black calligraphy on white and gray grounds, are tautness quintessential. He has stripped his art in order to make sure of it—not so much for the public as for himself. He presents only the salient points of his emotion. Three or four of the pictures in his two shows already serve to place him securely in the foreground of contemporary abstract painting, but one has the feeling that this gifted and accomplished artist still suppresses too much of his power. Perhaps, on the other hand, that is exactly the feeling one should have.[22]

Almost nine years after the publication of this initial critical encounter with Kline in *Partisan Review*, Greenberg significantly revised it for republication in *Art and Culture*. Although he acknowledged in his preface that many of the essays and reviews were edited, including noting the date of the revision after many of them, Greenberg apparently did not regard the changes he made to this review to be significant enough to warrant specific notification. And within the context of his agenda, he probably viewed such changes as insignificant. Whether considered by Greenberg to be important or not, however, these changes offer another perspective on the *modus operandi* of this century's most influential art writer.

> Kline's large canvases, with their blurted black and white calligraphy, have the kind of self evident tautness which has become identified with *modernist painting since Cézanne*. He, too, has stripped his art down, in order to be sure of it—but for his own sake, not for the sake of the public. His originality lies in the way in which he maintains a *Cubist contact* with the edges of his canvas while opening up a seemingly *un-Cubist or post Cubist ambiguity* of plane and depth elsewhere. Though presenting signs and marks floating free on a clear and expanding field, his pictures actually repeat—and in fact, succeed most when they do so most—the solid, one-piece *Cubist rectangle* with its emphatic enclosing shape. Three or four of the paintings Kline has shown already place him securely in the foreground of *contemporary abstract art*, yet I have the impression that the powers of this gifted and accomplished artist are still a little inhibited. But perhaps this is precisely what one should feel.[23] [emphasis mine]

Greenberg includes references to "Cubist" or "modern painting" six times, while in the original review they were not mentioned at all. Also added was a discussion of Cézanne, whom Greenberg now regarded as Kline's model when he "stripped his art down."

These heavily edited art reviews clearly reveal that Greenberg conceived of *Art and Culture* as a literary narrative, not as a record of his aesthetic experience, for it is precisely that experience—raw and tentative—that was edited out of these reviews. (I have often wondered whether readers of *Art and Culture* in the sixties actually believed that what they were reading was Greenberg's intuitive and remarkably prescient encounter with Franz Kline in 1952.) This collection of essays has done more than any other text to institutionalize and professionalize art criticism and the academic study of modern and contemporary art.

Ultimately, the subject of art criticism is the art critic. No less than Rosenberg's rhetorical riffs, *Art and Culture* is a literary narrative in which works of art and artists serve as characters in the unfolding drama, and it is the art critic (perhaps even as the fictional narrator of the story), the one who narrates this story, who ultimately is the hero. Greenberg's critical support for the abstract expressionists was tentative and temporary in relation to his constant, unwavering, and tenacious support of his authoritative role as an art critic to make such aesthetic judgments. For it was art criticism that defined for Greenberg the Western tradition in general and modernism more specifically, and its survival would ultimately signal the *triumph* of American high culture, a triumph that was virtually indistinguishable from the triumph of his own voice as a critic.

Histories of postwar art and art criticism have interpreted the debate between Greenberg and Rosenberg to be that of an object-based critic with a historical consciousness of continued relevance versus a poet whose fashionable rhetorical flourishes found a receptive, but ultimately temporary, audience. Since *Art and Culture*, Greenberg's reputation has increased dramatically even as Rosenberg's has slipped into the realm of historical curiosity. Greenberg is regarded as practicing "good" art criticism while Rosenberg practiced "bad" art criticism. But as I have argued, this perception is due to the institutionalization of art criticism as an academic discipline founded on—and ultimately circumscribed by—Greenberg's critical values that he advanced after the publication of *Art and Culture*. Consequently, even Greenberg's numerous detractors in the academy remain tangled in the theoretical net he cast.

It is tempting to offer a revisionist view of this critical debate as a manifestation of modernist and postmodernist critical perspectives: that Greenberg's ultra-formalist and universalist evolutionary theory of art is critiqued by Rosenberg's criticism that resists totalizations, emphasizes the contingencies of meaning, and stresses fissures and breaks, not to mention expresses a continental sensibility that respects (and exploits) the opacity of language.[24] Although I do not completely dismiss this perspective, the situation is more complex. Rosenberg continues to embrace certain modernist assumptions about the role of cultural criticism even while he recognizes the collapse of many of the sacred cows of modernism. He believes, for example, that the crisis of art criticism, the challenges of saying *anything* meaningful about a work of art in the mid-twentieth century, is best addressed through the modernist literary genre of cultural criticism. In the same way, Greenberg, who is the quintessential modernist critic, has also served as a foundation for postmodern critics. His "close readings"—influenced in part by the New Critics and T. S. Eliot—have in turn influenced deconstruction, what Edward Said once called the "new New Criticism."[25] Not only is much contemporary art criticism Greenbergian at its core but so too is the study of it. This therefore limits any attempt to move beyond it.

But it is important to understand that it is not the Greenberg of the forties and fifties, the practicing art reviewer, who had this massive institutional influence. It was the *Art and Culture* and the post-*Art and Culture* Greenberg (whom Thierry de Duve calls the "theorist" Greenberg[26]). After the publication of his book in 1961, Greenberg devoted the next three decades to criticizing Rosenberg's art criticism by lecturing in seminars in graduate art history departments and writing theoretical articles about what constitutes good art criticism. After 1961, Greenberg's efforts were almost exclusively concentrated on shaping the reception and expanding the range of *Art and Culture*. In sum, his art criticism for the next twenty-five years consisted of *context* not *content*.[27] Or, put differently, context became the content for Greenberg after 1961. And it is this context that offers the theoretical framework that shapes most historical work on postwar American art criticism.

In different ways, Rosenberg and Greenberg show that art criticism is as much, if not more, about the art critic and the literary genre of criticism than it is about recording or preserving an experience with art. This in no way diminishes the significance of art criticism. In fact, it reveals it to be a creative endeavor with its own genres and traditions that are parallel to—not derivative of—the art it engages. Both artist and critic are engaged in the act of creation, engaged in the act of discovery through their practice. If, however, the critic's task is, following Edward Said, "to advance human freedom and knowledge," the art critic's challenge is to use art to show how both art and criticism can serve these noble goals, to use criticism to demonstrate art's broader significance, and, finally, to model how art should be taken seriously.[28]

Academic Art Criticism versus Arts Journalism

Clement Greenberg's entrée into academia through the influence of his book *Art and Culture*, combined with the increasing professionalization of the intellectual since the Second World War, provided the opportunity for academia to co-opt art criticism as a scholarly practice limited to "specialists." This transformed art criticism from a predominately journalistic, amateurish practice derived from the nineteenth-century belles lettres and essayist tradition, practiced on the margins and that sought broad-ranging sociocultural and political influence, to a highly focused, specialized, and protected (not to mention endowed) realm of scholarship that came to be produced for other specialists.

As art criticism increasingly became part of the academic enterprise (getting tenure as opposed to establishing a readership), advocates of academic art criticism fabricated a sharp division, following Greenberg, between "authentic" art criticism and "mere" journalism. As academic critic Abigail Solomon-Godeau put it at a roundtable panel on art criticism: "I think there is an immediate problem when we scramble together the categories of arts journalism and art criticism, because I do not think they are the same thing."[29] Much of academic art criticism consists of maintaining this distinction.

But academic art critics are not the only ones who seek to separate the sheep from the goats. Many art critics outside academia are similarly concerned with separating themselves from the elitism of academic art critics. And given the poor reputation that academics have in the larger culture, it is a powerful dichotomy. An important example of how this distinction is worked out against academic art criticism is seen in a confrontation in the mid-1980s in *Artforum* between the art critic Hilton Kramer, editor of the neoconservative intellectual journal *The New Criterion,* and academic art critic Donald B. Kuspit.[30] Kramer was critical of the NEA-sponsored Criticism Seminar, in which several of the panelists were too political in their presentations (that is, represented politics Kramer disagreed with), and other panelists, of which Kuspit was one, whose presentations were obscure and unclear. Kramer's editorial was instrumental, apparently, in the decision by the NEA to do away with the art critics fellowship program. Kramer's criticism relied on the assumption that criticism should focus directly on the description and evaluation of individual works of art (thus ignoring "non-aesthetic" issues such as politics) and that it must be "clear," that is, written for a broad readership.

Kuspit's response is significant. First, he argues that criticism is, as Baudelaire argued, "passionate, political, and partisan," that art embodies all of the complexities of reality (including politics) in aesthetic form. Criticism's role is to reveal that. In addition, Kuspit observes that Kramer's argument against politics is that it is simply not the politics with which he agrees. This seems accurate, because Kramer is nothing if not politically ideological. Kramer simply objects to critics expressing political views at odds with (Reaganite) US public policy. Second, Kuspit suggests that Kramer himself is playing politics when he accuses art critics supported by the NEA of writing in an intentionally opaque manner that renders their writing unintelligible to a broader audience. Kuspit rightly observes that to argue against Kramer, then, becomes impossible, for it puts one in the awkward position of advocating for obscurity and unclarity. He suggests, again rightly, "Clarity in fact is relative, as much the burden of the reader as the writer, for it has as much to do with the reader's understanding of the concepts the writer uses as with the style the writer uses to articulate them. Clear thinking is the issue, not clear writing."[31] And clear thinking takes effort, sometimes considerable effort. Ironically, Kramer, who is an arch formalist art critic and follower of Greenberg, and has founded an art and cultural journal whose readership is no larger than any other academic journal, mobilizes a populist defense, which criticizes academic art criticism for being unpatriotic and elitist.

It is not a coincidence that this argument against academic art criticism dovetails almost seamlessly with a neoconservative political worldview that posits an elite cadre of liberal academia at odds with the conservative values of the "average person," which makes that ideological agenda appear *natural*, *intuitive*, and *commonsensical*. It also puts forth an elite cadre of intellectuals who are concerned with speaking on behalf of this "average person." Kramer, following Greenberg, clearly regards art criticism as a descriptive genre, with none of the creative potential with which it was invested by the likes of Baudelaire, Oscar Wilde, and even T. S. Eliot, for whom criticism was a distinctive and necessary form of artistic practice. It is also of note that although Kuspit wrote a book on Clement Greenberg, it is to Harold Rosenberg that he looks as a model for his practice as an art critic.[32]

Kuspit puts his finger on an important fact about Kramer: Kramer's criticism of art criticism is also criticism of the state of contemporary art—both contemporary art and contemporary art criticism are inextricable. In short, Kramer is fed up with contemporary art that takes as its subjects left-wing politics and social agendas that, to his mind, cater to the liberal elites in the academy. Kuspit observes: "Kramer is not only after art criticism, he is after art, and he is not only after art, he is after society. He attacks art under the cover of attacking art criticism, and he attacks the social challenge of critical opposition under the cover of demanding clarity and good writing, where both mean 'correct,' obedient thinking."[33]

Academic art critics are just as uncharitable as nonacademic art critics in trading in stereotyped profiles of their opponents. A significant example is a roundtable on art criticism sponsored by and published in *October*, an important journal for the publication of academic art criticism. For the academic art critics on the panel, such as Hal Foster, Rosalind Krauss, and Benjamin Buchloh (each holding important faculty positions at Ivy League schools), the popularity of such art critics as Arthur Danto and Dave Hickey is sufficient evidence to condemn them as tools of the market or as "rhapsodic substitutes" for authentic criticism, as Buchloh calls their writing, in a manner that is strikingly similar to how Harold Rosenberg's art criticism was characterized by Michael Fried,

Rosalind Krauss, and the other academic art critics who understood art criticism to be exemplified by Greenberg's *Art and Culture*.[34] Art criticism done by writers who are independent of the academy is regarded in this roundtable as subcritical, compromised, and incapable of offering the kind of independent judgment required of authentic criticism, since their *freedom* is compromised by their employers. But clearly this position simply assumes the academy is outside the market, that it is able somehow to produce more free criticism than arts journalism. This, of course, is overly idealistic. For academia, with its politics of publishing and promotion and its tendency to reward writing that addresses guild specialists who share in the academic rewards system, is no more *independent* than art critics who must meet the publishing deadlines of newspapers and magazines.[35] Moreover, the divide between journalists and academics is not nearly as wide as the rhetoric claims.

This is the context that Christian participation in art criticism must recognize and understand and within which it must participate and engage. But given the lack of Christian representation in the art academy, the neoconservative, populist, journalistic approach to art criticism, particularly with its antiacademy stand against *elitist* art and art criticism, has often functioned as the default key that Christian intellectuals tend to hit when attempting to engage contemporary art. It is through this neoconservative perspective that Christian intellectuals usually view contemporary art. Ironically, even Christian intellectuals who work from a largely left-wing perspective are remarkably right wing when it comes to modern and contemporary art. It is not uncommon for philosophers and theologians who take Nietzsche, Foucault, Lyotard, and Derrida seriously to dismiss out of hand the work of Marcel Duchamp, Jackson Pollock, and other extreme examples of modern art. Moreover, Christian representation in arts journalism is just as negligible and marginalized as it is in academia.

Christian intellectuals, then, should embrace their marginalized, "homeless" relationship to cultural power and resist the temptation to allow the neoconservative framework to define how modern and contemporary art is interpreted. An art criticism nourished by a robust Nicene Christianity, freed from its neoconservative captivity, can transcend the limitations of the unproductive and flawed dichotomy between "elitist" academic art criticism and "popular" arts journalism, between "elitist" nihilism or agnosticism on one hand and populist "Judeo-Christian" American values on the other.

Through the primary role of sacramental and liturgical practice expressed through the principle *lex orandi lex est credendi* (what we pray determines what we believe) the Nicene Christian faith offers a broad-based and robust aesthetics, embodied in and through the liturgy, that presumes the relevance of aesthetic practice for all human persons. No criticism of modern and contemporary art can overlook this fact. On the other hand, the Nicene Christian faith is the product of sustained, in-depth, and highly specialized thought, the result of which not only gave the faith its dogmatic shape but also had an important influence on philosophical discourse. Criticism of modern and contemporary art should not overlook these resources. Nicene Christianity thus offers a remarkably nuanced aesthetic and philosophical vocabulary from which art criticism can greatly benefit.

Alternatives

I became interested in studying modern and contemporary art through art criticism, in particular the art criticism of Donald B. Kuspit, with whom I studied at SUNY–Stony Brook from 1989 to 1991. Kuspit's writing is often difficult and sometimes opaque, but it reveals art as part of the process by which an artist learns about oneself and the world. In a short essay on art schools published in *Artforum*, Kuspit observed that "being an artist is about being a certain kind of subject, not just about making certain kinds of objects."[36] From Kuspit I learned that art and art criticism are practices in which the goal is to become a better person. Yet I never did agree with all of his conclusions. For example, Kuspit believes both Duchamp and Warhol are problematic at best and possibly destructive forces at the worst. His provocative perspectives on these artists taught me a considerable amount about both artists, even while I could still disagree with the conclusions he reached. For Kuspit, art criticism, like art, is a particular way of being in the world, a particular way of learning about the world, and an instrument of self-discovery.

Criticism is not merely an act of judgment or a mode of description. It is the practice of discerning reception. It sorts and sifts to find what is useful. It does not content itself with the surface appearance of things but probes their depths. It seeks to find unity in diversity and diversity in unity. Kuspit argues: "Art criticism, like criticism in general, is a way of making one aware of invisible significance behind visible reality, whether in art or anything else. Criticism teaches one not to parrot the given in description nor to exult about it in quasi-religious esthetic ecstasy."[37]

An important goal of this chapter has been to demonstrate that art criticism is a creative activity, one that often parallels and is thus not simply derivative of artistic practice. Art criticism takes many forms and consists of many options for the interpretation of art. Kuspit continues: "Criticism must not stay on the surface of the art it investigates, just as art must not stay on the surface of the reality it explores. Criticism appropriates the art, for its own sake as well as for an understanding of the art's intention, just as art appropriates and gives a 'reading' of reality."[38] Ultimately, criticism is a manifestation of the critic's sensibility, a record of art's effect on the critic. The real value of criticism is that it offers an opportunity to track this effect. To limit art criticism to judging what is *good* or *bad*, to write *for* an audience to tell them what to think of an artist's work, or even to claim to write *on behalf of* an audience, is to undercut the value of criticism itself, the value of individual reception and critical discernment. Following Baudelaire, "Criticism should be partial, passionate and political, that is to say, written from an exclusive point of view, but a point of view that opens up the widest horizons."[39]

If criticism, including art criticism, does not expand our experience of all aspects of art and life through the distinct subjectivity of the critic, then it is not worthy of the name of criticism. Although he defended academic art criticism against Hilton Kramer's neoconservative attacks in the mid-1980s, Kuspit was simultaneously critiquing some of the academic art critics, including Benjamin H. D. Buchloh, for failing to acknowledge the power of the German neo-Expressionist painters Georg Baselitz, Anselm Kiefer, and others because of their bias against figuration. Kuspit argues, "The new German painting was said to lack the critical character of modern art—as if Abstraction, with its tired strategies of negation, was still critical with respect to society and other art."[40] Kuspit does not stop there, but continues, "The new German painting is a convenient whipping boy for ineffectual, directionless criticism—a criticality that no longer really knows its goals. Indeed, it is too impotent to imagine any future for art other than the same modernist missionary position of 'classical' negation."[41] For Kuspit, German neo-Expressionist painting, which brought representation and the figure back into painting with a vengeance, revealed the failure of a modernist art criticism that was ill equipped to attend closely to the work itself. Kuspit's art criticism sought to sketch out a new way to understand the meaning and significance of representation in the new German painting.

Nourished by a robust and expansive Nicene Christianity, a Christian art criticism cannot be about maintaining airtight confessional boundaries or offering some narrowly defined "Christian perspective" that will painlessly and effortlessly define and sort out contemporary art. In contrast, Nicene Christianity's dogmatic foundation can open up the widest horizons for the experience of and reflection on contemporary art that reveals how artists discover what it means to be human through their artistic practice.

Art criticism nourished by a robust Nicene Christian faith can transcend the arts journalism versus academic art criticism dichotomy by appropriating the best of both practices. Following Edward Said, who argued that the role of the intellectual is best performed by an outsider—an alien—an art critic nourished by the Nicene Christian faith is perhaps most uniquely positioned to accomplish this task, for he or she is already "homeless," an alien in the world whose "citizenship is in heaven" (Phil. 3:20).

An important part of the Nicene Christian faith is that it possesses the aesthetic and intellectual resources to make the most sense of aesthetic experiences, such as Irving Sandler's experience standing in front of Franz Kline's *Chief*, to articulate the experience of art as contemplation of and communion with artifacts that are a hypostatic union of form and content, artifacts that, although they are the product of artistic intention, achieve their own identity separate from the artist. Therefore, art is not merely an image that needs to be decoded, explained, and assigned a philosophical, theological, or historical meaning, although it invites philosophical, theological, or historical reflection. As Alfred Barr once observed, "I believe that works of art, like human beings, thrive on the attention paid to them."[42]

In addition to Harold Rosenberg and Donald Kuspit, there are a number of art critics who can be enlisted as allies in such an expansive Christian vision of modern and contemporary art. Klaus Ottmann, Joseph Masheck, Eleanor Heartney, and Thomas McEvilley, to name just a few, have focused on philosophical, spiritual, and religious issues in contemporary art that are invitations for the Christian intellectual to study them and appropriate their insights. But art criticism need not even devote itself to religion or spirituality for it to be of potential use by Christian intellectuals. A good example is the work of Weldon Kees.[43]

Born in Beatrice, Nebraska, Kees attended the University of Nebraska, where he made a name for himself through publishing several stories in the *Prairie Schooner*. In the early 1940s Kees went to New York and became part of the circle of the New York Intellectuals, who gravitated toward the journals *Partisan Review* and *The Nation*. Throughout the forties Kees achieved literary distinction as a poet and even began painting in the manner of the abstract expressionists, to whom he was quite close, including William Baziotes, Hans

Hoffmann, and Robert Motherwell.[44] When Clement Greenberg abruptly resigned in 1949 as art critic for *The Nation*, Kees was selected to be his successor. Although he would serve in that capacity for only a year (he left New York for San Francisco to pursue photography and film), Kees presided over an important and transitional moment in the contemporary art world in the United States. New York would become by the end of the fifties the undisputed center of the international art world, and abstract expressionism would "triumph" as the first American modern art movement.[45] Kees took on Senator Dondero, who accused modern art of being communistic; he criticized the Metropolitan Museum of Art for its conservative exhibition policies; and he otherwise served as an advocate for artistic freedom and a champion of the new abstract expressionism as its embodiment.[46]

As important as these critical stands are, it is Kees's respect for and sensitivity to the complexities of the artistic process that distinguish his critical vision. Kees was remarkably prescient in observing that the price of success for the "triumph" of American modernism would result in pressure for artists to compromise their aesthetic development by cultivating a "look" that would sell. By the late forties, American modernism had already begun to take on a highly prized look, one that combined the geometric and bright color formats of Piet Mondrian (who lived in New York until his death in the mid-1940s) and the cubist-inspired compositions that seemed to be the official "progressive" style of the American Abstract Artists Group.

But Kees recognized that abstract expressionism was a way of painting that could promise further aesthetic development if artists were willing to take the risk. And as a poet and painter who was himself involved in this project, Kees focused considerable attention on its importance. In a review of the recent work of Bradley Walker Tomlin, Kees observed that "the middle-ground critic used to have a sizable stable of tasteful middle-ground painters in whose company he felt comfortable and assured; now there are not so many to provide comfort and assurance, and they are growing fewer. There is the avant-garde, and there is the great glowering world of the Academy."[47]

It was becoming more difficult for Kees to navigate between the two. He felt compelled to assume this position because Tomlin, one of those "tasteful middle-ground painters," had become a "recent convert to a manner of painting for which we still have no satisfactory name" and he had come under fire by critics for his experimental forays. "But it is dispiriting to find all the critical notices I have seen on Tomlin's show working overtime in questioning his altered manner."[48] A certain kind of modernism had become a good investment, both economically and symbolically, leaving little room for artists such as Tomlin, Hofmann, Motherwell, de Kooning and others who were hard at work developing their own aesthetic vocabularies.

The problem as Kees saw it was not outright rejection, but assimilation and condemnation through faint praise, each conspiring to keep artists from moving beyond their signature and marketable look. For example, Greenberg and other critics were surprised and deeply disappointed by de Kooning's return to figurative painting in the early 1950s after several years in the late forties of purely abstract painting. "If there was an heroic artist of the caliber of a van Gogh, he would be 'recognized,' would show annually on Fifty-seventh Street, be stroked, complimented, sell a few canvases, go to cocktail parties, and be tamed. Not tamed too much, however."[49]

Kees's conclusion? "One is continually astounded that art persists at all in the face of so much indifference, failure, and isolation." He went on to say, "With our obsessive regard for specialization—a regard that is ridiculously the common ground of those in business, in the arts, and in the professions—the shared understanding of a larger universe is a concept that generates the coldest light conceivable."[50]

It was this "shared understanding of a larger universe" that animated Kees's own creative and critical activities. In fact, his criticism focused particular attention on revealing this "larger universe" against which to view cultural life, including advanced art. Moreover, it was criticism that enabled Kees to overcome the limits of these "specializations," to find connections between his own diverse artistic practices including poetry, fiction, painting, music, photography, and film. If he felt limited as a poet or painter, his criticism could move freely between literature, visual arts, music, politics, film, and a host of other subjects and media that interested him. Kees did not engage in criticism to change the world, transform the arts, or participate in any other utopian or ideological movement. Criticism served much more modest, and personal, needs. "If we are beyond the point of hoping for a healthy culture, we can at least entertain a hope for a few small islands, crannies, nooks, here and there, where an art that is mature, serious, and unprovincial can come into being."[51]

Kees's criticism in general and art criticism more specifically were concerned primarily with finding precisely those "few small islands." Advanced art has been, and will always be, a challenge in whatever social, political, and economic context artists find themselves. These few small islands, the nooks and crannies "here and there," are not going to transform culture or society—Kees had no utopian illusions. This sense of the world, however, allowed Kees to speak truth to power, to risk unpopularity, and even to be funny and sarcastic where more deeply committed (i.e., invested) critics might have shied away.

Many commentators have recently bemoaned the transformation of criticism and art criticism into various forms of marketing and promotion. Kees's criticism offers a brief but potent demonstration of the preservation of the critical spirit and the costs involved in maintaining such a commitment. In a culture of professionalized criticism, Kees's critical writing is one of those "little islands." His melancholic "homeless" disposition made him extremely sensitive to the pressures artists feel to conform in a multitude of different ways. And Kees regarded it his own responsibility as a critic to help the artist in this regard by drawing attention to those aspects of his or her work that embody the risk needed to develop aesthetically.

Although his melancholy ultimately culminated in his suicide in 1955, by jumping off the Golden Gate Bridge, Kees's criticism can be useful for Christian critical reflection on contemporary art. Kees was keenly aware of the power of institutions to mold and shape thoughts and actions, and his criticism was devoted to fighting against such an inclination, an inclination that is more powerful not when it rejects an artist's work but when it accepts it. He was aware and concerned about the little compromises that are made along the way that ultimately inhibit the artist from achieving an authentic and powerful aesthetic expression, one that may or may not result in immediate market or critical success. Kees's critical approach shows how to proceed in a contemporary art world many would agree is dysfunctional, by looking for those "little islands." It is also a warning to those in the Christian community whose zeal is for bringing to fruition Rookmaaker's and Schaeffer's dream of an army of "Christian artists" who would transform the contemporary art world and abandon the ideals of artistic and critical practice for the sake of "success." Kees would ask: success, perhaps, but at what cost?

Conclusion

In the *October* roundtable, George Baker argued that criticism is concerned about "locating silences, articulating repressions, providing a space for certain types of work and certain artistic aspirations to continue to evolve."[52] There is nothing more silent and repressed than art's liturgical and sacramental dimension, due in large part to culture as a whole becoming insensitive to this aspect of human nature. Contemporary culture does not need "Christian artists." It needs critics and curators who have a rich vocabulary from which to revive the sacramental and liturgical identity of human practice and to demonstrate that this identity finds its most complete and profound embodiment in the Nicene Christian faith. The Christian community thus needs more critics, curators, and art historians who can creatively and critically bend and shape contemporary art toward Christ.[53] Not only are many artists pursuing work that has implicit and explicit spiritual and religious connotations but a growing number of critics and curators are also becoming sensitive to the religious and spiritual dimensions of modern and contemporary art.

Art critics nourished by the Christian faith must build bridges to these "little islands."[54] Art criticism nourished by the Christian faith should recognize that there is already support for the presence of the spiritual, for belief, even for the religious in the contemporary art world and build on that interest. For example, Ottmann's focus on the experience of a work of art—to contemplate it, to commune with it—is not to be dismissed as some romantically inflated notion of art's *spirituality* or critiqued as merely the manifestation of idolatry, but to be underwritten by the presence and reality of prayer, by our capacities and potential as human persons to commune with God, to partake of the divine nature. A Christian perspective that denies Ottmann's perspective ultimately denies this reality.

Clearly an important problem that faces the Christian intellectual community is that despite the interest and support for things spiritual in the contemporary art world, the understanding of Christianity in the art world is distorted and incomplete. The contemporary art world often reacts against the kind of Christianity that is used in the public arena by politicians, a Christianity that is more concerned with maintaining the "Judeo-Christian" foundations of the United States or the West, banning gay marriage, defeating evolutionists, getting prayer in the schools, and promoting "values." The Christian intellectual community must embody a Christian faith that is more robust, textured, and expansive than is operative in the public arena.

The Christian critic must continually show how wide and deep is the love of God and bring it to bear creatively and critically on contemporary art. As

St. Paul says, we are to "Test everything. Hold on to the good" (1 Thess. 5:21; see also Phil. 4:8). It might indeed be that for some artists and their art, the "good" that remains is just fragments. But that still is our critical responsibility, to show how all things—even those little fragments in the contemporary art world—hold together in Christ.

6

Art, Liturgy, and the Church

There is a great difference between *still* believing something and believing it *again*.

G. C. Lichtenberg, *The Lichtenberg Reader*

Taste and see that the Lord is good.

Psalm 34:8

The world is charged with the grandeur of God.

Gerald Manley Hopkins, "God's Grandeur"

Ideas for this chapter were worked out initially in a seminar on Christian scholarship on art and worship entitled "Visual Arts and the Church" led by Bill Dyrness at Calvin College, June and July 2006, and participation in the Visual Arts Summit hosted by the Calvin Institute of Christian Worship at Calvin College, March 2007.

Protestant Ambivalence with Respect to the Visual Arts

The Protestant church has come to believe in the visual arts again. And herein lies the problem. The increased presence of the visual arts in the Protestant church and the challenges that have come with it in the so-called worship wars are evidence that there does indeed exist a chasm between "still believing something" and "believing it again." Since the Reformation, the Protestant church in its myriad manifestations has attempted to strip itself of all but the most necessary of ingredients for worship, for fear that the purity and simplicity of the gospel is compromised by layers of unnecessary ornament. The clarity of the gospel, then, needs a minimalist church, a reductive, stripped-down, bare-bones church. Karl Barth exemplifies well this lean approach: "It is only the community met together for 'worship' in the strict meaning of the word—that is for prayer, preaching, baptism and the Lord's Supper—and above all the community in action in every day life, which corresponds to the reality of the person and work of Jesus Christ. No image and no symbol can play that role."[1] But after taking images and symbols out, different manifestations of Protestantism end up putting some objects, practices, dogmas, traditions, or teachings back in. This has indeed been the case with the visual arts. And it happened almost concurrent with the Reformation.

On March 6, 1522, Martin Luther beat a hasty return to Wittenberg after nearly a year in exile for the express purpose of putting an end to his successor Andreas Karlstadt's programmatic destruction of the city's religious images. Although he himself had campaigned vigorously against both the use of relics and icons and the excessive veneration of Mary and the saints, Luther initiated a series of sermons condemning Karlstadt's iconoclasm and offering his own support of religious images. Perhaps not insignificantly, Luther initiated his series of eight sermons on Invocavit Sunday, or the so-called Feast of Orthodoxy, that commemorates Nicaea II, which reasserted the necessity of the veneration of icons in Christian faith and practice. In these sermons Luther seems to side with the sacred tradition of the church over and against the excessive reforms under Karlstadt. Luther's turnabout five years after his Ninety-five Theses embodies the complexities of icons and visual imagery that have been a part of the rich but ambivalent history of the image in the Western church since the Reformation.

Joseph Leo Koerner's *The Reformation of the Image* is an in-depth analysis of the altarpiece for the City Church in Wittenberg. The altarpiece was painted by Lucas Cranach the Elder and his workshop as a means to embody the impact of the Lutheran Reformation on art, communication, the contours of Christian faith, iconoclasm, and the nature of belief itself. For this reason, Koerner's book is relevant for those concerned about contemporary art, evangelicalism, ecumenism, apologetics, and other forms of religious communication and practice that trace their spiritual roots to the Protestant Reformation. Koerner is fascinated by the ambiguity and paradox of Lutheran doctrine and imagery.[2]

For Koerner, "The Lutheran crucifix is both an icon and an iconoclasm. It does not simply restore, reactively, sacred pictures to a cleansed church. It maintains itself in a state of remove, asserting by visual means that what it shows is elsewhere and invisible."[3] Koerner's study reveals the unique, ironic, ambivalent, and ultimately "modern" approach to imagery taken by Luther and his disciples. Unlike John Calvin and his followers, Luther did not reject religious images out of hand. But unlike the Catholic Church in the East and West, Luther did not allow religious images to stand alone, as visual, aesthetic artifacts for contemplation and veneration.

For Luther, religious images needed to be accompanied by words; they needed explanation; they needed to be disenchanted for *communication*. The preached word was the means by which disenchantment rendered the religious images useful for the Lutheran church. And those uses were primarily didactic. What makes Lutheran art of this period so fascinating, according to Koerner, is that it carries with it its interpretation, just to make sure it does not get misinterpreted. It thus reduces the effect of aesthetic experience for the sake of visualizing an interpretation. Interestingly, Koerner turns to the didactic format of Luther's *Small Catechism*, with its focus on questions, *"Was ist das?"* (What is that?), which are followed by *"Das ist"* (It is), as a source for the Lutheran philosophy of art.

Therefore, the Christian faith is made a function of a series of simple questions and simple answers, defined by beliefs rather than practices, thus explaining, demystifying, and disenchanting the faith. "Luther invented religion," Koerner argues, "as an interpretive act: in the word, believers grasp the content that saves them."[4] Ultimately, "Didacticism required that the image become less rather than more: less visually seductive, less emotionally charged, less semantically rich. Deemed useless save as school pictures, images were built to signal the fact of their impotence."[5] He continues, "Do words teach more effectively than images simply because their content can be rephrased in other words? A structural relation between text and exegesis gives language the illusion of a referential centre, and distinguishing it from the round but hollow image."[6] This seems to be the crux of Protestant iconoclasm, the assumption that words are more effective communicators than images, practices, rituals, actions, and symbols. "Step by step," Koerner observes, "the sacred was 'linguistified.'"[7]

For Koerner, Lucas Cranach's Wittenberg altarpiece, dedicated on April 24, 1547, is a "disenchanted display of ceremony" that "marks and cancels church as a sacred place, the Eucharist as the real presence."[8] Koerner's focus is on the altarpiece's predella, the horizontal panel that serves as the backdrop for the priest on the table of the altar. The predella features an oddly positioned "floating" crucifix flanked by a congregation on the left and Luther himself preaching to them with an open Bible on the right. Luther gestures with an outstretched hand that directs the viewer's eye from his hand through the crucifix to the congregation. The crucifix, which is perched precariously on a single interior panel, is surrounded by empty space cleared of the clutter of artifacts, objects, icons, rituals, and gestures. Koerner convincingly argues that the crucifix is not really there. It is the crucifix of the heart, a depiction of a mental picture, to which Luther was intensely devoted; it is, furthermore, the believer's "visual image of verbal consent."[9] For the Reformers, the true church was invisible; consequently Cranach represents the invisible church, a church devoid of props and exterior accoutrements outside the preaching of the Word. For Luther, as Koerner rightly observes, Christ's kingdom is a *hearing* kingdom, not a *seeing* kingdom. The crucifix is the communication of a community, it is the "what" that is being preached and believed.

In an effort to suspend iconoclasm, to represent an icon of the preached Word, Cranach has visualized verbal communication. "By turning sacred rituals and objects into acts of language, image-breakers sanctified communication."[10] The Wittenberg altarpiece's predella has not only reformed the image—the icon—but has also constituted a social world dominated by communication, not ritual objects, behaviors, traditions, actions, and practices. Koerner argues that the reformation of the image constituted "the belief in belief itself."[11] "The collapse of all dogma and ritual into one belief," *sola fide*, "transformed the very character *of* belief."[12]

Koerner argues that the "I believe" of ancient Christian faith was transformed into an "I believe that," which constituted a specific *representation* of belief, "the belief together with its explanation, the word alongside its meaning, the communicative apparatus and the information it transmits."[13] Koerner's book is an important contribution to the study of the vast cultural transformations ushered in by the Protestant Reformation and an exploration of the ambiguities of iconoclasm. Koerner also succeeds in revealing the paradoxes of Lutheran art and its theology and Luther's struggle to "believe anew," a situation, ironically, for which he himself was chiefly responsible.

But despite his efforts, Luther could not go back. And so even while both Albrecht Dürer and Lucas Cranach are commemorated together with a feast day in the Lutheran calendar, the role of art (and the aesthetic) in the Reformational church was changed, from a primary means of spiritual contemplation and communion to a supportive function as a tool of education and communication. Even though "art" in the Lutheran tradition remains, it remains fundamentally changed.

Artistic Presence in the Protestant Church

Luther's example of the ebb and flow—of eliminating art and other "hard things" as evidence of papist superstition while at the same time railing against others for going too far—has been seared into Protestant consciousness. The result, as far as the Lutheran church is concerned, is the strong presence of visual imagery. But that imagery, in the service of "communication" and "education," has become so domesticated, muted, and didactic that crucifixes, festival banners, and even liturgical furniture are visually and aesthetically compelling *only* insofar as they are needed to *communicate* the point.

This harnessed aesthetic finds its way into other Protestant churches to differing degrees. For example, art has had a significant presence in recent evangelical movements. In savvy "seeker" Protestant churches, whether of the megachurch or the emergent conversation model, there is a much more sophisticated attitude toward art in the church. For the megachurch model, exemplified by Willow Creek, the arts are ways to make "doing church" more attractive and appealing, whether through music, drama, or exhibitions of art produced by the members of the congregation. For the emergent model, art finds its way into the church in several ways: first, through a renewed but selective interest in ritual objects, gestures, and practices that harkens back to a pre-Reformational Christianity; second, through the use of a design aesthetic to brand fellowships as hip, arty, and engaged in culture, which appeals to the "creative class"; and third, through artist residencies, providing opportunities for artists to work within the context of the church.

The loss of church patronage in the aftermath of the Reformation is often pointed to in order to explain the current situation of the visual arts and the church. On one hand, commentators bemoan this state of affairs, since the loss of church patronage has drastically diminished Christian presence in the visual arts. An effective way to rectify this situation is for the church once again to play a major role in artistic patronage. Other commentators, on the other hand, celebrate the fact that the church has gotten out of the art business, thereby freeing up art to pursue its destiny of celebrating the goodness of creation unhindered by the limits of ecclesial commissions. The church and culture inhabit two separate spheres (Abraham Kuyper) or kingdoms (Luther), and so art can flourish without the interference of the church.

Both sides of this debate do not take into sufficient account the aesthetic shift that occurred *within* the Protestant churches at the time of the Reformation, a shift that enabled Luther to continue to work with Lucas Cranach while changing the fundamental way the altarpiece functioned and consequently altering how the aesthetic works within the church. This shift has an impact on aesthetics in the secular realm. Since it is Christ's mystical body in the world and the pillar and foundation of Truth, the church offers a foundation for artistic and aesthetic practice, both within the church and in the larger culture. After the Reformation, the tendency has been either to conflate the aesthetics of the church and culture—implying that the latter should bear the explicit, visible imprint of the former—or to draw too sharp a distinction between the two.

The church's aesthetics underwrite aesthetics in the larger culture. But it underwrites them in a way that does not limit but expands the aesthetic potential in the larger culture, which ultimately offers the freedom of Christ that St. Paul observed was the liberating effect of the gospel that is wide enough, long enough, high enough, and deep enough to accommodate it (Eph. 3:18). In this context, there is nothing in the history of modern and contemporary art that can be dismissed out of hand because it violates some canonical norms of "Christian art." Therefore, abstract painting, performance art, conceptual art, and even the presentation of "ordinary objects" in art situations, such as Duchamp's readymades, are not only not violations of such normative standards but are in fact funded by the expansive aesthetics of the church. The task, then, is to articulate the expansive aesthetics of the church.

Theological Considerations

The church fathers were fond of saying that there is no salvation outside the church. The one holy, catholic, and apostolic church is ground for all human practices, which are contextualized and anointed as "good" within the church, even the most banal and mundane of material needs, from sex to eating and drinking.[14] The church is the witness to God's faithfulness to his people in the past, to the Jews first and also to the Greeks, and to his future salvation and redemption of all things under Christ, "so that God may be all in all" (1 Cor. 15:28). Orthodox liturgical theologian Alexander Schmemann observes: "All that exists is God's gift to man, and it all exists to make God known to man, to make man's life communion with God. It is divine love made food, made life for man. God blesses everything He creates, and, in biblical language, this means that He makes all creation the sign and means of His presence and wisdom, love and revelation."[15]

It is within the church that this reality is revealed, just as Asaph discovers God's sovereignty and the right order of the world after he goes into the sanctuary (Ps. 73:17). If all creation, then, is a sign of God's presence in and through the world, it follows that the world—the cosmos—is a temple and thus its contents are sacraments. The church is not a *religious* sphere separated from the *realities* of the world but reveals the world's true meaning and significance. "Our entrance into the presence of Christ is an entrance into a fourth dimension which allows us to see the ultimate reality of life. It is not an escape from the world, rather it is the arrival at a vantage point from which we can see more deeply into the reality of the world."[16]

Humanity has a unique responsibility in this sacramental world, which is underwritten, sustained, made visible, and mediated by the church, the sacramental reality of the world. This responsibility is first and foremost a priestly role, established through Christ's fulfillment of the priestly role given to Adam.

> The first, the basic definition of man is that he is the priest. He stands in the center of the world and unifies it in his act of blessing God, of both receiving the world from God and offering it to God—and by filling the world with this eucharist, he transforms his life, the one that he receives from the world, into life in God, into communion with Him. The world was created as the "matter," the material of one all-embracing eucharist, and man was created as the priest of this cosmic sacrament.[17]

Christ fulfills the divine calling for humanity to serve not only as prophet and king but also as priest. A sacramental worldview brings to the fore the importance of the priestly vocation, a vocation not limited to the clergy but intended for all members of the church, for our destiny is to be a kingdom of priests (Exod. 19:6). "Man's responsibility," John Zizioulas states, "is to make a Eucharistic reality out of nature, i.e., to make nature, too, capable of communion."[18] This is the "priesthood of all believers," which is not merely a glorification of the individual Christian's conscience, as in Protestantism. The clergy, as set apart from the laity, are so set apart only to reveal the priestly role of all those baptized into the body of Christ (1 Pet. 2:9) and to testify to the priestly destiny of all humanity, when "every knee shall bow." Protestant traditions often give less attention to the priestly role of humanity, seeking to explicate in far greater detail the dominion of kingship and the preaching of the prophetic role.

The priestly vocation presupposes that the entire cosmos is the temple of God and is thus sacred; all actions are liturgical and all artifacts are sacraments. As the Trisagion prayers declare: "O Heavenly King, O Comforter, the Spirit of Truth, who are in all places and fill all things . . ." The priestly vocation is characterized by reconciliation and healing, which testifies to the presence of the kingdom of God even in the midst of a broken world, a world governed by powers and principalities that deny the world its eucharistic identity. But it is a world in which God is "making everything new" (Rev. 21:5). This is the testimony and destiny of the church.

As the mystical body of Christ, the church becomes the church through the Eucharist. It is through the eating and drinking of Christ's body and blood that this mystical union is enacted, as we partake of the divine nature (2 Pet. 1:4). Alexander Schmemann again argues that "men understand all this instinctively if not rationally. Centuries of secularism have failed to transform eating into something strictly utilitarian. Food is still treated with reverence. A meal is still a rite—the last 'natural sacrament' of family and friendship, of life that is more than 'eating' and 'drinking.'"[19]

The church's identity as the mystical body of Christ, which is enacted corporately and individually through the Eucharist, thus imbues *all* eating and drinking with sacramental value. As Pavel Florensky's student Sergius Bulgakov states, "Eating represents the communion of human beings with the world that is external to them, a kind of identification with this world."[20] The liturgy is literally "the work of the people" (Greek: *leitourgos*) and thus,

God in the Gallery

as simultaneously "work" and "worship," it underwrites both work and worship in the world, for "the Christ of the Eucharist is revealed as the life and recapitualization of all creation."[21]

This expansive view of the liturgy, which has at its heart and soul the Eucharist, is also an important focus of Radical Orthodoxy, a group of British Anglo-Catholic theologians centered primarily around the work of John Milbank. Catherine Pickstock, who has played an important role in shaping Radical Orthodoxy, suggests that "liturgy transfigures our notion of genuine human action."[22] And even more, "The event of transubstantiation in the Eucharist is the condition of possibility for all human meaning."[23] Because it is eschatological, the liturgy not only makes human meaning and action possible, it is a powerful means of critique of the powers and principalities that govern "this world," whether it is a critique of "mundane time," as Pickstock suggests,[24] or the modern state, as asserted by William T. Cavanaugh.[25]

Radical Orthodoxy (hereafter RO) has had an important impact on contemporary theology, especially for those theologians concerned with engaging postmodern thought because of its tenacious critique of modernity, particularly its embodiment in theological liberalism and fundamentalism. Moreover, RO has sought to reintroduce the Platonic concept of participation into Western theology. This makes the RO theologians useful allies in this study, with their attention to an expansive aesthetic that can underwrite postmodern artistic practice. This reassertion has its origins in the Eucharist and, more specifically, as Graham Ward argues, the "ontological scandal" is the Words of Institution, "This is my body."[26] As James K. A. Smith observes, "RO proposes a participatory ontology that understands transcendence as an essential feature of material reality."[27]

The source of RO's participatory ontology is a revival of Greek neoplatonic thought, particularly the theurgical tradition of Iamblichus and Proclus, combined with controversial and idiosyncratic readings of Plato, St. Augustine, and St. Thomas Aquinas. But it is in many ways parallel to Eastern Orthodox mystical theology (especially the Russian philosophers of sophiology, Florensky, Bulgakov, and Soloviev), a theology that sees the Christian life as one of increased participation in communion with the divine nature, a participation and communion that is part of the sanctification process of deification, or theosis.[28]

Church Aesthetics

Pavel Florensky has emphasized the aesthetic dimensions of worship, suggesting that "church ritual being itself a musical drama on the aesthetic plane."[29] The liturgy, then, is the aesthetics of the church. And therefore any discussion of art and the aesthetic must take place first from within the context of the liturgy. It is the aesthetic dimension of the liturgy that underwrites aesthetic practice in the world. This does not mean, however, that the liturgy places limitations either in form or content on aesthetic and artistic practice. Quite the contrary, it opens up such practice. Just as the Eucharist does not limit eating and drinking to bread and wine, the liturgy does not limit artistic practice to icons, representational images, crosses, and the like.

Within the broader context of the liturgy, the aesthetic is not in the service of facilitating communication or teaching; it is not a pedagogical "help"; it is not speech pursued by other means. It facilitates veneration, contemplation, communion, and participation in Truth, and that Truth is not a proposition but Christ himself. Through the Eucharist truth is revealed in, and identified with, *communion*.[30] All aspects of the liturgy, from the text and its performance—through intonation or chant—to the gestures of the priest and the laity, to the incense, candles, and the presence of icons, focus attention on the experience *of* God, not just acquiring knowledge *about* God. As Florensky states, "In a church everything is interlinked."[31] And what is interlinked is the experience of God's presence in and through all its components, which encompasses all of creation. Christoph Cardinal Schönborn suggests the same when he observes: "A Church that in her liturgy, in her very life, draws vitality from the sense of awe in facing the mystery, will provide breathing space for any art whose primary purpose is not a breathless pursuit of outward success."[32]

This expansive notion of the church, its liturgy, and the Eucharist, defined and preserved through the councils and expressed dogmatically through the symbol of the Nicene Creed, with its comprehensive totality, does not suffocate artistic practice but instead gives it, as Schönborn suggests, "breathing space," precisely because it is so comprehensive, cosmic, and total in what it embraces. It thus can offer a foundation for artistic practice in the world. Installation art, conceptual art, performance art, abstract painting, ordinary objects presented in an artistic context—all these forms and more are underwritten by an ancient liturgy that embraces the aesthetic experience of objects, practices, and environments as constitutive of worship, and thus constitutive of who we are as human persons. The aesthetic power of much modern and contemporary art comes from this liturgical reality.

Minimalist Church versus Maximal Aesthetics

The Protestant tradition has often thought otherwise. Such an expansive liturgy—whether the Eastern rites of St. John of Chrysostom and St. Basil, or the Roman rite with its primitive rituals, the "bells and smells"—was thought to obscure, dilute, and obfuscate the simplicity of the truth of the gospel, the truth declared most clearly in preaching and supported or framed by two sacraments or "ordinances." The Protestant tendency, then, to limit the scope and reach of the church was intended, no doubt, to offer a more expansive engagement with the world free of the oppressive control of the church. A limited church was assumed to enable more freedom outside the church, a more developed secular world, within which Christians could carry out their vocations.

The reaction of a reductive and minimalist Protestant church to twentieth-century artistic practice has produced three responses. The first, what could be called the liberal response, has been to allow artistic practice in the secular realm to develop with virtually no theological formulation from the church. The implication is that the church has nothing to contribute to understanding and shaping contemporary artistic practice. The second response is a conservative one, one that is predicated on the assumption that the artistic forms of art in the church, defined as representational "church art," provide the norms for what contemporary artistic practice should follow. The third response is the most complex since it cuts across traditional conservative and liberal lines. It is the growing recognition that the Protestant church needs art as part of its worship. Whether liberal or conservative, there is a growing awareness that art is needed in the church.

The result is that Protestant (and Catholic) churches simply import secular artistic practices uncritically (whether more "fine art" for liberal churches and "popular art and commercial art" for conservative ones) with very little reflection on just what practices and patterns of belief are being brought in, since art works are not merely *objects* but products of institutional intention and belief, made under certain conditions and intended to be viewed in specific contexts.

Florensky, who was writing to preserve the entire church context for the icons under the Soviet regime, helps shed light on the significant differences between a church and a museum (or art gallery). "Here, in the church," Florensky states, "all of this exaggeration [in the icon] is softened and conveys a power unattainable by ordinary methods of representation."[33] He continues: "The finest blue veil of incense dissolved in the air brings to the contemplation of icons and frescoes a softening and deepening of aerial perspective, such as the museum neither knows nor can dream of."[34] Made for the special environment of the church, not just as a public display, icons are to be viewed, experienced, venerated, and contemplated amid the flickering candlelight, through the clouds of incense, and with the sounds of prayers and the psalms. In the same manner, works of art produced in and with the institutional patterns of the modern and contemporary art world are to be experienced in museums and gallery spaces, with electric track lighting, white walls, etc. Both icons and modern art have imbedded in them special conditions in order to maximize their aesthetic potential. Confusion can occur when artifacts produced for one context are uncritically displayed in the other.

A case in point is the blockbuster exhibition, organized by the Metropolitan Museum of Art in New York, called "Byzantium: Faith and Power" (1261–1557), which featured hundreds of icon panels, reliquaries, and other painted devotional objects from Orthodox churches throughout Eastern Europe.[35] In a review of the exhibition, medievalist Sharon E. J. Gerstel observes, "Set against porridge-colored and greenish blue walls, these devotional objects were presented as works of art largely decontextualized and subjected, many for the first time, to purely art historical appreciation and scrutiny." Gerstel continues: "The contrast between these common works and those that by any standard are indisputable masterpieces of painting introduced the critical issue of whether icons should be more properly considered works of art or primarily devotional objects."[36] The exhibition and the critical discourse it spawned offered an opportunity to reflect on precisely Florensky's point about art and context. What is surely accomplished art historically, achieved from the perspective of Western aesthetic reflection and accessibility, is purchased at some cost. It is the cost of decontextualization and recontextualization that must be considered by Protestant churches as they endeavor to incorporate the visual arts in their churches, whatever that might mean for them.

Without question the issue of "worship and the arts" is one of the more complex and challenging theological issues in contemporary evangelicalism.[37] I think about this subject each Sunday as my family sits in our customary front-row pew in our ninety-year-old traditionalist Lutheran church, with its ambitious and beautiful cycle of stained glass that envelops the sanctuary. But as I look at the altar, the lectionary, the baptismal font, and the preaching podium, my attention moves to the large crucifix that hangs on the back wall above the altar. As far as I know, no one looks at it. My fellow parishioners bow their heads in prayer, look down at the bulletin to follow the liturgy, read the pastoral prayers, read the Scripture texts prescribed for the day, and sing hymns. Each Sunday I try to train my eyes on that crucifix and think about art, think about what we as a congregation have in front of us. And, following Koerner, I've come to the conclusion that the crucifix, with its carved wood form, *resists* my gaze. It invites a distracted glance but moves my eye elsewhere, to more important places. I have no doubt that my fellow parishioners would protest vehemently if it, for some reason, were taken down so that we could focus on the crucifix in the heart or imagination, as Luther suggested. But I do not think that it wants to be looked at, really looked at—that is, contemplated. It would then become a distraction. But I remain confused and perplexed about why it is there, then. And so it hovers, oddly and uncomfortably, like Cranach's Wittenburg predella crucifix.

I offer this personal anecdote as a caveat that what follows in this section are merely some observations that can be helpful in negotiating the relationship between art in the church and art outside the church. Given the high value placed on icons in this study, it might be assumed that I advocate using only icons and the "hard things" of the Orthodox and Catholic tradition. But this is not the case. For good or ill, we must make our own way, step by step. It is my contention that clarity about the church's aesthetics—in the church—drawn creatively from the depths of a Nicene Christian faith must also be complemented by historical and theoretical clarity about modern and contemporary art in order even to begin the process. I have elsewhere written that it is in the context of the emergent conversation that such discussion can best take place, given its openness both to ancient Christianity and contemporary artistic practice.[38] I am, however, equally committed to the belief that this discussion will be best *practiced* elsewhere.

The Problematics of Church Art

In a short article entitled "Liturgical Art and Its Discontents," Gregory Wolfe, publisher and editor of *Image: A Journal of the Arts and Religion*, puts his finger on the complex problem of art and the church.

> Too many efforts to relate religion and the arts have stumbled because they attempt to channel the imagination into pious patterns. At the root of this failure is an underlying fear of the imagination itself—a force that can't be tamed or made to fit into comforting, predictable categories. Believers who fear the imagination prefer art that doesn't stray too far from the Church porch; they want to see things they already know gussied up with ornaments and flourishes. But art at its highest pitch tries to tell us things we don't know, or have forgotten, and that can be unsettling. Also, the majority of our waking hours are not spent in church, but in the world. And if religion is too important to be confined to church services, then so is art that grapples with religious themes.[39]

Wolfe's assessment is provocative and worth reflecting on in some depth because he not only isolates the basic problem of liturgical or church art but he also manifests a deeper problem: a continued reliance on some assumptions about art and the church that compromises his assessment.

While it is not a fair representation of the totality of his thought, Wolfe's observation suggests quite accurately that the problem with art and the church is that both are distinct institutional practices with their own norms and standards. The problem with Wolfe's assessment is that he does not differentiate clearly enough the institutions of church and (modern) art in his evaluation. Wolfe presupposes a reductive, minimalistic church whose role is to limit and put strictures on the "imagination" in order to serve "pious patterns," presumably church dogma and doctrine. Wolfe's church is already limited in the life of the modern person, a place (again, limited to a building) that plays a proportionally irrelevant role in the life of believers, who spend the vast majority of their time *not* in church. (My Orthodox and Catholic friends often observe how little time we Protestants actually spend in church on a weekly basis.) And so, Wolfe implies, the church, which plays such a minimal role in cultural life, should not be in a position to curtail, delimit, or otherwise stifle artistic imagination.

Wolfe's assessment, then, pits the church against the world, implying that the church cannot influence or sustain secular artistic practice theologically and dogmatically without being an overbearing patron. Wolfe also claims that the church's problems with art have much to do with the church's problem, not art's. Therefore, it is a "fear of imagination" in the church that prevents the visual arts from playing a more profound role in the church. But this is simply not the case. The church, with its liturgical practice, is most definitely not the place to incorporate art that forces the worshiper to "ask tough questions," "challenge previously held beliefs," and so on. Those are absolutely important practices, but not in the liturgy. As Mozart observed about a famous opera composer's attempt to write music for a Mass: "It is all fine, but not in church."[40]

Despite the complex theological and dogmatic implications that icons and their veneration have played in this study, their function within the context of the church is simple: to aid prayer. This is driven home in an account of the emperor's confessor, Gregory Melissenos, who objected to using a Latin rite church for Orthodox services during the Council of Ferrara (1438): "When I enter a Latin church, I do not revere any of the saints that are there because I do not recognize any of them. At the most, I may recognize Christ, but I do not revere Him either, since I do not know in what terms he is inscribed."[41] One cannot use icons as contemplative aids to communion with God through prayer unless the images can be recognized, their actions and gestures interpreted and understood. From a practical standpoint, *recognition* is an important— perhaps the most important—aspect of the veneration of icons. The recognition of the identity of the person depicted and the person's liturgical function is a key component of contemplation. Familiarity and comfort, those "pious patterns," do not hinder the imagination. They can facilitate it, deepen it.[42] Marcel Duchamp likewise relied on and exploited the notion of recognition in his readymades.

Wolfe would criticize both Mozart and Gregory Melissenos for their "pious patterns" and desire for "comforting, predictable categories." Wolfe appropriates the modern institutional understanding of art, demands that the church incorporate that understanding of art into its liturgy, and criticizes it as fearful of imagination when it will not. But the church and the art world have different audiences; participants in the church and in the art world have different expectations. The audience for the art world expects to be challenged, to question assumptions and accepted patterns of thought and practice; the audience for the church—the worshiper—on the other hand, expects first and foremost recognition. This does not mean that icons and other imagery in the church are simply passive artifacts "used" by the worshiper to facilitate his or her own needs. To the contrary, the economy of the icon is to exert pressure on the worshiper, to shape, develop, and discipline the imagination. But it is not clear that this kind of molding and shaping of the imagination can simply or always be identified with the *challenge* modern art offers the viewer.

And finally, Wolfe relies on the avant-garde myth of the artist as the locus of imagination and cultural leadership that the church desperately needs (a myth, let us remember, that is adapted, co-opted, even copied from the church). But Wolfe does not seem to raise the issue of what the artist might need from the church. Wolfe here conflates aesthetic with spiritual practice, making an aesthetic virtue within the context of the autonomous modern institution of art a spiritual one. It is commonly believed that the artist and his or her aesthetic practice in the studio have much to teach the church. But nothing is mentioned about how the church's spiritual practices and disciplines, including liturgical practice, can underwrite and sustain aesthetic practice, which was the case with iconographers in the ancient church and remains so even today in the East. The influence between artist and church for Wolfe seems to work just one way. The assumption is that the church would be far healthier if there were more artists making art for their churches, expanding their parishioners' imaginations, without asking why. The ancient church had some quite serious reservations about the conversion of pagan artists, poets, and intellectuals and, rather than shape the church to fit them, they subjected them to an even more rigorous testing of their faith. (Unlike Plato, they did not advocate banning the poets, but they certainly made sure they knew what they were getting into and who was calling the shots.)

Wolfe's assessment here simply does not go deep enough. He seems to assume that the primary role of the contemporary church is simply to serve as a patron for artists working in the world with little or no concern that the artist has been trained to practice art in a way that might indeed run counter to the liturgical framework of the church. Art in the church, Wolfe and his colleagues tend to believe, is merely museum art pursued by other means.

This finds its practical expression in the recent interest among megachurches that follow the Willow Creek model and develop schools of the arts under the assumption that the contemporary church must once again be a patron of the arts and encourage the artistic practice of their congregations.[43] The emergent conversation has gone a step further, and some communities actually employ "artists in residence."

But neither approach self-consciously develops and shapes an artistic practice that comes in and through the church. The practice of icon writing was indeed an adapted "secular" practice, but the ancient church appropriated it, shaped and molded it, and developed it over the centuries to make it a theological and dogmatic arm of the church, not something merely imported from the larger culture.

If Protestant churches are to develop artistically, they will have to evolve such practices over time, within and through the theological and dogmatic practice of their denomination or local congregation. This might result in little or no art being produced for quite some time. But it is important to recall that in Tarkovsky's cinematic masterpiece, *The Passion of Andrei Rublev* (1966), Rublev is never seen working on a single icon. There is so much more to art producing than its production, and that "more" must be provided for by the spiritual direction and dogmatic foundation of the church.

Ancient Church and Contemporary Art

The growing interest in the visual arts in Protestant and evangelical churches is part of a larger, important trend that seeks to engage the contemporary postmodern cultural condition through the development of an "ancient-future" faith that on one hand accepts and welcomes the postmodern critique of the myths of modernity—myths that the Western church has bought into—and on the other embraces a "premodern" Christianity, one that incorporates the wisdom of the ancient church of the East and West. The result has been greater awareness of the importance of spiritual and liturgical practices, including eucharistic piety. This has also brought a greater awareness of the dogmatic and spiritual content of the aesthetic. The development of the postmodern "missional" church has also sought to reach those engaged in contemporary art and music with the gospel. John Meyendorff says it well when he observes:

> The goal of mission is indeed that all men would know Christ and in Him find communion with God. But knowledge of Christ and communion with God (that which was called *theosis* by the Fathers) are not communicated to men so that they may in any way *replace* man's knowledge of himself and of the cosmos, but in order to fulfill that knowledge, to give it new meaning and a new creative dimension.[44]

It is the goal of "fulfilling that knowledge" and giving it "new meaning and a new creative dimension" that this study has as its own missional core, as it were.

The aesthetic dimension of the Nicene Christian faith is much wider and deeper than is often assumed by the cultured despisers in the Protestant and evangelical world, who see the ancient church as merely limiting, censoring, and stifling the artistic imagination, assuming that what is good for the secular world is good for the church: if this or that practice has a market in the world then it needs to be imported into the church. But the Nicene Christian faith can offer a firm foundation on which to build bridges toward culture—toward the secular world—in a more nuanced, discerning, and even expansive way. It was St. Paul's foundation in the life of the church that enabled him to engage culture, to look closely at the altars, to name the altar to the unknown gods, and to quote from pagan literature because these things can be bent, shaped, and molded in order to fulfill the knowledge implicit in them. (St. Paul's own conversion, or call, completed and fulfilled his knowledge of the Scriptures.) The missional movement goes from the church outward toward culture, not from culture to a passive, inert, irrelevant church.

Modern and contemporary art, particularly art made in the last fifteen to twenty years, needs for the church to be able to recognize altars to the unknown god and then be able to demonstrate how contemporary artistic practice finds its ultimate aesthetic and intellectual fulfillment through thought that lives and breathes and has its being in the life of the church. Much contemporary art—in its incorporation of practices, interest in utilizing sacred spaces, and psychological and aesthetic power of objects and artifacts—can benefit greatly from critical engagement with the sacramental and liturgical life as embodied by the Nicene, conciliar church. This is not merely an attempt to fortify a "Christian perspective" on art and culture but an attempt to experience and understand modern and contemporary art on its own terms in a context big and wide enough to accommodate those terms.

This does not "solve" the problem of the visual arts in the church or how Protestant churches utilize art in their worship, but it does serve to reactivate the church (Orthodox, Catholic, and Protestant), making it a proactive, shaping presence in the contemporary culture rather than a passive organization that merely adapts innovations developed elsewhere in culture, assuming tacitly (and sometimes not so tacitly) that the one hour a believer spends in worship at church each week is largely irrelevant for the remaining time in the world. Probe the theological, spiritual, and philosophical depth of church tradition and there will be powerful resources to speak aptly to contemporary art.

The divine liturgy, in its synesthetic dimension that engages all the aesthetic faculties, within which the veneration of icons occurs, is the analogical ground for all artistic practice. It offers a foundation that enables and encourages infinite freedom to explore its implications in culture as a means to understand artistic practices. This has a twofold purpose: first, it brings greater clarity and understanding to contemporary artistic practice; and second, it demonstrates the richness of the gospel that fulfills and completes rather than replaces or denies secular understanding and practice of art.

The aesthetic depth of the church, exemplified through the dogmas of the ecumenical councils, embodied in the divine liturgy of the Eucharist, and evidenced in the rich tradition of the veneration of icons, should be able to underwrite the work of the Reformational churches. The dogmas of the ecumenical councils, the divine liturgy of St. John Chrysostom and St. Basil, and the icons remain an important part of the Christian faith and thus can—and should—inform contemporary evangelical Protestant thinking on theological reflection, worship, and the arts. The task, perhaps, is not for evangelical churches to begin to use the divine liturgy of St. John Chrysostom, but to develop and elaborate on its aesthetic and dogmatic implications and appropriate them for their own worship services within the context of their own worship traditions, which has been the Protestant practice from the beginning.

Conclusion

The Search for Christian Art and the Christian Artist

Here I must say emphatically: art must never be used to show the validity of Christianity. Rather the validity of art should be shown through Christianity.

H. R. Rookmaaker, *Modern Art and the Death of a Culture*, 1970

Let me say firmly that *there is no such thing as a godly style or an ungodly style*. The more one tries to make such a distinction, the more confusing it becomes.

Francis Schaeffer, *Art and the Bible*, 1973

These essays have approached modern and contemporary art and Christian faith from a different vantage point in that they take for granted the existence of two things: first, the presence of modern and contemporary art as a legitimate cultural practice that requires critical, historical, and theoretical analysis and understanding; and second, the presence of a big and robust Christian faith, defined by the creeds (especially the Nicene-Constantinople), articulated and elaborated by the seven ecumenical councils, and embodied by the church, God's household, the "pillar and foundation of the truth" (1 Tim. 3:15). It is this Nicene Christian faith, in its maximal embodiment in the church, that offers an important framework for analyzing and understanding modern and contemporary art. From the vantage point of this Christianity, modern and contemporary art offers altars to the unknown god that we who embrace this faith can name. But such naming is not intended to simply offer a "Christian perspective" on contemporary art but to fulfill or deepen the integrity of these works as embodiments of significant cultural practices and to participate in the aesthetic world they project more deeply.

Although they emerged in response to my dissatisfaction with Christian approaches to the subject that have by and large been defined by the Reformed approaches of H. R. Rookmaaker and Francis Schaeffer, these essays do not seek to argue with them or pick fights with other manifestations of Christian approaches to modern and contemporary art. Engaging in prolonged argument over such points of contention can merely lock one's approach into the contours of the very scholarly consensus that one wants to avoid. Rather than attempt to fix things here and there, a completely new approach to the subject must be undertaken, with different theological preoccupations, aesthetic commitments, and art historical and art critical tools.

My intention, then, with these essays, is to offer an altogether different way to approach modern and contemporary art, with no apologies and caveats for doing so, an approach derived first and foremost from my perspective as a curator, critic, and historian of modern and contemporary art. The result is that this study appears to give short shrift to two important subjects held dear by conventional approaches. This is not because I believe these subjects are unimportant. But they have so dominated the literature on the subject that it is important to put them to the side, if only temporarily, so that other important questions and concerns can be addressed. The first is the relationship of the visual arts to the church. Chapter 6 thus offers an approach to this subject only after the study's preoccupations and concerns have been fully articulated.

The second subject, which is the focus of this conclusion, is the Christian artist and Christian art, a subject that has been defined largely through evangelical and Reformed approaches to art since H. R. Rookmaaker's *Modern Art and the Death of a Culture*, published in 1970, and Francis Schaeffer's *Art and the Bible*, published three years later.[1] This chapter, as a conclusion, reflects on the Christian artist, Christian art, and artistic practice that has indeed been shaped by Schaeffer and Rookmaaker and is manifest in the emergence of Christian arts organizations and institutions.

What Is a Christian Artist?

The Dutch art historian Hans R. Rookmaaker intended his *Modern Art and the Death of a Culture* for younger artists, particularly Christian artists.[2]

Rookmaaker concludes the book by addressing the Christian artist and Christian art. It is Christian art and the Christian artist that has, since Rookmaaker, become the primary preoccupation of most evangelical discussions of art. And that preoccupation has confused matters considerably.

What is Christian art? According to Rookmaaker, it is "art depicting biblical stories or subjects related to the Christian faith."[3] Since the Enlightenment in general and the nineteenth century most specifically, these subjects have become increasingly rare. Rookmaaker offers a spurious interpretation of such art that has replaced Christian art: "By removing Christ, or Mary, or other Christian themes from the picture itself, leaving them outside the picture-frame, it is as if Christ Himself, and the reality of the things Christians believed in, were placed outside the world."[4] The Christian artist, then, presumably is concerned with restoring to art biblical themes, subjects, and stories.

However, the Christian artist must stand for much more than Christian content in his or her art. For Rookmaaker, writing at the height of the global crisis of communism, the Christian artist must stand for freedom: "In his art he is free from the past, the present and the future."[5] The Christian artist must also stand for humanity.[6] (It is significant that the Marxist medievalist Meyer Schapiro, writing during the Cold War in the fifties, identified abstraction with freedom.[7]) The Christian artist is also to speak prophetically to and be critical of culture. "Our calling," Rookmaaker concludes, "is to live in freedom and love, to fight against sin; to stand for freedom and humanity."[8] But the Christian artist also needs a community. "The way may be long and hard. And an artist is virtually never able to succeed alone. He needs a community to back him up: if he fails it may be his fellow-Christians who are at fault, failing to give him the positive response he needs. But without this creativity we shall not be able to show the real validity of an art and life based on Christ our Lord."[9] The Christian artist's responsibility is to participate in the revitalization and renewal of contemporary culture through the embodiment of freedom, love, and hope in Christ.

The distinctive role of the Christian artist and his or her need for a Christian community to support his or her work has slanted evangelical Christian reflection on the visual arts toward the development of the Christian artist who can produce Christian art. Rookmaaker's focus in the late sixties, which culminated in the publication of *Modern Art and the Death of a Culture*, was intended to plant seeds of an artistic revolution and fan the flames of a Christian art movement. Rookmaaker's history of Western art in general, and modern art more specifically, was crafted not so much to maximize understanding of the history of modern art but to maximize space for the Christian artist.

Modern Art and the Death of a Culture, then, is a manifesto for a younger generation of evangelical art students. The history of modern art that it presents is intended to serve as a rhetorical tool that demonstrates culture's need for the Christian artist. If Rookmaaker's strategies seem vaguely familiar, it is because they borrow from the avant-garde tradition, which posits a powerful role for the artist as cultural leader. For an evangelical Christian community that had been largely marginalized from contemporary culture, Rookmaaker's manifesto offered hope and opportunity for cultural leadership through the arts. The Christian artist, as vaguely defined by Rookmaaker, served primarily as an imaginative ideal that shaped and guided the imagination of those committed to his vision.

Rookmaaker's manifesto has come to exert an important influence in the evangelical intellectual community, especially through his assertion of the importance of developing a community to support the Christian artist. Tapping into his Dutch Calvinist roots, Rookmaaker's manifesto found an audience among neo-Kuyperian intellectuals eager to build alternative arts and educational institutions. As such it has shaped such organizations as Christians in the Visual Arts (CIVA). Founded in 1979 and now based out of Gordon College in Wenham, Massachusetts, CIVA includes over thirteen hundred members. Rookmaaker's conception of the Christian artist provides a role and function with which CIVA member artists can identify.

The ideology of the concept of the Christian artist causes numerous problems, problems that have not gone unnoticed. But such criticism has yet to displace the authority of this role in evangelicalism.[10] First, this ideology legitimizes and empowers virtually every kind of artistic practice, provided one self-identifies as a "Christian artist." Second, it does not make sufficient distinctions between artistic practices. Is Christian art liturgical art? Is it art made by a Christian? Is it art that has as its subject matter Bible subjects? The power of Christian art and the Christian artist rests in its vagueness as well as its capacity to tap into common assumptions about what constitutes the way Christian and art relate.

Far from becoming dated, the idea of the Christian artist not only lives on nearly forty years after Rookmaaker's influential book was published but it also seems to have been given new life through the evangelical embrace of postmodernism. Rookmaaker observes: "As Christians today we realize that we are living in hard times. It is hard to keep to the right path; temptations are legion. And as we look around, it is hard to see a great culture breaking down around us, even though, as we have seen, it is not really based on Christian principles, but on those of the Enlightenment."[11] The Christian artist, then, is not concerned with gaining assimilation into modern art, which is based on Enlightenment assumptions, but with hastening its defeat. The inheritors of Rookmaaker's legacy celebrated the demise of modernism because it signals the end of the modernist narrative of high art, from which Christian art and the Christian artist have been marginalized.

Embracing Arthur Danto's "end of art" thesis, the advocates of Christian art celebrate postmodern pluralism, which not only entitles the Christian artist (to their mind) a seat at the artistic table but also justifies the development of alternative art communities that provide the interpretive framework for Christian art and the legitimacy of the role of the Christian artist. Faced with a challenge similar to Gustave Courbet's at the Universal Exposition in 1855, self-described Christian artists who produce Christian art run the risk of having their work interpreted as failed attempts to make autonomous modern art rather than successful attempts to make Christian art, which has its own distinct criteria for evaluation. This is why advocates of Christian art have worked so diligently to deprive modern and contemporary art of its historical roots in the art of the Middle Ages, Renaissance, and even Reformation, seeking to demonstrate that it is Christian art and not autonomous modern art that is the true legacy of Western artistic practice. In many ways, CIVA and the Coalition of Christian Colleges and Universities (CCCU) function, then, as part of an alternative institutional framework for interpreting and legitimizing Christian art.

The contemporary art world is a complex institution. It is not defined entirely by *Artforum*, Chelsea art galleries, the Museum of Modern Art, and the auction houses. There are times when my curatorial work is mainstream and other times when it is deeply and profoundly marginalized. Successful artists working firmly and comfortably within the institution of high art may never have an exhibition at a commercial gallery in Chelsea, have work included in an exhibition at a New York museum, or have their exhibitions reviewed by *Art News* or *Artforum*. For a variety of reasons, the institution of high art is not located exclusively on the East and West coasts but is dispersed in commercial galleries, museums, contemporary art centers, and the like throughout the country, so that an artist might never have to spend considerable time in New York or Los Angeles to develop a successful career.

This diversity has been facilitated and accentuated through academia. The explosion of art departments and art schools throughout the country since the 1960s also provides more opportunities to engage the contemporary art world in different ways. Academia does not merely provide full- and part-time jobs for working artists but also offers more venues for the presentation of their artwork through departmental art galleries and college and university museums, as well as other opportunities for their work to be written about and funded as part of scholarly research.[12]

The elusive ideal of the Christian artist has benefited considerably from this explosion and fragmentation of a diffuse, pluralistic art world. Rookmaaker's Christian artist is the heart and soul of CIVA, which serves as a congested intersection of the diversity of Christianity and visual art. CIVA provides workshops, newsletters, journals, and biennial conferences; sponsors projects and programs; and, perhaps most importantly for its membership, offers opportunities for artists to exhibit their artwork in traveling exhibitions.

Rookmaaker's Christian artist also has a palpable presence in art departments in Christian colleges and universities. Not only is Rookmaaker's manifesto often used as a textbook for a variety of art history classes but his Christian artist is the role that is most often communicated by faculty to students and celebrated by administrators. Art department art galleries are a primary venue for many CIVA traveling exhibitions, and CIVA's conferences become opportunities for art students to learn and assimilate the role of the Christian artist.

These developments might indeed give the impression that Christianity and the visual arts, particularly as embodied in a Reformed evangelicalism that dominates the CCCU, are thriving. And neither this book in general nor this conclusion in particular will contradict such a position. I have participated in several CIVA conferences and lectured at a number of art departments of CCCU-affiliated colleges, and it is my observation that Rookmaaker's Christian artist is primarily responsible for significant success. But this success does come at a price. What follows, then, is an analysis of this cost and how the framework that produced the essays in this book can offer another way to achieve Rookmaaker's aspirations.[13]

Limitations of the Christian Artist

Rookmaaker's Christian artist is underwritten by the neo-Kuyperian urge to transform secular cultural practices for Christ's lordship, an urge that often consists of building alternative institutions as part of a "pillarizing" strategy. This is given further legitimacy through postmodernist pluralism and relativism. From the perspective of George Dickie's institutional theory of art, articulated in chapter 1, this strategy resulted in developing an alternative institution of art, with its own role for the artist, work of art, and audience, and underwritten by its own history and theory of art as well as its own publications and criteria for success.

There are two potential problems with this approach. First, it tends to marginalize Christianity, reducing it to merely another theory or "ism" or identity, like Marxism or feminism; and second, it tends to reduce these communities merely to consumer brands, a form of niche marketing. The result is isolation. Artists find their own niche, and their practices are intended to have meaning only within the narrow confines of this community, although the very existence of the community is predicated on a certain interpretation of the other, "autonomous" modern and contemporary art. Christianity is thus reduced to yet another worldview and, although it has a seat at the table, it is unable—or unwilling—to engage other participants in meaningful conversation and speak to the table at large, as it develops its own exhibiting and publishing venues.

Christianity thus loses its relevance to the secular contemporary art world even while Christian art and the Christian artist thrive in their own institutional domain. Christian artists can have long and successful careers in this context, but their work often has viability only within the CIVA and Christian college institutional axis. Second, and much more problematic, particularly within the framework of these essays, is that in building such alternative institutional frameworks, apologists have to create maximum space for not merely the existence of such a framework but its utter necessity. Therefore, the tendency has been, at least since Rookmaaker, to paint as dire a picture as possible of the history of modern art and the contemporary art world. The temptation is to do exactly the opposite of St. Paul at Mars Hill with modern and contemporary art because it might reduce the necessity of such alternative ventures as Christian arts organizations such as CIVA, publishing and exhibiting venues, and the like.

The development of alternative Christian practices is not a problem in and of itself. There are times when such alternatives are necessary and important, and even within the expansive framework that the essays in this book sketch out, Rookmaaker's Christian artist and the worldview it requires are useful. There is indeed much in the history of modern and contemporary art that is problematic; engagement in the contemporary art world does not require complete adherence to all it produces. (Most contemporary artists I have worked with express deep antipathy for the contemporary art world.) But the Christian artist strategy cannot be considered the only way to negotiate modern and contemporary art. And Rookmaaker's manifesto, in which the ultimate goal is to drive a significant wedge between the past of nihilistic modern art and a future where Christian artists can shape culture, can create problems because it is rarely an either/or proposition.

The contemporary art world cannot easily and simply be pitted against a Christian alternative. It is not, as Douglas Campbell assumes, simply a mainstream art world of twentieth-century modernism versus "artists of faith."[14] The sheep and goats cannot be so easily separated.[15] Christian artists who have graduate degrees are trained exclusively in secular graduate studio art programs.[16] They do not reject offers to exhibit their work in secular college art galleries and university museums, nor do they refuse to exhibit in secular art museums when invited or turn down opportunities to have their exhibitions reviewed by the secular media. In fact, when Christian artists do accept such invitations, they are often celebrated as evidence of Christian art "having an impact" in the secular world. And so, in a backhanded way, the authority of the secular art world creeps in the back door. But by and large, Rookmaaker's Christian artist functions in an alternative art world, initiated by the fall of modernism and the emergence of postmodern pluralism, that requires a nihilistic, elitist, anti-Christian history of modern art and an impenetrable, corrupt, and inaccessible contemporary art world against which to react.

But the institutional theory of art cannot offer a complete view of artistic practice, since it does not address the cognitive meaning and significance of making and experiencing a work of art. In this way, as outlined in chapter 1, Paul Crowther's transhistorical and transcultural concept of art, which affirms the transcendent character of all visual representation, augments Dickie's institutional concept. Rather than be content with multiple definitions of art that operate institutionally and are largely mutually exclusive, Crowther's concept cuts across and through these institutional differences to evaluate transcendence as an aesthetic category. If both making and experiencing aesthetic artifacts is an inherently transcendent experience, it enables the use of spiritual and religious language for all artistic practice, including mainstream modern art and not only work produced by Christian artists. Moreover, Crowther's perspective allows transcendence itself to be the critical criteria for evaluating art; that is, the power of a work of art is found in its distinctive embodiment of this transcendent experience. The challenge is to experience art's transcendence, not simply to *interpret* it, *decode* it, or *define* it.

Douglas Campbell suggests that modern art has "left no room, at least within the mainstream, for art to image forth a transcendent God."[17] The essays in this book suggest otherwise and provide ways to conceptualize an alternative understanding of modern and contemporary art. This study concludes by considering Christian art and the Christian artist within this expansive conceptual framework, which forces us to consider the difficult question of whether or how Christian art actually does "image forth a transcendent God."

Beyond Christian Art

Art is a form of communication. But it is a specific kind of communication. And this poses certain problems and challenges for the Christian art/ secular mainstream art antithesis for those, particularly evangelicals, who embrace Rookmaaker's Christian artist as an ideal. Because evangelicalism is a reform and revival movement within Protestantism, it is predicated on a populism that is pathologically leery of elitism, whether it is embodied in the form of the clericalism and sacramentalism of high church traditions or takes the form of a cultural elitism manifest in rarified aesthetic taste. In addition, evangelicalism has been so successful since the nineteenth century because it makes significant use of popular forms of communication and, as David Morgan argues, has even pioneered those forms.[18] Therefore, artistic practice that is unable to conform to these forms of communication and is accessible to the "ordinary person" is greeted with skepticism.

For most evangelical art writers, art follows the conventional *sender-receiver* model of communication, in which the form of the communication disappears in order for the content, the message, to be received clearly and without alteration from the sender. Evangelicalism tends to treat art as speech, or dogma, conducted by other means. And when its "message" is ambivalent, complex, and difficult, yielding different interpretations, it is considered suspect. As Pavel Florensky observes, "True art is a unity of content and the means of expressing that content."[19] Form, then, is as important as the content.

Art is not a visual illustration of a truth, idea, thought, or worldview *already formulated*, cloaked in aesthetic form, and then "sent" to the receiver. Truth, an idea, a thought, or even a worldview emerges through the relationship between the viewer and the work, which cannot be limited and defined by the intentions of the artist, even though the artist's intentions (conscious or not) are the impetus of the work. Artists make art not because they have knowledge they want to "express" but because they want to discover or learn something through the practice of art. Communion and contemplation, then, are disciplines not merely for viewers but also for artists as they make their work.

Furthermore, the meaning of a work of art evolves over time. It shifts, changes, and gains breadth and texture as the viewer reflects on it. As discussed in chapter 6, Koerner demonstrates that Luther sought to replace sacramental devotion and contemplation, which he considered to be papist superstitions, with the communicative directness and predictability of the sermon that, according to the rationalist logic of the Reformers, sends the same message to all hearers. The veneration of the Host or the veneration of an icon do not always have the same results for all participants and do not always result in a mystical vision or new "information." The experience of art is best understood not from the perspective of "reading" or "decoding" but in contemplation and communion, metaphors that derive from the veneration of icons, which is itself grounded in prayer, in communion with God, the ultimate goal of our lives.[20]

In contrast, Campbell exemplifies the Protestant view when he states that, as far as the gospel is concerned, "art is one very effective way of communicating these truths."[21] Despite Rookmaaker's belief that the Christian artist needed to use the artistic language of the time, Christian art is almost exclusively defined by its content. Campbell says, "I am an advocate of visual art, including art that involves itself with Christian imagery, subjects, or content."[22] Christian art is defined not as a union of form and content but as content alone. Therefore, no critical distinctions are made within the genre of Christian art, only between Christian art and "mainstream" modern and contemporary art. The possibility of what would make an excellent or poor work of Christian art is not broached. Gregory Wolfe's observations about the poor quality of what he calls liturgical or religious art, discussed in chapter 6, reveals the problem. Consequently, to critique Christian art exhibitions, for example, is to risk being accused of betraying the cause and aiding and abetting the enemy. Art criticism from a Christian perspective, then, is assumed to be a form of promotion of Christian art.

Considering art as simply another form of communication risks making artistic practice conform to standards and expectations that it not only cannot achieve but also does not intend to achieve. The result is that modern and contemporary art is often dismissed for being elitist because its message is not clear and univocal. In the introduction to his widely read book on art, *World* magazine culture editor and academic dean of Patrick Henry College Gene Edward Veith simply states as a matter of fact that "art has become elitist, cut off from actual human life."[23] The notion of modern and contemporary art's elitism is based on the assumption that art used to be accessible to the "average person" when the church was the patron for the visual arts at some point before the Reformation. But this is a red herring. The average person during the Middle Ages and the Renaissance, for example, experienced art in the churches as part of the liturgy, as part of worship. The average person in fifteenth-century Florence may or may not have been literate and may or may not have understood all the iconography and symbolism of an altarpiece, for example, but that person would have recognized the main contours of the imagery because it was part of the liturgical life of the church that worshipers absorbed. It was what defined their experience from birth. It was not because art was somehow more accessible to them than it is now.

Moreover, the "average person" in contemporary American society is literate, educated, and devotes a tremendous amount of time to learning new skills, whether on the Internet or the bike path, in the boardroom or the kitchen. But art is rarely a part of this continuing education because people believe that art needs no preparation. It should simply "speak" to them, clearly and right away, or else it is "elitist." Moreover, there is a view that art, somehow, *should* communicate to this average person, who often has no real interest in putting in the time and effort required to understand and appreciate the hard-won results of artistic practice.

In addition, Christian commentators often indulge this presupposition when they claim that modern artists such as Marcel Duchamp and Andres Serrano actively "thumb their noses" at the average person, or make such works as *Fountain* or *Piss Christ* in order to shock them. But the average person figures nowhere in either Duchamp's or Serrano's concept of their intended audience. The avant-garde had as part of its ideology *l'épater les bourgoisie*, but this bourgeoisie fancied themselves consumers of high culture and the avant-garde went about poking holes in their inflated aesthetic sophistication. This was not merely "shocking" their artistic sensibilities but revealing that they did not even understand the traditional art they claimed to appreciate. The average person often delighted in such avant-garde practices because of the spectacle it offered.

Not communicating with the average person does not, therefore, entail elitism, nor does it mean that the modern or contemporary artist is mocking this average person. For better or worse, modern and contemporary artistic practice evolved its aesthetic criteria outside the Western church. Therefore, unlike the average person in fifteenth-century Florence, who was baptized in the Roman Church and from infancy was shaped by the symbolic cultic life of the church, the average person of the early twenty-first century, which is in many ways a fabrication of post-Reaganite American politics, is not trained to recognize and understand modern and contemporary art beyond being mocked as elitist and silly by popular culture. Therefore, the learning curve is steeper and, as Varnedoe observes in the epigraph to chapter 1, it requires considerable work.

The ultimate distinction, then, is not between Christian art and autonomous modern art but between art that in its union of form and content can bring forth or testify to an embodied transcendence, revealing our "amphibious existence," and art that denies such transcendence. It is thus quite possible and indeed quite probable that some of what is understood as Christian art is in fact a profoundly anti-transcendent art, presupposing a world hermetically sealed off from the contemplation of the Son, a purely immanent world in which communication consists solely of *messages*, sent and received, not of contemplation of and communion with the Divine. In the Christian artist's zeal to express a Christian message, Christian art—in the bitterest of ironies—can further contribute to denying Christ's presence in the world.

Conclusion

> Men of Athens! I see that in every way you are very religious. For as I walked around and looked carefully at your objects of worship, I even found an altar with this inscription: to an unknown God. Now what you worship as something unknown I am going to proclaim to you. (Acts 17:22–23)

St. Paul's approach to the altar of the unknown god at the Areopagus on Mars Hill inspired my approach to these essays. It presumes that the mystery of God is Christ "in whom are hidden all the treasures of wisdom and knowledge" (Col. 2:3). These essays also presume that modern and contemporary art requires understanding from a Christian perspective that is big enough to bend and shape it in service of making Christ known to contemporary culture. The whole earth is indeed full of God's glory (Isa. 6:3), and modern and contemporary artistic practice can reveal this presence even with work that is not explicitly religious or spiritual or, in fact, even work that might seem at first glance to contradict our assumptions about God's presence in the world. But we are called to penetrate the surface of things, revealing how all things hold together in Christ, even if this is not immediately apparent.

The economy of icons also plays an important role in the essays in this book. If the postmodern church has sought a renewed relationship with the premodern church in order to engage contemporary culture and society, then Nicaea II, with its reaffirmation of the veneration of icons, could serve as an important ecclesial resource for those ancient-future Christians who have an interest in an aesthetic witness in contemporary culture. The theory and practice of icons, however, need not limit artistic practice according to their form and content, but can underwrite an expansive aesthetic, one that is big enough to include modern and contemporary artistic practice.

Icon veneration is a christological practice embodied in and through the aesthetic. But it also has important ethical implications as well, since Christ is an icon of the living God (Col. 1:15). Christ is then the face of the Lord we seek (Ps. 27:8). Moreover, we also participate in this iconic image and likeness from creation (Gen. 1:26) as well as through Christ, so that when we look into the faces of our neighbors, strangers, and enemies, we see the face of Christ himself (Matt. 25:40). These ethical implications are affirmed and strengthened in and through the economy of the icon.

The essays in this book sketch only the broadest and faintest contours of an alternative approach to modern and contemporary art nourished by Nicene Christianity. They reflect the limitations of my own particular preoccupations and interests. There are many more artists, critics, and aspects of modern and contemporary art that require attention. Moreover, there are many other aspects of Nicene Christianity than the theory and practice of icons that can and should be brought to bear on contemporary artistic practice.

Therefore in no way do these essays represent anything resembling a comprehensive history, theory, or theology of modern and contemporary art. And perhaps in the last analysis, the value of this book lies in its peculiarities and idiosyncrasies. It is the record of a complex journey through modern and contemporary art. When these essays are read in conjunction with other art historical, critical, and theological resources, it is my hope that they will encourage further thinking on the subject and open up new ways to bring Christ to bear on artistic practice, within and outside the church.

Despite its limitations, Rookmaaker and Schaeffer's approach to modern and contemporary art was primarily intended to stimulate a sustained engagement in artistic practice. This had a significant influence on such art writers as

Calvin Seerveld, Nicholas Wolterstorff, John Walford, and Bill Dyrness, among many others, even if that influence at times consists of reacting against the details of their arguments. It is my hope that parts of the essays in this book might likewise encourage and provoke a deeper interest in and commitment to modern and contemporary art. Despite my disagreements with some of their arguments, Schaeffer and Rookmaaker's expansive vision has been a constant presence throughout the writing of these essays. It is my hope that they extend their legacy and fulfill their wishes for a deeper commitment to contemporary art.

> Oh, the depth of the riches of the wisdom and knowledge of God!
> (Rom. 11: 33)

Notes

Preface

1. Daniel A. Siedell, "Modern Art and the (Evangelical) Church," *Perspectives on Religious Studies* 32/2 (Summer 2005): 183–91. See also Daniel A. Siedell, "Art and the Practice of Evangelical Faith," *Christian Scholar's Review* 34/1 (Fall 2004): 119–31.

2. William Dyrness, *Visual Faith: Art, Theology, and Worship in Dialogue* (Grand Rapids: Baker Academic, 2001), 10.

Introduction

1. I use "Nicene Christianity" as shorthand for this robust Christian faith. By referring to the Christian faith as Nicene and conciliar, my only intention is to affirm a Christianity that is as big and wide and deep as possible where Catholic, Orthodox, and Protestant alike can draw, which nonetheless recognizes the decisive contribution the East played in the christological controversies that raged between Nicaea I and Nicaea II. See Robert W. Jenson, "With No Qualifications: The Christological Maximalism of the Christian East," in *Ancient and Postmodern Christianity: Paleo-Orthodoxy in the 21st Century, Essays in Honor of Thomas C. Oden*, ed. Kenneth Tanner and Christopher Hall (Downers Grove, IL: InterVarsity, 2002), 13–22.

2. The depth and breadth of the Christian faith is the embodiment of what Vincent of Lérins, in the fourth century, observed: "We must hold what has been believed everywhere, always, and by all." Quoted in George Florovsky, "The Function of Tradition in the Ancient Church" (1963), in *Eastern Orthodox Theology: A Contemporary Reader*, ed. Daniel B. Clendenin (Grand Rapids: Baker Academic, 2003), 98.

3. See Michael Kelly, *Iconoclasm in Aesthetics* (Cambridge: Cambridge University Press, 2003).

4. George Steiner, *Real Presences* (Chicago: University of Chicago Press, 1989).

5. My experience of ancient Christian dogma and practice finds common cause with several trends in evangelicalism, including the work of Thomas Oden on patristic biblical commentaries; Robert Webber's concept of an "Ancient-Future" faith, including his *The Younger Evangelicals* (Grand Rapids: Baker Books, 2002); and Webber and Phil Kenyon's, "A Call to an Ancient Evangelical Future," in *Christianity Today* (September 2006): 57–58.

6. For similar conclusions, see James K. A. Smith, *Who's Afraid of Postmodernism? Taking Derrida, Lyotard, and Foucault to Church* (Grand Rapids: Baker Academic, 2006).

7. The phrase comes from Graham Ward, "The Beauty of God," in John Milbank, *Theological Perspectives on God and Beauty* (Harrisburg, PA: Trinity Press International, 2003), 35–65.

8. Smith, *Who's Afraid of Postmodernism?* 25.

9. See Ward, "The Beauty of God," 35–65; Catherine Pickstock, "Liturgy, Art and Politics," *Modern Theology* 16 (2000): 159–80; John Milbank, *Being Reconciled: Ontology and Pardon* (New York: Routledge, 2003); James K. A. Smith, *Speech and Theology* (New York: Routledge, 2002).

10. Alexander Schmemann, *For the Life of the World: Sacraments and Orthodoxy* (Crestwood, NY: St. Vladimir's Seminary Press, 2000), 113.

Chapter 1: Overture

1. Richard Florida, *The Rise of the Creative Class and How It's Transforming Work, Leisure, Community, and Everyday Life* (New York: Basic Books, 2002).

2. Perhaps the only situation that is approximate is the relationship between lawyers and the "average person" with common sense. However, an important difference is that, as despised as lawyers are, they are still recognized as necessary—unlike art experts.

3. To say that "modern art is museum art," however, is not to overlook the other artistic strategies and aesthetic practices that emerged in the twentieth century as implicit and explicit critiques of the museum and museum art. This tradition, initiated by the Dadaists and recontextualized in the United States by Fluxus, happenings, and performance and conceptual art movements of the sixties, utilized the framework of high (museum) art as a transactional process of cultural critique. Although this tradition lies slightly (but not entirely) outside the pale of these essays, I hope that the perspective articulated here opens onto this fruitful and compelling artistic tradition. See Stephen C. Foster, "Event Structures and Art Situations," in *"Event" Arts and Art Events,* ed. Stephen C. Foster (Ann Arbor, MI: UMI, 1988), 3–10; and Stephen C. Foster, "Disaster and the Habits of Culture," in *Dada: The Coordinates of Cultural Politics,* ed. Stephen C. Foster (New York: GK Hall, 1996), 1–6.

4. Nicholas Wolterstorff, *Art in Action: Toward a Christian Aesthetic* (Grand Rapids: Eerdmans, 1980).

5. See David Carrier, *Museum Skepticism: A History of the Display of Art in Public Galleries* (Durham, NC: Duke University Press, 2006). For an art museum symposium that takes Carrier's book as a point of departure, see Daniel A. Siedell, ed., "The Future of the Art Museum: Curatorial and Educational Perspectives," *Journal of Aesthetic Education* 41/2 (Summer 2007): 1–24.

6. Quoted in *Realism and Tradition in Art 1848–1900,* ed. Linda Nochlin (Englewood Cliffs, NJ: Prentice-Hall, 1966), 34–36.

7. T. S. Eliot, "Tradition and the Individual Talent" (1917), in *Collected Essays, 1917–1932* (New York: Harcourt, 1999).

8. Jerrold Levinson, "Defining Art Historically," *The British Journal of Aesthetics* 19 (1979): 232–50.

9. This view is similar to George A. Lindbeck's "cultural-linguistic" approach to religion. "[T]o become religious—no less than to become culturally or linguistically competent—is to interiorize a set of skills by practice and training." See George A. Lindbeck, *The Nature of Doctrine: Religion and Theology in a Postliberal Age* (Philadelphia: Westminster, 1984), 35.

10. Pavel Florensky, "The Church Ritual as a Synthesis of the Arts" (1918), in *Beyond Vision: Essays on the Perception of Art,* ed. Nicoletta Misler (London: Reakton Books, 2002), 106.

11. Arthur Danto, "The Artworld," *Journal of Philosophy* 61/19 (October 15, 1964): 580.

12. See George Dickie, *The Art Circle: A Theory of Art* (New York: Haven, 1984).

13. See Daniel A. Siedell, "The Other Warhol," *Books & Culture* (November–December 2002): 39.

14. See Robert Wuthnow, *All in Sync: How Music and Art Are Revitalizing American Religion* (Berkeley and Los Angeles: University of California Press, 2003), 236–47.

15. Danto, "The Artworld," 580.

16. Noel Carroll, "Historical Narratives and the Philosophy of Art," *The Journal of Aesthetics and Art Criticism* 51/3 (Summer 1993): 313.

17. See George Dickie, "What is Anti-Art?" *The Journal of Aesthetics and Art Criticism* 33/4 (Summer 1975): 419–21.

18. Paul Crowther, "Art Making: Why Aesthetics Matters to Art History," unpublished manuscript. See also "Cultural Exclusion, Normativity, and the Definition of Art," *The Journal of Aesthetics and Art Criticism* 61/2 (Spring 2003): 121–31; and "Defining Art, Defending the Canon, Contesting Culture," *British Journal of Aesthetics* 44/4 (October 2004): 361–77.

19. Paul Crowther, *Art and Embodiment: From Aesthetics to Self-Consciousness* (Oxford and New York: Oxford University Press, 1993), 5.

20. Ibid., 6.

21. See William Desmond, *Art, Origins, and Otherness: Between Philosophy and Art* (Albany: SUNY Press, 2003), 1–17.

22. Philostratus, *The Life of Apollinarius of Tyana*, VI, 19. Quoted in Gilbert Dagron, "Holy Images and Likeness," *Dumbarton Oaks Papers* 45 (1991): 23.

23. See Algis Valiunas, "Spirit in the Abstract," *First Things* 159 (January 2006). Valiunas assumes abstract art is a distorted and broken form of representation, which means that he radically misconceives and misreads such paintings as Willem de Kooning's masterpiece, *Excavation* (1950).

24. For a more finessed exploration of the mimetic role of art, one that sees representation as a dynamic relationship between the copy and original, see William Desmond, *Philosophy and Its Others: Ways of Being and Mind* (Albany: SUNY Press, 1990), 87–93.

25. Joseph Brodsky, "Foreword," in *Winter Dialogue: Poems by Tomas Venclova* (Evanston, IL: Hydra Books, 1997), ix.

26. Jean-Luc Marion, *The Crossing of the Visible,* trans. James K. A. Smith (Palo Alto, CA: Stanford University Press, 2004), 87.

27. Daniel J. Sahas, *Icon and Logos: Sources in Eighth-Century Iconoclasm* (Toronto: University of Toronto Press, 1986); Ernst Kitzinger, "The Cult of Images in the Age Before Iconoclasm," *Dumbarton Oaks Papers* 8 (1954): 83–150; Gerhart B. Ladner, "The Concept of the Image in the Greek Fathers and the Byzantine Iconoclastic Controversy," *Dumbarton Oaks Papers* 7 (1953): 1–34; George Florovsky, "The Iconoclastic Controversy" (1950), in *Christianity and Culture*, vol. 2: *Collected Works,* 14 vols. (Belmont, MA: Nordland, 1972–89), 101–19; Sixten Ringbom, *Icon to Narrative: The Rise of the Dramatic Close-Up in Fifteenth-Century Devotional Painting* (Abo, Finland: Abo Akademi, 1965); Hans Belting, *Likeness and Presence: A History of the Image Before the Era of Art,* trans. Edmund Jephcott (Chicago: University of Chicago Press, 1994).

28. St. John of Damascus, *Three Treatises On the Divine Images,* trans. and intro. Andrew Louth (Crestwood, NY: St. Vladimir's Seminary Press, 2003), 96–100.

29. Milton V. Anastos, "The Ethical Theory of Images Formulated by the Iconoclasts in 754 and 815," *Dumbarton Oaks Papers* 8 (1954): 151–60; Joseph Leo Koerner, *The Reformation of the Image* (Chicago: University of Chicago Press, 2003).

30. Florovsky, "The Iconoclastic Controversy," 118–19.

31. Ibid., 115–16.

32. Robert E. Webber, *Ancient-Future Faith: Rethinking Evangelicalism for a Postmodern World* (Grand Rapids: Baker Academic, 1999).

33. Michel Quenot, *The Resurrection and the Icon* (Crestwood, NY: St. Vladimir's Seminary Press, 1997); Leonid Ouspensky and Vladimir Lossky, *The Meaning of Icons* (1952; Crestwood, NY: St. Vladimir's Seminary Press, 1999); Victor Bychkov, *The Aesthetic Face of Being: Art in the Theology of Pavel Florensky* (Crestwood, NY: St. Vladimir's Seminary Press, 1993); Pavel Florensky, *Iconostasis*, trans. Donald Sheehan and Olga Andrejev (Crestwood, NY: St. Vladimir's Seminary Press, 1996).

34. St. John of Damascus, *Three Treatises on the Divine Images*, 29.

35. The concept of participation is facilitated through the patristic distinction between God's "essence" and his "energies." It is the latter that we are, through grace, enabled to participate in. God's essence remains utterly transcendent. Through love, God's energies invite us into communion with him. This distinction is further facilitated through the largely Eastern orientation of the Trinity as first and foremost a hypostatic union of three distinct persons whose participation with each other create and sustain the union. (Western Nicene Christianity, through St. Athanasius and St. Augustine, has worked largely through emphasizing God's unity first and then to articulate God's diversity in three persons.) The Eastern focus on the diversity of the trinitarian persons made the acceptance of the Nicene language of "consubstantiality" (Greek: *homoousios*) much more difficult than in the West. Consequently, it is this debate in the East over consubstantiality and the hypostatic union that has generated significant insights for approaching the aesthetic experience. See John Meyendorff, "The Council of 381 and the Primacy of Constantinople," in *Catholicity and the Church* (Crestwood, NY: St. Vladimir's Seminary Press, 1983), 121–42. See also John Meyendorff, *Christ in Eastern Christian Thought* (1975; Crestwood, NY: St. Vladimir's Seminar Press, 1987).

36. St. John of Damascus, *Three Treatises on the Divine Images*, 43.

37. Martin Luther, "Against the Heavenly Prophets in the Matter of Images and Sacraments" (1525), in *Luther's Works*, vol. 40 (Philadelphia: Muhlenberg Press, 1955), 69–101. It is not a coincidence that Luther initiated his series of eight sermons on Invocavit Sunday, or the Feast of Orthodoxy, which celebrated the affirmation of the Second Council of Nicaea in 787.

38. See Ringbom, *Icon to Narrative*, 11–39.

39. Joseph Masheck observed that this historical fact "invalidates the opening sentence" of Clement Greenberg's influential essay "The Crisis of the Easel Picture" (1948). "The easel painting, the moveable picture hung on a wall, is a unique product of the West, with no real counterpart elsewhere." "Iconicity," *Artforum* 17 (1979), 40n14.

40. Ibid.

41. Bruno Latour and Peter Weibel, eds., *Iconoclash: Beyond the Image Wars in Science, Religion, and Art* (Cambridge, MA: MIT Press, 2002); Alain Besançon, *The Forbidden Image: An Intellectual History of Iconoclasm,* trans. Jane Marie Todd (Chicago: University of Chicago Press, 2000); Dario Gamboni, *The Destruction of Art: Iconoclasm and Vandalism Since the French Revolution* (New Haven: Yale University Press, 1997). See David Morgan, "The Vicissitudes of Seeing: Idolatry and Iconoclasm," *Religion* 33/2 (April 2003): 170–80.

42. See G. Jeffrey MacDonald, "Reformed Protestants No Longer See Images as Idolatrous," *Christianity Today*, http://www.christianitytoday.com/ct/2004/decemberweb-only/12-6-12.0.html.

43. Graham Ward, *Cities of God* (London and New York: Routledge, 2000), 173.

44. Alexander Schmemann, *For the Life of the World: Sacraments and Orthodoxy* (Crestwood, NY: St. Vladimir's Seminary Press, 2000), 15.

45. Quoted in Meyendorff, *Christ in Eastern Christian Thought*, 161.

Chapter 2: A History of Modern Art

1. T. J. Clark, *Farewell to an Idea: Episodes from the History of Modernism* (New Haven: Yale University Press, 1999), 3.

2. "The only works of art America has given are her plumbing and her bridges." Quoted in Pepe Karmel, "Marcel Duchamp, 1917: The Not So Innocent Eye," in *Modern Art and America: Alfred Stieglitz and His New York Galleries*, ed. Sarah Greenough et al. (Washington: National Gallery of Art, 2000), 224.

3. See Milton W. Brown, *The Story of the Armory Show* (Greenwich, CT: New York Graphic Society, 1963); Erika Doss, *Twentieth-Century American Art* (New York: Oxford University Press, 2002); Wanda Corn, *The Great American Thing: Modern Art and National Identity, 1915–1935* (Berkeley: University of California Press, 1999).

4. Quoted in Doss, *Twentieth-Century American Art*, 56, 75.

5. See William Inness Homer, *Robert Henri and His Circle* (Ithaca, NY: Cornell University Press, 1980).

6. Charles Brock, "The Armory Show, 1913: A Diabolical Test," in Greenough, ed., *Modern Art and America*, 127–43. See also Debra Bricker Balken, *Debating American Modernism: Stieglitz, Duchamp, and the New York Avant-Garde* (New York: American Federation of the Arts, 2003).

7. Jennifer R. Gross, ed., *The Société Anonyme: Modernism for America* (New Haven: Yale University Press in association with the Yale University Art Gallery, 2006).

8. Sybil Gordon Kantor, *Alfred H. Barr, Jr. and the Intellectual Origins of the Museum of Modern Art* (Cambridge, MA: MIT Press, 2002). For a selection of Barr's writings, see Irving Sandler, ed., *Defining Modern Art: Selected Writings of Alfred H. Barr, Jr.* (New York: Abrams, 1988).

9. Quoted in Kantor, *Alfred H. Barr, Jr.*, 6. For a biography of Barr that uses his Christian upbringing as a means to describe his "evangelistic" activities as an advocate of modern art, see Alice Marquis, *Alfred H. Barr, Jr.: Missionary for the Modern* (Chicago: Contemporary Books, 1989).

10. Quoted in Sally M. Promey, "Interchangeable Art: Warner Sallman and the Critics of Mass Culture," in *Icons of American Protestantism: The Art of Warner Sallman*, ed. David Morgan (New Haven, CT: Yale University Press, 1996), 172–74.

11. Promey, "Interchangeable Art," 172.

12. Barr's diary was published for the first time in Alfred H. Barr Jr., "Russian Diary 1927–28," *October* 7 (Winter 1978).

13. Kantor, *Alfred H. Barr, Jr.,* 165.

14. Alfred H. Barr Jr., "Russian Icons," *Arts* 17 (Feb. 1931): 297–313, 355–62.

15. Robert Storr, *Modern Art despite Modernism* (New York: Museum of Modern Art, 2000), 25. The following discussion leans heavily on Storr's working definitions.

16. Hal Foster, Rosalind Krauss, Yve-Alain Bois et al., *Art Since 1900: Modernism, Antimodernism, Postmodernism* (London: Thames and Hudson, 2004); Charles Harrison, *Modernism* (Cambridge: Cambridge University Press, 1997).

17. Storr, *Modern Art despite Modernism*, 28.

18. Clark, *Farewell to an Idea*, 235.

19. The scholarly literature on the importance and implications of linear perspective is vast. See Erwin Panofsky, *Perspective as Symbolic Form*, trans. Christopher Wood (New York: Zone

Books, 1991); and James Elkins, *The Poetics of Perspective* (Ithaca, NY: Cornell University Press, 1994).

20. For the definitive study of representation as a pictorial device, see E. H. Gombrich, *Art and Illusion: A Study in the Psychology of Pictorial Representation* (Princeton: Princeton University Press, 1960).

21. Pavel Florensky, "Reverse Perspective" (1920), in *Beyond Vision: Essays on the Perception of Art*, ed. Nicoletta Misler (London: Reakton Books, 2002), 202.

22. This is the conclusion of Algis Valiunas, "Spirit in the Abstract," *First Things* 159 (January 2006).

23. Storr, *Modern Art despite Modernism*, 28.

24. Clark, *Farewell to an Idea*, 253.

25. The discussion of the avant-garde relies heavily on Donald Drew Egbert, "The Idea of the 'Avant-Garde' in Art and Politics," *American Historical Review* 73/2 (December 1967): 339–66; Egbert, *Social Radicalism and the Arts* (New York: Alfred A. Knopf, 1970); Peter Berger, *Theory of the Avant-Garde* (Minneapolis: University of Minnesota Press, 1984); and Renato Paggioli, *The Theory of the Avant-Garde* (Cambridge: Belknap Press, Harvard University Press, 1968).

26. Keith Taylor, ed. and trans., *Henri Saint-Simon: Selected Writings on Science, Industry, and Social Organization* (London: Croom Helm, 1975), 281.

27. Ibid.

28. See James H. Rubin, *Realism and Social Vision in Courbet and Proudhon* (Princeton, NJ: Princeton University Press, 1980).

29. Quoted in Linda Nochlin, ed., *Realism and Tradition in Art, 1848–1900* (Englewood Cliffs, NJ: Prentice-Hall, 1966), 37.

30. See Dana Tiffany, "Jarry's Inner Circle and the Public Debut of Père Ubu," in *"Event" Arts and Art Events*, ed. Stephen C. Foster (Ann Arbor, MI: UMI, 1988), 135–58.

31. For a discussion of the avant-garde text, see the special issue of *Visible Language* 21/3–4 (Summer/Autumn 1987).

32. Quoted in Nochlin, *Realism and Tradition in Art, 1848–1900*, 35.

33. "New Christianity: First Dialogue" (1825), in Taylor, *Henri Saint-Simon: Selected Writings*, 289.

34. Egbert, *Social Radicalism and the Arts*, 160.

35. See Rodney Stark, "Secularization, R.I.P.," *Sociology of Religion* 60/3 (Fall 1999): 249–73. This section relies heavily on this essay.

36. Peter Berger, ed., *The Desecularization of the World: Resurgent Religion and World Politics* (Grand Rapids: Eerdmans, 1999).

37. Graham Ward, *True Religion* (Malden, MA: Blackwell, 2002), 21.

38. Graham Ward, *Cities of God* (London and New York: Routledge, 2000), 71.

39. Clark, *Farewell to an Idea*, 253.

40. Quoted in Carol Mancusi-Ungaro, "Material and Immaterial Surface: The Paintings of Rothko," in *Mark Rothko* (Washington, DC: National Gallery of Art; Yale University Press, 1998), 299.

41. The collecting activities of John and Dominique de Menil warrant special attention within the context of the religious and spiritual character of modern art. The de Menils had a collection of well over fifteen thousand objects of tribal, medieval, Byzantine, and twentieth-century art (particularly surrealism). The de Menils were deeply attracted to this aspect of modern art. They developed a significant collection of Byzantine icons, and in 1997, through the leadership of Dominique and the Menil Foundation, the Byzantine Fresco Chapel Museum was dedicated. It has the only intact Byzantine fresco in the Western hemisphere. The fresco was stolen and

dispersed from Cyprus and recovered and restored through the work of the Menil Foundation, and is on loan with the approval of the Church of Cyprus. It is significant that one of the de Menils' closest advisers was Father Marie-Alain Couturier, a Dominican priest.

42. Barbara Novak and Brian O'Doherty, "Rothko's Dark Paintings: Tragedy and Void," in Mancusi-Ungaro, *Mark Rothko*, 277.

43. Ibid., 273.

44. I spent some time at the Rothko Chapel for the first time in April 2007 and was surprised by my reaction to the space. My experience of these large dark works in a dimly lighted chapel space was oppressive, thick with the weight of a spiritual experience that bore little resemblance to the soft, fluffy, and largely inconsequential and "uplifting" spirituality that is so characteristic of the new age. The kind of spirituality embodied in the Rothko Chapel was a struggle, perhaps even "a dark night of the soul," about which the Spanish poet and Carmelite priest St. John of the Cross wrote in the sixteenth century.

45. Novak and O'Doherty, "Rothko's Dark Paintings," 275. For a more detailed analysis of the Rothko Chapel, see Seldon Rodman, *The Rothko Chapel Paintings: Origins, Structure, Meaning* (Austin: University of Texas Press, 1997).

46. Donald B. Kuspit, "Symbolic Pregnance in Mark Rothko and Clyfford Still," in *The Critic Is Artist: The Intentionality of Art* (Ann Arbor, MI: UMI, 1984), 205.

47. Ibid., 207.

48. Quoted in Mancusi-Ungaro, *Mark Rothko*, 368.

49. A more in-depth and thorough treatment of nineteenth- and twentieth-century modern art is beyond the pale of this essay, but will be addressed in a forthcoming collaboration with William Dyrness entitled "Modern Art and the Life of a Culture."

50. Thomas G. Guarino, "'Spoils from Egypt' Yesterday and Today," *Pro Ecclesia* 15/4 (Fall 2006): 405.

51. See William Dyrness, "Contemplation for Ecstatically Challenged Protestants: Where the Reformed Tradition Went Wrong," lecture delivered at Dubuque Seminary, April 2006.

Chapter 3: Enrique Martínez Celaya's *Thing and Deception*

1. Dario Gamboni, *The Destruction of Art: Iconoclasm and Vandalism Since the French Revolution* (New Haven: Yale University Press, 1997), 336. See also Alain Besançon, *The Forbidden Image: An Intellectual History of Iconoclasm,* trans. Jane Marie Todd (Chicago: University of Chicago Press, 2000).

2. The two stanzas that Martínez Celaya has inscribed on the back of the painting from Baudelaire's "Danse macabre" are:

Viens tu troubler avec ta puissante grimace, / La Fête de la Vie? Ou quelque vieux désir,
Espêronnant encore ta vivante carcasse, / Te pousse-t-il, crédule, au sabbat du Plaisir?
Aux chants des violins, aux flames des bougies, / Espéres-tu chaser ton cauchemar moqueur,
Et viens-tu demander au torrent des orgies / De rafraichir l'enfer allumé dans ton coeur?

3. See Daniel A. Siedell, "Forum: In Defense of Curatorial Irrelevance," *Curator: A Museum Journal* 47/4 (October 2004): 375–81.

4. See Daniel A. Siedell, *Enrique Martínez Celaya: The October Cycle, 2000–2002* (Lincoln, NE: Sheldon Art Gallery; Marquand Books, 2003).

5. This evaluation of Martínez Celaya's relationship to the Latin American experience in Southern California comes from Martínez Celaya. Although it falls outside the scope of this chapter, Martínez Celaya's critical reception in Germany warrants special attention.

6. Donald B. Kuspit, *The Rebirth of Painting in the Late Twentieth Century* (Cambridge, MA: Cambridge University Press, 2000), 4.

7. Quoted in Fergus Kerr, *Theology After Wittgenstein* (Oxford: Basil Blackwell, 1986), 33.

8. Personal e-mail correspondence from Martínez Celaya, May 2002.

9. For an interesting and informative comparative study of Santeria and Christianity, see Miguel A. de la Torre, *Santeria: The Beliefs and Rituals of a Growing Religion in America* (Grand Rapids: Eerdmans, 2004).

10. Personal e-mail correspondence from Martínez Celaya, May 2002.

11. Ibid.

12. Ibid.

13. James Jensen, ed., *Enrique Martínez Celaya, 1992–2000* (The Contemporary Museum, Honolulu; Köln: Wienand Verlag, 2001), 136.

14. Enrique Martínez Celaya, *Guide*, vol. 1 (Los Angeles: Whale & Star, 2002), 75, 23, 21.

15. E-mail from Martínez Celaya, November 24, 2004. Subsequently, Martínez Celaya observed: "I was wrong. I found a picture of this work in a catalog showing that the silk rose, which also included a small hummingbird at rest, preceded the black tulip. Sorry for the confusion. But it proves your assertion about my memory in relation to stages of the work" (e-mail from Martínez Celaya, July 8, 2005).

16. The brilliant Russian Orthodox theologian and martyr Pavel Florensky once bemoaned that few Christians use the most powerful apologetic of their Orthodox faith: "There exists the icon of the Holy Trinity by St. Andrei Rublev, *therefore God exists*" (emphasis mine), Pavel Florensky, *Iconostasis,* trans. Donald Sheehan and Olga Andrejev (Crestwood, NY: St. Vladimir's Seminary Press, 1996), 68.

17. Transcribed by me at the exhibition, February 2004.

18. Ludwig Wittgenstein, *Tractatus Logico-Philosophicus*, trans. C. K. Ogden (London: Routledge & Kegan Paul, 1981), 6.54.

19. "Author's Preface," in ibid., 3.

20. Quoted in Klaus Ottmann, *The Genius Decision: The Extraordinary and the Postmodern Condition* (Putnam, CT: Spring Publications, 2004), 32. See also Daniel A. Siedell, "Art and Failure," *The Journal of Aesthetic Education* 40/2 (Summer 2006): 105–17.

21. For an informative discussion of the influence of Buddhism on contemporary art, see Jacquelynn Baas and Mary Jane Jacobs, eds., *Buddha Mind in Contemporary Art* (Berkeley: University of California Press, 2004).

22. See Tom W. Boyd, "Is Spirituality Possible Without Religion? A Query for the Postmodern Era," in *Divine Representations: Postmodernism and Spirituality,* ed. Ann Astell (New York: Paulist Press, 1994), 83–101; and Robert Wuthnow, *All in Sync: How Music and Art are Revitalizing American Religion* (Berkeley: University of California Press, 2003).

23. I was present at the opening at Griffin Contemporary, Venice, California, at which Margo Timmins performed, and I visited with Martínez Celaya about his intentions and their implications before and after the performance.

24. Martínez Celaya has discussed Hilma Af Klint's work at length with me numerous times. See also Ake Fant, "The Case of the Artist Hilma Af Klint," in *The Spiritual in Art: Abstract Painting, 1890–1985,* ed. M. Tuchman (Los Angeles County Museum of Art; New York: Abbeville Press, 1986), 155–63.

25. Ludwig Wittgenstein, *Philosophical Investigations* (Oxford: Blackwell, 1967), sec. 217.

26. Edward Said, "Introduction to Erich Auerbach's Mimesis," in *Humanism and Democratic Criticism* (New York: Columbia University Press, 2004), 103.

27. Quoted in John Meyendorff, *Christ in Eastern Christian Thought* (Crestwood, NY: St. Vladimir's Seminary Press, 1987), 161.

28. Quoted in Harold Rosenberg, "Twilight of the Intellectuals" (1958), in *Discovering the Present: Three Decades in Art, Culture, and Politics* (Chicago: University of Chicago Press, 1973), 166.

Chapter 4: Embodying Transcendence

1. Rodney Stark, "Secularization: R.I.P.," *Sociology of Religion* 60/3 (Fall 1999): 249–73. For an alternative perspective on secularization, see Timothy Larsen, "Dechristendomization as an Alternative to Secularization: Theology, History, and Sociology in Conversation," *Pro Ecclesia* 15/3 (Summer 2006): 320–37.

2. John Caputo, *On Religion* (London and New York: Routledge, 2001), 63.

3. Graham Ward, *True Religion* (Malden, MA: Blackwell, 2002), vii.

4. Ibid., viii.

5. Robert Wuthnow, *All in Sync: How Music and Art are Revitalizing American Religion* (Berkeley: University of California Press, 2003).

6. Thierry de Duve, *Look, 100 Years of Contemporary Art,* trans. Simon Pleasance and Fronza Woods (Brussels: Ludion, 2001), 14.

7. At an Art Seminar panel discusson on re-enchantment, organized by James Elkins at the School of The Art Institute of Chicago, de Duve reiterated his commitment to the Enlightenment project of secularism and suggested that since it is only three centuries old, it needs more time. The panel discussion will be published in *Re-Enchantment*, ed. James Elkins and David Morgan (New York and London: Routledge, 2008).

8. James Elkins, *On the Strange Place of Religion in Contemporary Art* (New York and London: Routledge, 2004), 115, 116.

9. Sally M. Promey, "Warner Sallman and the Critics of Mass Culture," in *Icons of American Protestantism: The Art of Warner Sallman,* ed. David Morgan (New Haven: Yale University Press, 1996), 172–74. See also Sybil Gordon Kantor, *Alfred H. Barr, Jr. and the Intellectual Origins of the Museum of Modern Art* (Cambridge, MA: MIT Press, 2002).

10. See Sally M. Promey, "The 'Return' of Religion in the Scholarship of American Art," *The Art Bulletin* 85/3 (September 2003): 581–603. See also David Morgan: "Toward a Modern Historiography of Art and Religion," in *Reluctant Partners: Art and Religion in Dialogue,* ed. Ena Heller (New York: The Gallery at the American Bible Society, 2004), 16–47.

11. David Morgan, "Visual Religion," *Religion* 30 (2000): 51. For more in-depth work by Morgan, see *Visual Piety: A History and Theory of Popular Religious Images* (Los Angeles: University of California Press, 1998); and *The Sacred Gaze: Religious Visual Culture in Theory and Practice* (Los Angeles: University of California Press, 2005).

12. Maurice Tuchman, ed., *The Spiritual in Art: Abstract Painting, 1890–1985* (LACMA; New York: Abbeville Press, 1986). See also Lynn Gamwell, *Exploring the Invisible: Art, Science, and the Spiritual* (Princeton, NJ: Princeton University Press, 2002).

13. Kirk Varnedoe, *Pictures of Nothing: Abstract Art Since Pollock* (Princeton, NJ: Princeton University Press, 2006).

14. Richard Francis, ed., *Negotiating Rapture* (Chicago: Museum of Contemporary Art, 1996).

15. Christian Eckart, Harry Philbrick, and Osvaldo Romberg, eds., *Faith: The Impact of Judeo-Christian Religion on Art at the Millennium* (Ridgefield, CT: The Aldrich Museum of Contemporary Art, 2000).

16. John Ravenal, ed., *Vanitas: Meditations on Life and Death in Contemporary Art* (Richmond, VA: Virginia Museum of Fine Arts, 2000); Jeff Fleming, *Magic Markers: Objects of Transformation* (Des Moines, IA: Des Moines Art Center, 2003).

17. Lynn M. Herbert, ed., *The Inward Eye: Transcendence in Contemporary Art* (Houston: Contemporary Arts Museum, 2001).

18. John Baldessari and Meg Cranston, eds., *100 Artists See God* (New York: ICI, 2004). See the symposium on this exhibition, "100 artists see god: a forum," *Material Religion* 3/1 (2007): 120–42.

19. "Ways of Seeing God," in Baldessari and Cranston, *100 Artists See God*, 12.

20. David Morgan, "exhibition review, the critical view: visuality and the question of god in contemporary art," *Material Religion* 3/1 (2007): 142.

21. See Jacquelynn Bass and Mary Jane Jacob, eds., *Buddha Mind in Contemporary Art* (Berkeley: University of California Press, 2004). For a review of this book see Daniel A. Siedell, "Buddha Mind in Contemporary Art," *Curator: A Museum Journal* 49/3 (July 2006): 313–19.

22. My understanding of transcendence in transition has been wrought in my particular museum context, the Sheldon Memorial Art Gallery and Sculpture Garden at the University of Nebraska–Lincoln. The Sheldon's collection is housed in a magnificent temple to modern art designed by Phillip Johnson in the early sixties. With its glass and travertine, the Sheldon is a monument to a kind of transcendence that is purely and autonomously aesthetic.

23. Personal communication with Ottmann.

24. Klaus Ottmann, "The New Spiritual" (1989), in *Thought Through My Eyes: Writings on Art, 1977–2005* (Putnam, CT: Spring Publications, 2006), 103.

25. Klaus Ottmann, "Firstness: On the Possibility of Art," in *Still Points in a Turning World* (Santa Fe: SITE Santa Fe, 2006), 9.

26. Ibid., 11.

27. Ibid., 16. See also Ottmann, *The Genius Decision: The Extraordinary and the Post-Modern Condition* (Putnam, CT: Spring Publications, 2004).

28. For a discussion of Ottmann's book and its religious implications, see Daniel A. Siedell, "Art and Failure," *The Journal of Aesthetic Education* 40/2 (Summer 2006): 105–17.

29. Ottmann, "The New Spiritual" (1989), 103–4.

30. Ibid., 104.

31. Klaus Ottmann, "Spiritual Materiality" (2002), in *Thought Through My Eyes*, 184.

32. See Emmanuel Levinas, *Totality and Infinity*, trans. Alphonso Lingis (Pittsburgh: Duquesne University Press, 1969). See also Emmanuel Levinas, "The Trace of the Other," trans. A. Lingis, in Mark C. Taylor, ed., *Deconstruction in Context: Literature and Philosophy* (Chicago: Chicago University Press, 1986), 345–59. In this essay Levinas explores the implications of liturgy for ethical practice.

33. Ottmann, *Still Points of a Turning World*, 21.

34. Ibid., 185.

35. Ottmann's work finds support from William Desmond, *Art, Origins, and Otherness: Between Philosophy and Art* (Albany: SUNY Press, 2003).

36. Edith Wyschogrod, "God and 'Being's Move' in the Philosophy of Emmanuel Levinas," *Journal of Religion* 62/2 (April 1989), 149.

37. The aesthetic concept of "embodied transcendence," as articulated by Ottmann, following his interest in the Eastern European Levinas and Jewish mysticism, has some relevant connections with (Slavophile) Russian religious philosophy, especially sophiology, which is the speculative study and exploration of Divine Wisdom (Sophia), particularly in the work of Sergei Bolkagov, his mentor Pavel Florensky, and Vladimir Soloviev. See Victor Bychkov, *The Aesthetic*

Face of Being: Art in the Theology of Pavel Florensky (Crestwood, NY: St. Vladimir's Seminary Press, 1993); Pavel Florensky, *The Pillar and the Foundation of the Truth* (1914; Princeton, NJ: Princeton University Press, 1997); Sergei Bulgakov, *Sophia, The Wisdom of God: An Outline of Sophiology* (Hudson, NY: Lindisfarne Books, 1993).

38. Jean-Luc Marion, *The Crossing the of Visible,* trans. James K. A. Smith (Palo Alto, CA: Stanford University Press, 2004), 87.

39. Rosalind Krauss, "Overcoming the Limits of Matter: On Revising Minimalism," *Studies in Modern Art: American Art of the 1960s,* vol. 1 (New York: Museum of Modern Art, 1991), 128.

40. Pavel Florensky, "The Church Ritual as a Synthesis of the Arts" (1918), in *Beyond Vision: Essays on the Perception of Art,* ed. Nicoletta Misler (London: Reakton Books, 2002), 102.

41. Ibid., 107.

42. Christoph Schönborn, *God's Human Face: The Christ-Icon,* trans. Lothar Krauth (1976; San Francisco, Ignatius Press, 1994), 239–40.

43. Robert Storr, "A Piece of the Action," in *Jackson Pollock: New Approaches,* eds. Kirk Varnedoe and Pepe Karmel (MoMA; New York: Abrams, 1999), 33.

44. *Life* magazine (August 8, 1949). See Kirk Varnedoe, *Jackson Pollock* (New York: Museum of Modern Art, 1997), 59.

45. See Donald B. Kuspit, "To Interpret or Not to Interpret Jackson Pollock," in *The Critic Is Artist: The Intentionality of Art* (Ann Arbor, MI: UMI, 1984), 161–69. For new scholarship on Pollock, see Stephen Polcari, "Pollock and America, Too," in *Abstract Expressionism: The International Context,* ed. Joan Marter (New Brunswick, NJ: Rutgers University Press, 2007), 182–95.

46. Kuspit, "To Interpret or Not to Interpret Jackson Pollock," 167.

47. Florensky, "The Church Ritual as a Synthesis of the Arts," in *Beyond Vision,* 105.

48. R. R. Reno, "Origin and Spiritual Interpretation," *Pro Ecclesia* 15/1 (Winter 2006): 108–26. Reno observes, "To read Origen's exegesis is like standing beneath a waterfall" (108).

49. Emily Genauer, *New York World-Telegram* (February 7, 1949).

50. Varnedoe, *Pictures of Nothing,* 99.

51. Harold Rosenberg, "The American Action Painters" (1952), in *The Tradition of the New* (New York: Horizon Press, 1959), 25.

52. A powerful and influential moment I experienced as a graduate student at SUNY–Stony Brook (1989–91) was to visit Pollock's home in The Springs, Long Island, and to spend time in his studio-barn. This property is owned by Stony Brook, and so my experience of Pollock consisted, very early on, of much more than just viewing his paintings but in the actual, concrete place in which they were made and with how they were made. It is of note that Varnedoe's 1997 retrospective included a full model of the interior of the barn.

53. Quoted in Helen Molesworth, "Duchamp: By Hand, Even," in *Part Object Part Sculpture,* ed. Helen Molesworth (Columbus, OH: Wexner Center for the Arts; University Park, PA: Pennsylvania State University Press, 2005), 182.

54. In a recent blog about the contemporary art world on the *First Things* Web site, theologian R. R. Reno claimed that with *Fountain,* Duchamp was "giving the finger" to the public. For a similar view, see Hilton Kramer, "Duchamp and His Legacy" (1995), in *The Triumph of Modernism: The Art World, 1987–2005* (Chicago: Ivan R. Dee, 2006), 185–91.

55. William Camfield, *Marcel Duchamp: Fountain* (Houston: The Menil Collection and Houston Fine Arts Press, 1989), 13–14.

56. Ibid., 38.

57. Quoted in David Joselit, "Molds and Swarms," in Molesworth, *Part Object Part Sculpture*, 161.

58. "The photographs make it look like anything from a Madonna to a Buddha." Quoted in Camfield, *Marcel Duchamp: Fountain*, 34–35.

59. H. R. Rookmaaker writes, "The spirits took their abode in the minds of men like Duchamp, and brought a whirlwind of anarchy, nihilism and the gospel of absurdity." *Modern Art and the Death of a Culture* (Downer's Grove, IL: InterVarsity, 1970), 130.

60. See Tosi Lee, "Fire Down Below and Watering, That's Life: A Buddhist Reader Response to Marcel Duchamp," in *Buddha Mind in Contemporary Art,* 123–38; Jacquelynn Baas, *Smile of the Buddha: Eastern Philosophy and Western Art from Monet to Today* (Berkeley: University of California Press, 2005), 78–95.

61. Graham Ward, *Cities of God* (London: Routledge, 2000), 173.

62. The inextricable relationship between the creator and his creation is an important aspect of the Russian philosophers of Sophia, or Holy Wisdom, and is also the reason their thought was criticized as "pantheistic" even by Orthodox theologians Alexander Schmemann, John Meyendorff, and Georges Florovsky. For a strong argument in defense of these thinkers, see Robert Slesinski, "The Relationship of God and Man in Russian Religious Philosophy from Florensky to Frank," *St. Vladimir's Theological Quarterly* 36/3 (1992): 217–35.

63. C. S. Lewis, *The Screwtape Letters* (New York: Collier, 1982), 36. I owe this citation to R. R. Reno, *The Ordinary Transformed: Karl Rahner and the Christian Vision of Transcendence* (Grand Rapids: Eerdmans, 1995), 23. Reno observes: "Betwixt and between, we enjoy an amphibious form of existence which resists strict categorization within this world or the next, refuses labels such as material and immaterial, sets aside the conceptual clarity which follows from clear distinctions between temporal and eternal, finite and infinite."

64. Quoted in David Joselit, "Molds and Swarms," in Molesworth, *Part Object Part Sculpture*, 158.

65. The following is based in part on conversations with Antoni.

66. Martha Buskirk, *The Contingent Object of Contemporary Art* (Cambridge, MA: MIT Press, 2003), 7.

67. Conversation with Antoni.

68. Klaus Ottmann, "The Solid and the Fluid: Perceiving Laib," in *Wolfgang Laib: A Retrospective* (American Federation of Arts; Ostfildern/Ruit, Germany: Hatje Cantz, 2000), 20.

69. Ibid.

70. Ibid., 13.

71. See Margit Rowell, "Modest Propositions," in Ottmann, *Wolfgang Laib,* 25.

72. Max Hollein, "Preface," in *James Lee Byars: Life, Love, and Death,* eds. Klaus Ottmann and Max Hollein (Ostfildern/Ruit, Germany: Hatje Cantz, 2004), 9.

73. Shinto functions as the interpretive framework for Matthew Barney's film *Drawing Restraint 9* (2005).

74. Klaus Ottmann, "Epiphanies of Beauty and Knowledge: The Life-World of James Lee Byars," in *James Lee Byars,* 17.

75. For more information on Fluxus, see Elizabeth Armstrong and Joan Rothfuss, eds., *In the Spirit of Fluxus* (Minneapolis: Walker Art Center, 1993); and Estera Milman, ed., *Fluxus: A Conceptual Country, Visible Language* 26 1/2 (Winter/Spring 1992).

76. Ottmann, "Epiphanies of Beauty and Knowledge," 39.

77. Ibid.

78. Quoted in Phyllis Rosenzweig, "Gabriel Orozco: Photographs," in *Gabriel Orozco: Photographs* (Hirshhorn Museum and Sculpture Garden; Gottingdam, Germany: Steidl Publishers, 2004), 11.

79. Molly Nesbit, "The Tempest," in *Gabriel Orozco* (Los Angeles: The Museum of Contemporary Art, 2000), 163.

80. Quoted in Rosenzweig, "Gabriel Orozco: Photographs," 12.

81. Quoted in Hal Foster, "American Gothic," *Artforum* (May 2005): 223.

82. Quoted in brochure for Venice Biennale, 2001.

83. Foster, "American Gothic," 224.

84. Ibid.

85. Ibid.

86. Brenda Richardson, *A Robert Gober Lexicon*, vol. I (New York: Matthew Marks Gallery, 2005), 10.

87. Ibid., 36.

88. Ibid., 55–73.

89. I had the opportunity to view Gober's installation at Matthew Marks Gallery in New York, and my experience of the installation was indeed informed by a sense of being in a sacred, ritualized space within which the headless crucifix functioned like an antique fragment rescued from the trash.

90. Quoted in Matthew Drutt, *Robert Gober: The Meat Wagon* (Houston: The Menil Collection, 2006), 20.

91. For a critical exploration of the relationship between these two environments, see Daniel A. Siedell, "*Coming Home* Before and After *Schneebett*," *ArtUS* 16 (January–February 2007): 10–13.

92. Enrique Martínez Celaya, lecture at the American Academy in Berlin, October 19, 2004.

93. Quoted in "Schneebett," in *Martínez Celaya: Early Work* (Delray Beach, FL: Whale and Star, 2006).

94. My recent work on these two environments has begun to explore the role of time, both as *Chronos* (sequential time) and *Kairos* (sacred time), as it is embodied in a distinctly liturgical dimension in these works.

Chapter 5: Art Criticism

1. Irving Sandler, *Sweeper-Up After Artists* (New York: Thames and Hudson, 2003), 10.

2. George Steiner, *Real Presences* (Chicago: University of Chicago Press, 1989), 185.

3. Stephen C. Foster, "Making a Movement Modern: The Role of the Avant-Garde Critic," *Art International* 20 (October–November 1976): 59.

4. There are a few graduate programs in art criticism, such as SUNY–Stony Brook and the School of Visual Arts, New York.

5. See Tobin Siebers, *Cold War Criticism and the Politics of Skepticism* (New York: Oxford University Press, 1993); Edward W. Said, *Representations of the Intellectual* (New York: Pantheon Books, 1993); and Russell Jacoby, *The Last Intellectuals: American Culture in the Age of Academe* (New York: The Noonday Press, 1987).

6. For an analysis of how the interpretation of this debate formed the foundation of the discipline of art criticism in the sixties, see Daniel A. Siedell, "Contemporary Art Criticism and the Legacy of Clement Greenberg: How Artwriting Earns its Good Name," *The Journal of Aesthetic Education* 36/4 (Winter 2002): 15–31.

7. For a sensitive analysis of Greenberg's and Rosenberg's early criticism, see Stephen C. Foster, *The Critics of Abstract Expressionism* (Ann Arbor, MI: UMI, 1980), 13–33. This book was deeply influential to me, particularly since I studied with Foster from 1991–94 at the University of Iowa, where he served as my doctoral adviser.

8. For evidence of the important role that the Greenberg-Rosenberg debate played in the development of the discipline of art criticism in the sixties, see Amy Newman, *Challenging Art: Artforum, 1962–1974* (New York: Soho Press, 2000).

9. Allan Kaprow, "The Legacy of Jackson Pollock," *Art News* 57 (October 1958): 24–26, 55–57; Jacques Barzun, *Classic, Romantic, Modern* (Garden City: Doubleday, 1961).

10. For a discussion of Thomas Hess's criticism in this context, see Daniel A. Siedell, "Re-Reading De Kooning's Critics," *Art Criticism* 10/1 (December 1994): 29–46.

11. Clement Greenberg, "How Artwriting Earns Its Bad Name," *Encounters* 17 (December 1962): 67–71.

12. Newman, *Challenging Art*, 41.

13. Quoted in ibid., 59.

14. Harold Rosenberg, "The American Action Painters" (1952), in *The Tradition of the New* (New York: Horizon Press, 1959), 25.

15. Harold Rosenberg, "Action Painting: A Decade of Distortion," *Art News* 61 (December 1962): 42.

16. Hilton Kramer, "A Critic on the Side of History: Notes on Clement Greenberg," *Arts Magazine* 37 (October 1962).

17. All of the above-mentioned essays are included in Harold Rosenberg, *Discovering the Present: Three Decades in Art, Culture, and Politics* (Chicago and London: University of Chicago Press, 1973).

18. Rosenberg, "The American Action Painters," 28.

19. For a more in-depth analysis of the narrative structure of Greenberg's *Art and Culture*, see Daniel A. Siedell, "Art Criticism as Narrative Strategy: Clement Greenberg's Critical Encounter with Franz Kline," *Journal of Modern Literature* 26/3–4 (Spring 2004).

20. Donald B. Kuspit, "Foreword," to Foster, *The Critics of Abstract Expressionism*, ix.

21. These texts are dealt with in greater depth in Siedell, "Art Criticism as Narrative Strategy."

22. Clement Greenberg, "Art Chronicle: Feeling is All," *Partisan Review* 19 (January–February 1952): 101.

23. Glement Greenberg, *Art and Culture: Critical Essays* (Boston: Beacon Hill, 1961), 151–52.

24. See Jerome Klinkowitz, *Rosenberg/Barthes/Hassan: The Postmodern Habit of Thought* (Athens: University of Georgia Press, 1988). T. J. Clark's *Farewell to an Idea: Episodes from a History of Modernism* (New Haven: Yale University Press, 2000) is based on Greenberg's definition of modernism. In addition, T. J. Clark and Michael Fried engaged in a series of discussions about "how modernism works," and the interpretation of Greenberg's criticism was the central focus. For Clark's essay, Fried's response, and Clark's rejoinder, see *The Politics of Interpretation,* ed. W. J. T. Mitchell (Chicago: University of Chicago Press, 1983).

25. The apologists for Greenberg over against Rosenberg make for strange and ironic bedfellows. Hilton Kramer, the insightful art critic and editor of *The New Criterion,* an influential neoconservative periodical of art and culture, is in agreement with the very postmodernist academy of tenured radicals against whom he and his colleague Roger Kimball never tire to rail. For Kramer's views on Greenberg and Rosenberg, see "Jackson Pollock and the New York School" (1995) and "Clement Greenberg in the Forties" (1987), in *The Triumph of Modernism: The Art World, 1985–2005* (Chicago: Ivan R. Dee, 2006).

26. Thierry de Duve, *Greenberg Between the Lines,* trans. Brian Holmes (Paris: Editions Dis Voir, 1996), 8. De Duve identifies three "Greenbergs": the "doctrinaire" Greenberg of the late thirties, the day-to-day "art critic" Greenberg of the forties and fifties, and the "theorist" Greenberg of the seventies. Although he says he "likes" the "art critic" best and wants to see him emulated, the "theorist" Greenberg interests him the most.

27. Clement Greenberg, "Modernist Painting," *Art and Literature* 4 (Spring 1965): 193–201; "Necessity of 'Formalism,'" *Art International* 16 (October 1972): 105–6. Greenberg published nine "seminars" (originally presented as lectures at Bennington College in 1971) from 1973–78 in *Art International, Arts Magazine,* and *Studio International.* These and other dogmatic texts are reprinted in Clement Greenberg, *Homemade Esthetics: Observations on Art and Taste* (New York: Oxford University Press, 1999).

28. Said, *Representations of the Intellectual,* 17.

29. Quoted in "The Art Seminar," in James Elkins and Michael Newman, eds., *The State of Art Criticism* (London and New York: Routledge, 2008). My response to the seminar is published in the "Assessments" section, 242–45.

30. See Hilton Kramer, "Criticism Endowed: Reflections on a Debacle," *The New Criterion* (November 1983), and Donald B. Kuspit, "Forum: Art Critics Grants," *Artforum* (May 1984): 78–79. Reprinted in Donald B. Kuspit, *Redeeming Art: Critical Reveries* (New York: Allworth Press, 2000).

31. Kuspit, "Forum," 5.

32. Donald B. Kuspit, *Clement Greenberg: Art Critic* (Madison: University of Wisconsin Press, 1979). See Kuspit, "Two Critics: Thomas B. Hess and Harold Rosenberg," *Artforum* 17/1 (September 1978): 32–33.

33. Kuspit, "Forum," 5.

34. Roundtable, "The Present Conditions of Art Criticism," *October* 100 (Spring 2002): 206.

35. See Daniel A. Siedell, "After Abstract Expressionism: Mapping the Coordinates of the Critical Discourse, 1962–1977," in Stephen C. Foster, *An American Odyssey, 1950–1980: Debating Modernism* (Madrid: Circulo de Bellas Artes, 2004).

36. Donald B. Kuspit, "FORUM: Art Students" (1984), in *Redeeming Art,* 10.

37. Donald B. Kuspit, "Art Criticism: Where's the Depth?" in *The Critic Is Artist: The Intentionality of Art* (Ann Arbor, MI: UMI, 1984), 81–82.

38. Kuspit, "Art Criticism: Where's the Depth?" 79.

39. Charles Baudelaire, "What Good is Criticism?" in *The Salon of 1846,* ed. David Kelly (Oxford: Oxford University Press, 1975), 44.

40. Donald B. Kuspit, "Flak From The 'Radicals': The American Case Against Current German Painting," in *Expressions: New Art from Germany,* ed. Jack Coward (The Saint Louis Art Museum; Munich: Prestel-Verlag, 1983), 43.

41. Ibid., 44.

42. Alfred H. Barr Jr., "Research and Publication in Art Museums" (1946), in *Defining Modern Art: Selected Writings of Alfred H. Barr, Jr.,* ed. and intro. Irving Sandler (New York: Abrams, 1986), 209.

43. See Daniel A. Siedell, "The Art Criticism of Weldon Kees," in *Weldon Kees and the Arts at Mid-Century,* ed. Daniel A. Siedell (Lincoln and London: University of Nebraska Press, 2004), 75–104.

44. I curated an exhibition of Weldon Kees's paintings and collages in the spring of 1998, which traveled to the University of Iowa Museum of Art in the fall of 1998.

45. See Irving Sandler, *The Triumph of American Painting: A History of Abstract Expressionism* (New York: Praeger Publishers, 1970). See also Daniel A. Siedell, "An Excavation of Tenth Street: The Failure of Modernism and the Politics of Postwar Historiography," PhD dissertation, University of Iowa, 1995.

46. For a collection of Kees's art and cultural criticism, see James Reidel, ed., *Weldon Kees: Reviews and Essays, 1936–55* (Ann Arbor, MI: UMI, 1988).

47. Quoted in Siedell, "The Art Criticism of Weldon Kees," 94.

48. Ibid.

49. Ibid.

50. Ibid., 99.

51. Ibid.

52. Roundtable, 210.

53. For attempts to suggest such an expansive approach to art criticism nourished (implicitly) by a Nicene Christian faith, see Daniel A. Siedell, "Heavenly Real Estate," *ChristianityToday .com*, http://www.christianitytoday.com/books/features/bookwk/051017.html; and Daniel A. Siedell, "Always Distinguish," *ChristianityToday.com*, http://www.christianitytoday.com/books/features/bookwk/061127.html.

54. See Steve Fuller, *The Intellectual* (Thriplow, England: Icon Books, 2005).

Chapter 6: Art, Liturgy, and the Church

1. Karl Barth, "The Architectural Problem of Protestant Places of Worship" (1959), in André Biéler, *Architecture in Worship: The Christian Place of Worship* (Philadelphia: Westminster, 1965), 92–93.

2. Joseph Leo Koerner, *The Reformation of the Image* (Chicago: University of Chicago Press, 2003), 12.

3. Ibid., 11.

4. Ibid., 36.

5. Ibid., 28.

6. Ibid., 150.

7. Ibid., 151.

8. Ibid., 73.

9. Ibid., 152.

10. Ibid., 85.

11. Ibid., 93.

12. Ibid., 256.

13. Ibid., 307.

14. For publications that situate ancient Eastern and Western theology and doctrine of the church in a postmodern evangelical context, see Kenneth Tanner and Christopher Hall, eds., *Ancient and Postmodern Christianity: Paleo-Orthodoxy in the 21st Century, Essays in Honor of Thomas C. Oden* (Downers Grove, IL: InterVarsity, 2002); Daniel B. Clendenin, ed., *Eastern Orthodox Theology: A Contemporary Reader*, 2nd ed. (Grand Rapids: Baker Academic, 2003); Robert E. Webber, *Ancient-Future Faith: Rethinking Evangelicalism for a Postmodern World* (Grand Rapids: Baker Academic, 1999).

15. Alexander Schmemann, *For the Life of the World: Sacraments and Orthodoxy* (Crestwood, NY: St. Vladimir's Seminary Press, 2000), 14.

16. Ibid., 27.

17. Ibid., 15.

18. John Zizioulas, *Being and Communion: Studies in Personhood and the Church* (Crestwood, NY: St. Vladimir's Seminary Press, 1997), 119.

19. Schmemann, *For the Life of the World*, 15–16.

20. Sergius Bulgakov, *The Holy Grail and the Eucharist* (1930; Hudson, NY: Lindisfarne Books, 1997), 86.

21. Zizioulas, *Being and Communion*, 119.

22. Catherine Pickstock, *After Writing: On the Liturgical Consummation of Philosophy* (Oxford: Blackwell, 1998), 192.

23. Ibid., xv.

24. Ibid., 222.

25. William T. Cavanaugh, "The City: Beyond Secular Parodies," in *Radical Orthodoxy: A New Theology,* eds. J. Milbank, C. Pickstock, and G. Ward (London: Routledge, 1999), 182. Cavanaugh writes, "The Eucharist, which makes the Body of Christ, is therefore a key practice for a Christian anarchism."

26. Graham Ward, *Cities of God* (London and New York: Routledge, 2000), 82.

27. James K. A. Smith, *Introducing Radical Orthodoxy: Mapping a Post-secular Theology* (Grand Rapids: Baker Academic, 2004), 185.

28. For an example of this unconventional reading of St. Thomas Aquinas, see John Milbank and Catherine Pickstock, *Truth in Aquinas* (London: Routledge, 2001). The concepts of participation, *theosis*, and deification are not simply an alien influence from the Eastern Church but has theological warrant in the West. It has even had an impact on Martin Luther scholarship. See Tuomo Mannermaa, "Justification and *Theosis* in Lutheran-Orthodox Perspective," in *Union with Christ: The New Finnish Interpretation of Luther,* eds. Carl Braaten and Robert Jenson (Grand Rapids: Eerdmans, 1998), 25–41.

29. Pavel Florensky, "The Church Ritual as a Synthesis of the Arts" (1918), in *Beyond Vision: Essays on the Perception of Art,* ed. Nicoletta Misler (London: Reakton Books, 2002), 109.

30. Zizioulas, *Being and Communion*, 101. Zizioulas states that the Greek Fathers' main achievement was the "identification of truth with communion."

31. Florensky, "Church Ritual as a Synthesis," 109.

32. Christoph Schönborn, *God's Human Face: The Christ-Icon,* trans. Lothar Krauth (1976; San Francisco: Ignatius Press, 1994), 239–40.

33. Florensky, "Church Ritual as a Synthesis," 108.

34. Ibid.

35. See the beautiful catalogue of the exhibition, Helen C. Evans, ed., *Byzantium: Faith and Power (1261–1557)* (Metropolitan Museum of Art; New Haven: Yale University Press, 2004).

36. Sharon E. J. Gerstel, "Exhibition Review: The Aesthetics of Orthodox Faith," *Art Bulletin* 87/2 (June 2005): 331.

37. See Robert Webber, "The Crisis of Evangelical Worship: Authentic Worship in a Changing World," in *Ancient and Postmodern Christianity*, 140–54.

38. See Daniel A. Siedell, "Aesthetic Practice and the Postmodern Church," *The Church and Postmodern Culture* 1.1 (August–December 2006): 51–53, http://churchandpomo.typepad.com/conversation/2006/11/aesthetic_pract.html.

39. Gregory Wolfe, "Liturgical Art and its Discontents," in *Intruding Upon the Timeless* (Baltimore: Square Halo Press, 2003), 92.

40. Quoted in Hans Küng, *Mozart: Traces of Transcendence,* trans. John Bowden (Grand Rapids: Eerdmans, 1993).

41. Quoted in Gerstel, "Exhibition Review," 336.

42. In fact, in the mystical tradition of the Orthodox Church, believers who are visited, comforted, and encouraged by the departed saints are able to recognize them as saints based on their likeness to the icons they have venerated. This has important ramifications for a more nuanced reflection on representation, copies, and originals than is currently assumed. For such guidance, see William Desmond, *Art, Origins, Otherness: Between Philosophy and Art* (Albany: SUNY Press, 2003), 19–51.

43. My observation comes from participating in such art initiatives and conversations in several local area churches.

44. John Meyendorff, *Living Tradition: Orthodox Witness in the Contemporary World* (Crestwood, NY: St. Vladimir's Seminary Press, 1978), 93.

Conclusion

1. See Ronald W. Ruegsegger, ed., *Reflections on Francis Schaeffer* (Grand Rapids: Zondervan, 1986). *Art and the Bible* was republished by InterVarsity in 2006. See Laurel Gasque, *Art and the Christian Mind: The Life and Work of H. R. Rookmaaker* (New York: Crossway, 2005). Gasque has also edited Rookmaaker's complete works.

2. Hans R. Rookmaaker, *Modern Art and the Death of a Culture* (Downers Grove, IL: InterVarsity, 1970), 9. For insightful discussions of the Kuyperian neo-Calvinist tradition and Rookmaaker's place in it, see Peter S. Heslam, *Creating a Christian Worldview: Abraham Kuyper's Lectures on Calvinism* (Grand Rapids: Eerdmans, 1998), 196–223; Henry Luttikhuizen, "Serving Vintage Wisdom: Art Historiography in the Neo-Calvinian Tradition," in *Pledges of Jubilee: Essays on the Arts and Culture, in Honor of Calvin G. Seerveld*, ed. Lambert Zuidervaart and Henry Luttikhuizen (Grand Rapids: Eerdmans, 1995), 78–104; Jeremy Begbie, *Voicing Creation's Praise: Towards a Theology of the Arts* (Edinburgh: T&T Clark, 1991), 127–41; William Dyrness, *Visual Faith: Art, Theology, and Worship in Dialogue* (Grand Rapids: Baker Academic, 2001), 95–97; William Edgar, "Why All This? Rediscovering the Witness of Hans Rookmaaker," *Books & Culture* (January–February 2006): 12–13.

3. Rookmaaker, *Modern Art*, 67.

4. Ibid., 70.

5. Ibid., 243.

6. Ibid., 248.

7. See Meyer Schapiro, "The Liberating Quality of Avant-Garde Art," *Art News* 56 (Summer 1957): 36–42.

8. Rookmaaker, *Modern Art*, 250.

9. Ibid., 245.

10. Douglas G. Campbell, *Seeing: When Art and Faith Intersect* (Lanham, MD: University Press of America, 2002), 31–36.

11. Rookmaaker, *Modern Art*, 250.

12. For an analysis of the impact of academia on artistic practice, see Howard Singerman, *Art Subjects: Making Artists in the American University* (Los Angeles: University of California Press, 1999).

13. For another approach to this subject, see Daniel A. Siedell, "Passionately Ambivalent," *ChristianityToday.com*, 2006, http://www.christianitytoday.com/ct/2006/februaryweb-only/107 -22.0.html.

14. Campbell, *Seeing*, xi.

15. See my comments on Campbell's book in Daniel A. Siedell, "Art and the Practice of Evangelical Faith," *Christian Scholar's Review* 34/1 (Fall 2004): 119–31. For Campbell's response,

see *Christian Scholar's Review* 34/3 (Spring 2005). If there is any doubt as to the fact that the stakes are high for the survival of Rookmaaker's Christian artist within the academic institutional network of CCCU schools and its funding and publishing venues, including *Christian Scholar's Review* (*CSR*), consider the fact that I was not allowed an opportunity to respond to Campbell's response, which devoted more time to telling the reader how angry he was with my essay than in clarifying the discourse and extending the discussion. I will allow the reader to come to his or her own conclusions about what Campbell's response, *CSR*'s willingness to print it, and *CSR*'s unwillingness to print my response reveal about the state of contemporary art discourse in the Christian academic community.

16. There is only one MFA program offered by a CCCU college, and that program, started by Azusa Pacific University, was initiated only in the summer of 2006. There is another program, sponsored by Bethel University—a CCCU member—that approaches undergraduate art education in a provocatively expansive way, offering a one-semester program in New York City for primarily art students at CCCU-affiliated colleges and universities. The program, called the New York Center for Art and Media Studies (NYCAMS), immerses the student in the contemporary art world. Both of these programs, in very different ways, offer significant potential to reshape the contours of Christian studio art education.

17. Campbell, *Seeing*, xi.

18. David Morgan, *Protestants and Pictures: Religion, Visual Culture, and the Age of American Mass Production* (New York: Oxford University Press, 1999). For a review of the book, see Daniel A. Siedell, "Protestants and Pictures," *Books & Culture* (September–October 2000): 31–35.

19. Pavel Florensky, "The Church Ritual as a Synthesis of the Arts" (1918), in *Beyond Vision: Essays on the Perception of Art*, ed. Nocoletta Misler (London: Reakton Books, 2002), 105.

20. This is the view of William Dyrness in his recent paper, "Contemplation for Ecstatically Challenged Protestants: Where the Reformed Tradition Went Wrong," Dubuque Seminary Lectures, April 2006.

21. Campbell, *Seeing*, 9.

22. Ibid., xii.

23. Gene Edward Veith, *State of the Arts: From Bezalel to Mapplethorpe* (Westchester, IL: Crossway, 1991), xv.

Index

Numbers in italic indicate plate numbers.

freedom, 155
Fried, Michael, 115, 180n24

Gallery 291, 37
"genius decision," 79
Gnaw (Antoni), *pl. 9*, 93–94
Gober, Robert, *pl. 2*, 101–5
Graham, John, 33
Greenberg, Clement, 111, 113–20, 180n24,
181n26
Guide (Martínez Celaya), 59–60, 64

Heartney, Eleanor, 126
Henri, Robert, 36, 37
Herbert, Lynn, 77
Hess, Meyer, 111
"How Artwriting Earns Its Bad Name" (Green-
berg), 115
human development, 26
humanity, as microcosm, 34, 68–69

iconoclasm
Celaya's meditation on, 52
history of, 31, 32, 134–36
relevance of art and, 52
soft, 14
icons
function of, 147, 184n42
implications of veneration of, 165
Luther and, 134–36
and modern art, 33–34, 82–85
objecthood of, 94
representation *vs.* abstraction, 29
and Second Council of Nicaea, 30
setting of contemplation, 144
and spiritual power in avant-garde, 32–33
icon writing, 96
imagination, artistic, 146–47
incarnation, 65–66, 68
installations, approaches to, 100–107
interpretation, by creators, 62
"Inward Eye, The" (2001), 77
Island within an Island (Orozco), *pl. 6*, 100

Jarry, Alfred, 43
John of Damascus, Saint, 30, 31–32, 34, 68
Johnston, Robert, 11

Kandinksy, Wassily, 32
Karlstadt, Andreas, 32, 134
Kees, Weldon, 126–29
Kinkade, Thomas, 46
Kline, Franz, *pl. 13*, 110, 117–18

Koerner, Joseph Leo, 134–36, 162
Kramer, Hilton, 121–23, 180n25
Krasner, Lee, 85
Krauss, Rosalind, 84
Kuhn, Walter, 36
Kuspit, Donald B., 121–23, 124–25

Laib, Wolfgang, *pl. 5*, 94–95
Levinas, Emmanuel, 80, 82
*Look, One Hundred Years of Contemporary
Art* (de Duve), 74
Los Angeles County Museum of Art, 76
love, 27
Luther, Martin, 32, 83, 134–35

"Magic Markers: Objects of Transformation"
(2003), 77
Malevich, Kasimir, 32
Marion, Jean-Luc, 30, 82
Martínez Celaya, Enrique, *pl. 3*, *pl. 4*, *pl. 11*, *pl.
12*, 51–69, 105–7
Masheck, Joseph, 33, 126
McEvilley, Thomas, 77, 126
Merleau-Ponty, Maurice, 27
Metropolitan Museum of Art, 38, 144
Milbank, John, 141
milk stone (Laib), *pl. 5*, 94
mimesis, 28–29
*Mimesis: The Representation of Reality in
Western Literature* (Auerbach), 65–66
mission, 149
modern and contemporary art
aesthetic practice and human development
through, 26
art after 1945, 85–91
beginnings of, 35–38
Christian artists and, 158–61
commentators' roles and positions, 13–15
definitions, 38–45
elitism of, 162–63
historical tradition of, 23–24
institutional framework of, 24–30
popular views of, 22–24
and rise of religion and spirituality, 73–74
secularization and, 45–49
theological reflections regarding, 30–34
Modern Art, 13
Modern Art and the Death of Culture (Rookmaaker), 154–56
modernism, 36, 38
Morgan, David, 75–76, 77
Museum of Art (Fort Lauderdale), 61
Museum of Contemporary Art (Chicago), 76

God in the Gallery

A CHRISTIAN EMBRACE
OF MODERN ART

Daniel A. Siedell